Media Sociology

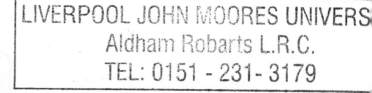

Media Sociology:
A Reappraisal

Edited by Silvio Waisbord

polity

First published in 2014 by Polity Press

Polity Press
65 Bridge Street
Cambridge CB2 1UR, UK

Polity Press
350 Main Street
Malden, MA 02148, USA

ISBN-13: 978-0-7456-7055-3
ISBN-13: 978-0-7456-7056-0(pb)

A catalogue record for this book is available from the British Library.

Typeset in 10.5 on 12 pt Plantin by
Servis Filmsetting Ltd, Stockport, Cheshire
Printed and bound in Great Britain by TJ International, Padstow, Cornwall

The publisher has used its best endeavours to ensure that the URLs for external websites referred to in this book are correct and active at the time of going to press. However, the publisher has no responsibility for the websites and can make no guarantee that a site will remain live or that the content is or will remain appropriate.

Every effort has been made to trace all copyright holders, but if any have been inadvertently overlooked the publisher will be pleased to include any necessary credits in any subsequent reprint or edition.

For further information on Polity, visit our website: www.politybooks.com

Contents

Introduction:
Reappraising Media Sociology

Silvio Waisbord

As a sociologist working on media, journalism, and politics, I often ponder how sociology shapes my work. Call it the recurrent preoccupation of the academic émigré, bound to frequently interrogate matters of academic identity. I am a sociological refugee in media studies. Sociology is my intellectual mothership, but it isn't my academic home. I rarely attend sociological meetings or publish in sociology periodicals. Despite my institutional distance from academic sociology, I regularly go back to the sociological well. The discipline remains a rich source of ideas for my work on different issues in communication and media studies. As editor-in-chief of the *International Journal of Press/Politics*, I regularly read submissions by psychologists, political scientists, and international relations and communication scholars (and a small number of sociologists) addressing a range of issues located at the intersection between news/journalism and political actors and processes. And, inevitably, I am reminded of the influence of disciplinary, theoretical, and methodological traditions on research questions and arguments.

Given this biographical trajectory, I was drawn to recent argument about the relation between communication/media studies and sociology. Jeff Pooley and Elihu Katz (Katz 2009; Pooley and Katz 2008) offer a much-needed, thought-provoking reassessment of the paths of media sociology.[1] They argue that sociology "abandoned" communication due to internal and external processes half a century ago. Although the Chicago School had laid the groundwork for communication studies during the interwar period, sociology eventually shifted attention away from communication. Early press studies were the province of sociologists on both sides of the Atlantic. Robert Park notably raised questions about the press and social identity and the formation of communities/publics/crowds amidst social change driven by industrialization, international migration, and urbanization. Although questions about communication remained central to the symbolic interactionism tradition of sociological research represented by George Mead, Herbert Blumer, and Erving Goffman, sociology increasingly lost interest in media effects and public opinion research. This shift happened simultaneously with the ascent of public opinion and persuasion studies in the postwar years. This line of inquiry, identified with the "propaganda" studies at the height of the Cold War, obtained substantial government and philanthropic funding and conquered a field originally grounded in sociology. This double academic/geographical move led to several intellectual shifts. Questions about short-term media effects overshadowed interest in the role of the media in social integration, collective identities, and structural issues. Positivism and quantitative methodologies prevailed over qualitative and ethnographic approaches. Sociopsychological questions and theories displaced sociological concerns rooted in foundational theories. Simultaneously, the opening of journalism and communication departments in subsequent decades offered a home to media sociologists who found that their discipline was becoming uninterested in communication/media research. The institutional consolidation of media studies in various departments across US colleges cemented the growing distance between sociology and communication. Although they try to find signs of a possible rapprochement between sociology and media/communication research, Katz and Pooley are "skeptical (if not resigned)" (2008: 776) to the prospects of media sociology. As long as the institutional infrastructure remains weak (the lack of journals or divisions in the American Sociological Association devoted to media issues) and mainstream sociology remains largely uninterested, prospects are dim for a reconciliation.

Other scholars have similarly concluded that sociology is missing in public opinion/political communication studies. As editor of a special issue devoted to sociology in the journal *Political Communication*, Schudson (2004) observed that few sociologists were working in the field. In the same issue, Benson (2004) shared Schudson's observation, calling for sociology's return to the study of political communication.

Manza and Brooks (2012) argue that sociology "lost" public opinion research at the hands of social psychology and political science due to the structural, anti-functionalist turn in political sociology in the 1970s. Interest in long-term structural processes and collective action drove attention away from "public opinion" which became identified with the problematic explanations of democracy and social change advanced by functionalist-cultural theorists in the postwar years. Media, communication, and public opinion were not central to seminal works by Charles Tilly, Theda Skocpol, and Michael Mann that outlined the analytical contours of political and historical sociology's study of revolutions and collective action. This tradition found problematic "political culture" arguments identified with modernization theories that dominated the literature in previous decades. Media and opinion research was caught in the functionalist, culturalist, and positivist side of the argument that lost ground vis-à-vis structural positions in neo-Marxist and neo-Weberian variants. Consequently, political sociologists have paid virtually no attention to issues that had been central to early studies of politics and communication. They are guided by the notion that structural, socioeconomic and political processes and "movements from below" are critical for understanding massive social change. Public opinion, and consequently the role of the news media in shaping beliefs and attitude changes, seemed superfluous for understanding the origins and consequences of large-scale social transformations such as democracies, revolutions, labor markets, protest and insurrection, state formation, and social movements.

The absence of sociology in public opinion/political communication research troubles scholars. Vliegenthart and van Zoonen (2011), as well as Carragee and Roefs (2004), note the limitations of news framing research, mainly lack of attention to power, which they attribute to refusal to engage with sociological questions. By ignoring power, the literature sidelines a key reason why news frames are analytically important: they perpetuate specific ideologies grounded in social and political inequalities and fail to understand how frames are opportunities for organized publics to contest interpretations over events and policies. The absence of sociological analysis particularly in news frames studies is remarkable, considering that sociologists (Gamson and Modigliani 1989; Gitlin 1980; Goffman 1974) produced landmark writings and that the sociology of social movements has extensively dealt with this question (Benford and Snow 2000). Unlike communication researchers and political scientists who primarily deal with the "effects" of news frames on knowledge, attitudes, and beliefs, sociologists were interested in news frames to address questions about hegemony, control, and domination.

Arguably, the absence of power in frame analysis is not only the consequence of sociology's weak presence in communication research. It also reflects the absence of questions about power within a line of political communication research primarily concerned with discussing media effects on public opinion. By failing to contextualize. frame analysis within contemporary politics and media organizations in capitalist societies, "media effects" research not only overlooks sociological studies, but also sidelines critical work by political scientists such as Entman (2004) and Wolfsfeld (1997) who raise questions about links between news frames and power inequalities. As long as narrow questions about "media effects" prevail, the links between the news media, public opinion, and political and social power remain neglected.

In my mind, the argument about the rift between sociology and communication/media studies raised the question whether "media sociology" is a unique case, given sociology's long history of producing and pushing specializations out. Sociology has been described as an "exporter discipline" (Holmwood 2010) with a distinguished academic progeny. A host of interdisciplinary fields that exploded in the post-1960s US academe are rooted in sociology. An incomplete list includes criminology, gender studies, race and ethnicity studies, women's studies, urban studies, health policy, cultural studies, education, and science and technology studies. Although these fields became meeting points for scholars from diverse disciplines, their origins are grounded in sociology (J. Turner 2006). Their analytical parameters, central questions, and conceptual baggage are sociological. Their interest in power, control, structure, institutions, class, and community are indelibly sociological (Rosenfeld 2010).

The case of media sociology seems symptomatic of sociology's specialization (Smelser 1988), the constant shedding of areas of study driven by its long-standing, thematic omnivorousness and US academe's institutional and programmatic fragmentation in past decades. Sociology's interests have been wider than other social sciences such as political science and economics (Calhoun 2007; Calhoun, Rojek, and Turner 2005; Holmwood 2010). Its wide-ranging theoretical stock provides research questions and insights relevant for various fields of study. Thematic and analytical dispersion has fueled balkanization (Cole 2001). From Bourdieu to Weber, sociology's theoretical canon provides common reference points, but it doesn't create a collective corpus or research enterprise. Instead, competing visions and interests continue to characterize sociology (Patel 2010).

Additionally, the academic drive towards specialization offered the "pull" factors for sociologists' migration. Proliferation of interdisciplinary programs and specialized journals built the necessary professional scaffolding and appealing institutional incentives for departure. Sociology was not the only (or main) source of employment or intellectual community. From urban studies to gender programs, the opening of academic units dealing with contemporary social problems and issues offered opportunities for sociologists to migrate. Although social sciences' fragmentation and specialization encourages social scientists to leave home disciplines, sociology's fissiparous tendency (Lamont 2009; Turner 2012) provided "push" factors. Sociologists became academically nimble, taking their highly portable specific interests, their slice of the broad sociological universe, across the social sciences and humanities.

These dynamics suggest that the case of "media sociology" may not be exceptional. Instead, it reflects the "fractal" character of sociology (Abbott 2001), permanently subjected to secessions and recombinations. The evolution of media sociology may be symptomatic of this tendency to generate and export new fields of study. Sociology's "abandonment" of media/communication research can be interpreted as reflecting broad internal movements: just as "gender," "science/technology," and "crime" sociologists moved to new programs in the 1970s and 1980s, media sociologists similarly found congenial the growing numbers of departments of communication, media, and journalism.

Katz and Pooley's argument raises other questions: Is the process they observed generally indicative of media sociology? Or does it apply to specific lines of inquiry in communication/media research, namely, media effects and opinion research? Has sociology as a whole abdicated from communication/media studies? Or are some branches of media sociology still attached to it? Does it reflect the unique experience of media sociology in US academe?

Parsimonious answers to these questions are difficult to offer because communication and media studies are disjointed fields. The contours of communication/media studies permanently shift. They are hardly what they were when media sociologists interrogated the field's analytical directions and theoretical strands in the 1970s (Gitlin 1978; Tunstall 1970). At the crossroads of the social science and humanities, communication/media studies neither have central, unifying questions nor single, theoretical, or disciplinary entry points. Ongoing transformations of the analytical object (whether "communication" or "media") are doubtless partially responsible for fragmenting communication/media studies. In the case of media studies, its expanding analytical reach reflects the conceptual instability of "media" understood as platforms for production and consumption of symbolic content (Couldry 2012). Originally identified with specific and separate technologies and institutions consolidated during the twentieth century (broadcasting, print, audiovisual, recording, and telecommunications), "media" became more fluid with recent technological innovations. Digital technologies' dominance and the multiplication of channels (from computers to mobile platforms) challenge old industrial/technology divisions. Global expansion of portable, digital, and interactive platforms not only heralds a "post-broadcast" era, but also transforms the meanings of "media." "Media" are not simply what people consume when not working or sleeping; they are interwoven in social life, making "mediation" integral to everyday life. Therefore, the analytical subjects of media sociology are broader than ever, as it incorporates questions that were once the purview of technology studies. New media have, if not completely abolished, certainly reduced the distance between interpersonal and mass communication. If sociology, particularly after relinquishing media effects/public opinion research, once focused on "mass communication," such clear-cut differentiations are no longer tenable: digital technologies blur separations between personal, interpersonal, and mass communication (Peters and Pooley 2012).

As communication/media studies are analytically dispersed, it is worth examining the proposition that sociology may be absent in some lines of research but present in others.

Ron Jacobs's (2009) position on this issue seems right, namely that the relationship between media studies and sociology is more nuanced than Katz and Pooley suggest. Jacobs affirms that narrow focus on the impact of messages on society in communication/media studies pushed sociology out. For Jacobs, renewed centrality of cultural research in sociology in past decades attests to the durability of questions and relevance of arguments originally developed by the Chicago School in the 1920s. Thus, there is no complete separation but a narrow interest in media research about sociological ideas and themes. His argument for this complex relationship is supported by other scholars. Silverstone (2005) described it as "paradoxical," characterized by analytical ebbs and flows across the sociological universe. In a similar vein, Couldry (2010a) and McQuail (2008) outlined the ambiguities of the relationship and recognized that in some disciplines, such as cultural studies, sociology underpinned critical studies of communication, culture, information, and media.

Perhaps Katz and Pooley referred to a particular set of questions and issues that were abandoned by sociology during the postwar years rather than to media/communication issues at large. Undoubtedly, psychology, social psychology, and political psychology have colonized public opinion and media effects research, areas in which sociology has a meager presence. It is also reasonable to suggest that sociology turned away from communication, as reflected by limited numbers of articles published in leading sociological journals and the few media sociologists in the faculty of (particularly US) sociology departments.

This position confirmed my knowledge of specific areas of research in communication/media studies, as well as my impression based on reading journals and attending conferences. Journalism studies is filled with references to the sociology of news, and ideas such as "risk," "field," and "liquid modernity" that reference, respectively, the work of prominent sociologists such as Ulrich Beck, Pierre Bourdieu, and Zygmunt Bauman. Sociological themes of globalization are central in international media studies about the changing political economy of media industries, the dynamics and hybridization of media cultures, and national and cosmopolitan identities anchored in global media flows.

I came to think, then, that sociology has a different presence in areas of communication/media inquiry. Despite the dearth of media sociologists in US sociology departments and journals, one finds scholars across academe who think sociologically about media/ communication issues. Just as there is neither unified sociology nor communication/media studies, no single coherent media sociology exists, but rather sociologists engage differently with communication/ media issues. The state of media sociology may look different for scholars interested in different issues.

The book

With this in mind, I decided to put this book together. My interest is threefold: to take stock of media sociology, map out current lines of communication/media research embedded in sociological thought, and highlight the contributions of sociological thought to media studies. By "media sociology," I understand the study of media processes and phenomena anchored in classic and contemporary sociological questions and methods. Media sociology interrogates the relevance of the media to understand "how society works" – specifically, by linking the media to fundamental social processes such as stratification, organizations, identity, autonomy, individualism, community, social influence, and power. It also draws from theories and arguments about these key dimensions of social life to analyze various aspects of the media – industries, institutions, audiences, content, and policies. Media sociology assumes that unpacking the complexity and multidimensionality of "the media" is critical to understanding fundamental aspects of societies, and that sociological theories offer critical questions and conceptual frameworks to analyze media processes and dynamics. Media sociology is guided by a double conviction: sociological understanding of the media helps us foreground important questions about how the media work and their impact on multiple aspects of social life; and the study of "the media" illuminates key areas to explain significant trends and transformations in contemporary societies.

Several questions drove my interest in this project: Are sociological approaches relevant in communication/media studies? What does sociology bring to media studies? What classic and contemporary sociological questions remain important? What has media sociology contributed to sociological research? A collective approach seems suitable to answer these questions. If my own experience is correct, specializations in the vast world of media sociology offer incomplete perspectives. Because answers may vary according to where sociologists stand in the fragmented landscape of communication/media studies, a collection of reflections could provide a better, comprehensive view. An edited book featuring contributions from media sociologists working on different research areas seemed appropriate to review the historical path and current whereabouts of media sociology. The goal of this book is not to discuss the institutional position of media sociology in academia measured by departments, conferences, funding, and journals. Instead, it seeks to provide snapshots of media sociology by scholars interested in various communication, media, and sociological questions.

The book is divided into four thematic sections: media, institutions, and politics; media industries and audiences; media representations; and technologies, self, and society. Each section features three original chapters. Although these sections do not capture the full range of subjects in media sociology, they reflect key areas of interest in media studies embedded in sociological theories and questions.

The first section addresses the study of media, institutions, and politics. Rod Benson revisits the study of structure and agency, particularly regarding comparative research about news and politics. He demonstrates the problems of continuing to talk about "the media" as if they were institutionally monolithic. Such a commonplace, offhand concept ignores divisions and multiple articulations of media institutions within social fields. Benson doesn't just remind us that "institutions matter." Reviewing comparative studies, he shows why media sociologists need to examine how different institutional logics embedded in politics, culture, and economics shape media dynamics and content. Michael Schudson similarly argues that political institutions are crucial to understanding the performance of media organizations and their contributions to democracy. He discusses four developments that have changed the political context of the news media in contemporary democracies: the rise of the administrative state, the multiplication of opportunities for active citizenship, the strengthening of monitoring mechanisms, and the consolidation of globalization to assess models. His interest is to examine institutional changes in order to reexamine classic questions and arguments in the analysis of press, journalism, and democracy. Questions about watchdog journalism, representation, activism, and control cannot be understood as they were fifty years ago. Democratic institutions have changed. Scholars therefore must be sensitive to substantial differences in the institutional context in which news media operate. Howard Tumber's chapter examines the contemporary relevance of classic sociology of news and journalism from the 1970s and 1980s in order to understand major changes in the news industry and journalistic practice in intervening years. Tumber demonstrates the importance of sociological methodologies and theoretical frameworks to identify questions and the complexity of news production. So-called "golden age" studies laid out arguments about structures and agency in news-making that should be critically examined in news landscapes transformed by technology, economics, and politics.

The second section discusses the contributions of sociological analyses of media industries and audiences. The sociological themes of structure and agency are central to Richard Butsch's discussion of audience studies. Butsch offers a comprehensive genealogy of audience studies that attests to the continuous presence of sociological interests. Issues such as social action and identity have been central to various scholarly approaches. Indeed, central themes in this research directly emerged from sociological debates on both sides of the Atlantic. Audience studies not only demonstrate the prevalence of the media in contemporary societies; they also show the impossibility of understanding sociological questions about identity, class, and collective action without integrating the study of the media. Tim Havens traces the sociological inspirations of various terms used to define "media industries" and reviews the central assumptions and arguments of three dominant perspectives. Tidying concepts is not simply a matter of semantics, for they reflect different assumptions about the existence of and links between "the media" and "society." No consensus exists on how to study "media industries." Markets, culture, and power are often viewed in contrasting terms, such that sociological approaches render different pictures about the state and functioning of "media industries." Havens identifies areas for further research to move analysis forward and test old arguments in light of major transformations. Toby Miller's chapter reassesses the state of the political economy of "media work" to account for recent developments in terms of ownership, control, and political struggle. He underscores why critical political economy is vital to uncover capitalist domination in "media industries," strip neoliberal truisms, and illuminate matters of labor, corporatization, globalism, and collective action. His chapter foregrounds issues long defining critical sociology of the media: relations of production, commoditization, social and ecological exploitation, and cultural domination. Eschewing cliché, dichotomic approaches that envision either full control by industries or absolute individual autonomy, Miller directs attention to areas where corporate strategies meet audience activism. He urges media sociologists to reveal patterns of domination and challenge relations between media industries and power.

The third section focuses on sociological analyses of media representations. Media representations are, as Shani Orgad writes in her chapter, "the images, narratives, accounts and frames that circulate in the media and carry symbolic content." Although various disciplines study media representations, sociologists have been particularly interested in understanding their links to specific social contexts and questions about power and inequality. Orgad reviews the "social work" of media representations – how they simultaneously promote certain understandings of society and specific groups and issues and discourage other interpretations and views. Sociologists are also concerned with how media representations solidify certain notions of order and acceptability and help certain groups to manage dissent and reify values. Orgad reminds us about the multiple, open, and subtle ways in which media representations are constitutive of social orders in a globalized world. She neither embraces a deterministic view, according to which media representations *are* reality nor subscribes to the position that they are naturally open and ambiguous. Instead, she suggests that sociological analysis needs to examine the dynamic nature of media representations by addressing actions to control and contest meaning and uses. Several of these issues, particularly the symbolic and material force of media representations, are discussed by Laura Grindstaff and Andrea Press. Their chapter examines the relationship between feminist sociology and feminist media studies. It argues that the relationship has not been as close as it should have been. This gap is grounded in the different trajectories of both fields and the eclectic disciplinarity and theoretical underpinnings of feminist media studies. In a crowded field of study, sociology's unique contribution is to pay close attention "to the people, practices, and institutional contexts at stake in the production and consumption of media texts in addition to the texts themselves." They enumerate several lines of research which could not only promote a sociological mindset in feminist media studies, but also critically address contemporary debates about multiple waves of feminism and post-feminism. Ron Jacobs's chapter offers further insights into media representations by discussing the relevance of classic sociological studies on media and race, particularly the portrayals of African Americans during the past decade. In line with arguments presented in this section, Jacobs argues that it is necessary to consider a range of mediated representations, to ground the analysis in political and social matters, and to search for domination and resistance in texts and meanings. The changing politics of language and narratives, demonstrated by contrasting portrayals of race in the US media in recent years, cannot be comprehended outside sociological concerns such as stratification, marginalization, and conflict. Furthermore, the production of texts, as well as the interaction between representations and audiences, needs to be placed within changing conditions for public expression, such as the proliferation of digital spaces for representing and contesting race, which pushes sociological studies in new directions.

The final section features sociological studies on technologies, self, and society. The three contributions show the relevance of a range of sociological questions in the contemporary study of technologies. Debates about media technologies and societies are embedded in classic sociological interests – domination, identity, difference, and representation – which have attracted attention from several theoretical perspectives. Graeme Kirkpatrick discusses the impact of social changes in late capitalism on technological design, purpose, and aesthetics. Society shapes digital media technology and is shaped by specific technological developments in unpredictable ways. Because of this conflictive relationship, technology should not be narrowly seen as the handmaiden of capital intended to achieve instrumental

goals, as orthodox critical approaches contend. Capitalist rationality and aesthetics are rather articulated in dynamic, ever-changing
relations between society and technology. By showing the reality
and potential of the aesthetic critique of capitalist uses of technology, Kirkpatrick identifies conflictive assessments about control and
autonomy. He avoids both sociological techno-pessimism and ingen-
uous techno-optimism by focusing on areas such as ludification/
ludefaction, demonstrating the ambiguous relationship between
society and digital technologies. Rich Ling's chapter draws on a different set of sociological theories and questions to produce a critical
survey of the social consequences of mobile communication. Ling
makes a persuasive case for why classic sociological questions about
belonging and coordination are critical in the study of portable
technologies. Global ubiquity of mobile communication means we
cannot analyze social interactivity without addressing the role of
technology. Mobile platforms have rapidly transformed interpersonal
communication as they are central to the conduct of social activities,
from safety to daily logistics. The interweaving of mobile technologies
into everyday life reminds us about the significance of classic sociological themes, namely, the inherent tension between autonomy and
dependency, individualism and community. Some of these themes
are also discussed in Jeff Pooley's chapter, which carefully dissects
the burgeoning literature on digital social networks. It concludes that
sociological analyses are scarce and marginal. Pooley's concern is
not to defend sociology vis-à-vis prevalent psychological approaches.
He rather wants to alert us to important analytical lacunae resulting
from individualistic, ahistorical and pre-social frameworks. One way
to properly address these issues is to move sociological approaches
concerned with "interactional, institutional, and historical" questions to the center, lest communication studies remain limited by the
epistemological assumptions of psychological approaches. As social
media are embedded in critical questions about community, self and
social experience, sociology has much to contribute to this growing
field of study.

In all, these twelve chapters provide a panoramic yet nuanced
examination of key themes, questions, and theories at the intersection between sociology and media studies. This book doesn't
pretend to offer an exhaustive survey of media sociology. Any table
of contents would inevitably be incomplete, given the expanding and
porous borders of communication/media studies.

One absence is the lack of assessments about the state of media
sociology outside the West. The question "where is media sociology?"

can be approached *thematically*, analyzing areas of specialization in media/communication studies, and *geographically*, comparing academic traditions around the world. This book takes the former approach, given that the debate that originated my interest in this project focused on the evolution of media sociology in US academe. Moreover, no criteria were obvious for selecting one country/region over others. As the traditions of sociology, communication, and media studies have particular trajectories in the global South (see Sreberny 2008; Tomaselli 2009; Yu 2011), a global comparative analysis of media sociology requires a separate study beyond the scope of this volume.

Another omission is thematic. The book doesn't have contributions on important contemporary themes, such as media and collective action/social movements (McCurdy 2012; Mische 2008; Van Aelst and Walgrave 2002), media and risk (Anderson 2009; Tulloch and Zinn 2011), media consumption and rituals (Couldry 2003), media and surveillance (Fuchs 2011), and political identity and communication (Schlesinger 1991). Space constraints made it impossible to cover comprehensively the rich variety of issues at the intersection of sociology and media/communication studies.

Sociology in communication/media studies

Aside from critically reviewing the literature on specific themes, the chapters reflect on how sociology informs current thinking in various lines of research. The authors raise a range of sociological theories and arguments – from cultural sociology to the sociology of technology and aesthetics, from postfeminism to post-structuralism, from neo-Marxism to neo-Durkheimianism.

The emerging picture suggests that the relationship between sociology and communication/media studies cannot be categorically summarized in terms of estrangement or rapprochement. A sociological sensibility is present in several lines of research. Sociological questions continue to be important, despite the weak position of media sociology in sociology, as Butsch observes in his chapter on media audiences. Tumber also shows that the rich legacy of sociological works informs contemporary studies of journalism. Research on the adaptation of news organizations to digital technologies attests to the vitality of sociological questions about organizational values, routines, and norms. Sociology is also present in contemporary studies of media and technology, as Kirkpatrick and Ling demonstrate in their chapters. From the critical views of Marcuse to arguments about everyday sociability by Goffman, theoretical frameworks and questions identified with macro- and micro-sociology are central to current research on media, technology, and society. Likewise, as shown by Miller and Havens in their respective chapters, sociological insights about power, capitalism, commodification, autonomy, and stratification are central in the analysis of media industries. Butsch, Jacobs, and Orgad also demonstrate that sociological questions are central in the study of media representations and audiences.

A different picture is presented about the state of media sociology in other areas of communication/media studies. Grindstaff and Press lament the marginalization of sociological analysis in feminist media studies, as well as the fact that feminist sociology has largely ignored the media. For them, a drift still exists as "the two arenas of scholarship seem to run on parallel rather than intersecting tracks." They call for the incorporation of sociological approaches to power and social justice into feminist media studies. Pooley finds a persistent rift in his nuanced analysis of the voluminous literature about communication studies on social media. Psychological questions and methodologies are dominant. Sociological issues are notably absent, such as the social and historical embeddedness of subjectivity, including matters of social stratification and inequalities, as well as the political economy of "social" platforms/companies. Ignoring these issues, psycho-communication studies ignore questionable western-centric assumptions about individual self-identity, the significance of gender, class and race self-presentation in digital platforms, and the social context of technology and its uses. Although he confirms that communication questions are still anchored in the psychological paradigm, Pooley remains hopeful that sociological questions could gain more attention.

It is difficult to explain concisely why sociology has had a different presence across communication/media studies. Explanations may need to address the position of sociology and the presence of other disciplines within the particular genealogy of fields of research. Sociology has been able to maintain its original lead position in the study of media organizations/industries, technology, and cultural studies – all interdisciplinary fields studied by economists, historians, psychologists, and humanities scholars. For example, Havens argues that the material and historical analysis of media organizations' "creative industries" has drawn from sociology (also, see Starr 2004). Kirkpatrick confirms that studies of the social impact of technology have been traditionally informed by sociological questions. Instead, the analytical boundaries of research on health communication (Kreps and Maibach 2008), media effects, and political communication have been shaped by psychology and political science. There may be self-perpetuating cycles at work. Theories and empirical questions shape the analytical contours of certain specializations in communication/media studies. Just as disciplines that originally defined a certain field shaped its analytical parameters and early direction, questions that eventually became central tilted research in favor of specific disciplinary and theoretical directions.

The chapters also help us unpack the meanings of having a "sociological sensibility," or "sociological imagination" to use C. Wright Mills's (1959) well-known expression, in communication/media studies. Contributors offer various ideas for understanding "sociological sensibility" and its contributions. Orgad suggests that media sociology is driven by an interest in the social role and the social "work" of media representations in particular contexts. For Butsch, media sociology is attentive to the complexity of the social and political dimensions of the media. Benson asserts that media sociology constantly reminds communication/media scholars about the importance of political, economic, and social structures, and that it serves as a necessary mediator between different disciplinary and theoretical traditions. Havens argues that media sociology brings up questions about social power and the relation between fields and actors.

In lieu of a succinct definition, a sociological sensibility can be characterized as the interest in linking the analysis of media industries, text, and audiences to questions about stratification, order, collective identity, sociability, institutions, domination/control, and human agency. It seeks to examine both the significance of media developments for the study of contemporary social trends and transformations, and the relevance of sociological questions for understanding communication/media issues (e.g. the functioning of media industries and occupation, the mobilization and contestation of media meanings, the context of media labor including engagement with media texts, or the characteristics and dynamics of media systems). Sociology places communication/media questions within important transformations in contemporary societies, such as the affirmation of "the network society" (Castells 1996), labor conditions in media industries (Mayer 2011), and the emergence of innovative forms of political action (Van Aelst and Walgrave 2002; Walgrave et al. 2011). It links communication and media to urgent social problems such as the environment (Maxwell and Miller 2012) and health (Seale 2003). Sociological analysis reflects on the materiality and symbolic dimensions of the social processes of mediation – how individuals, groups, and societies integrate media texts, technologies, and forms in everyday experience and definitions of private and public spaces, and local and global (Livingstone 2009; Silverstone 1999).

What does a sociological sensibility add to communication/media studies? What is missing if sociological issues aren't addressed? The chapters offer several insights into these questions.

One argument is the fallacy of thinking about "the media" as an institution driven by a single, unified logic. The media are everywhere in contemporary societies, but they are not regulated by a coherent, integrated logic, a point made by Benson and Butsch. Research needs to flesh out this question by examining and comparing the inner workings of media industries and organizations. This conclusion finds further support in the chapters by Havens and Tumber. Whether in traditional audiovisual or news industries, the study of power dynamics, status, socialization, and values finds the presence of different rationalities and influences in decision-making processes. Informed by the sociology of work, organizations, and professions, the analysis needs to be sufficiently nuanced to examine similarities and differences in the functioning of media industries and occupations in late capitalism. Matters of occupational autonomy, labor conditions, and organizational adaptation to changing social/technological/economic/political environments need to be put at the center of analysis.

Another argument is that communication/media studies need to pay attention to the interplay between structure and agency. From Marx's notion about the constraints on human action to Durkheim's social facts to Giddens's concept of "structuration," this line of thinking has a long tradition in sociological thought. It remains helpful to ascertain the interaction between structural forces (economic, political, cultural) and human action in myriad processes, such as changes in media policies/industries/texts, and the uses of media in processes of social and political change. Media studies need to be grounded in the analysis of social process and forces that shape the dynamic interaction between structures and agency. Structures, whether market forces, institutional settings, or cultural traditions, are shaped by policy traditions, cultural repertoires, and forms of socialization. Although they may not determine present and future decisions and practices, they affect the way people, for example, find opportunities for public expression, define self- and collective identity, and use media for everyday interaction. Media definitions of social issues, consumption and contestation of media content, and oppositional publics are inextricably linked to opportunities and inequalities shaped by social structures, as discussed by Benson, Jacobs, Lin, and Orgad. While warning communication/media research, particularly embedded in psychological traditions, about the perils of forgetting social structures, sociologists also emphasize the importance of agency in communication/mediated processes.

Communication/media studies should be equally sensitive to the infrastructure of public expression as to citizens/audiences' meaning-making and interaction. Just as structures don't close media dynamics, human action doesn't happen in a social vacuum. Infrastructure can be understood in terms of sociological concepts such as Habermas's public sphere, Castells's network, Bourdieu's field and Marx's labor/political economy. A dynamic, actor-centered media sociology should integrate structural issues in the study of how citizens mobilize social, cultural, and media resources to create/challenge media content and promote political and cultural democracy, as discussed by Orgad and Schudson.

Another important contribution of sociological approaches has been to foreground social questions in the study of media technologies. No matter what the technology is or does, whether digital news-gathering and news-disseminating platforms (or mobile telephony), research should socially and historically contextualize media and technology. Following recent studies (Anderson 2012a; Murthy 2012; Pinch 2010; Wajcman 2008), several contributors suggest that sociologists offer a corrective to psychological and nonsocial interpretations permeating recent thinking about digital technologies in the humanities and social sciences. Ling believes that matters of self-representation, social cohesion, autonomy, and interpersonal communication are critical to understanding the transformation of social life by mobile technologies. Mobile connectivity is central to the way people establish and renew social bonds and develop expectations about social interactivity. Pooley argues that sociology brings out important social dimensions missing in recent analysis of "social media." Kirkpatrick emphasizes the importance of sociological questions about power and labor to assess the innovations and limitations of digital media.

The authors offer plenty of evidence to explain why sociology matters for communication/media studies. Without "bringing sociology in," questions about capitalism, history, power, inequality, control, institutions, autonomy, and human agency may not be foregrounded. They don't simply heap praise for sociology; some recognize several limitations. For example, Schudson argues that although media sociologists have made important contributions, they have not properly recognized changes in governance and democratic participation in past decades. The workings of news organizations and the role of journalism in democracy cannot be understood outside the evolving institutional architecture of democracy. In what he calls a "post-legislative democracy," citizens use news and information technologies in novel and sophisticated ways. The multiplication of advocacy organizations that constantly produce news and commentary indicates important changes in the information landscape that need to be considered. Newsrooms, the traditional analytical focus of the sociology of news, aren't the only or dominant sources of information. Sensitivity to the interplay between media institutions and processes and political and social transformations is necessary. Sociology should not forget one of its own critical points: the value of a historical sensitivity to media institutions and political conditions. Historicizing media institutions and comparing media systems/practices across time are necessary for solid theory-building.

Media sociology and its futures

To recapitulate, sociology isn't completely absent from the study of media/communications but its presence is uneven. Media studies' multi-thematic foci and disciplinary cross-pollination has diluted, rather than displaced, sociological perspectives. Sociology has a weak presence in certain areas of research. Contemporary studies about media effects and public opinion are more attuned to questions in cognitive psychology and political science. Textual analyses informed by psychoanalytical, anthropological, and literary theories aren't sufficiently concerned with sociological dimensions such as social power, stratification, and collective agency. Yet other lines of research, such as studies on media organizations, industries, audiences, technologies, and citizenship, attest to the persistent influence of sociology.

These mixed results make it difficult to talk about media sociology as a single field with core questions. There appears to be neither a common past nor a common future for all areas within media sociology. Some branches had "golden" eras and foundational moments – the sociology of public opinion in mid-twentieth century or the sociology of news and journalism in the 1970s – but other offshoots grew differently. Sociologists may deem it necessary to introduce, "bring back," or expand sociological analysis in different areas of inquiry, depending on the particular dominant analytical parameters in specific literatures.

Sociologists reasonably argue that communication and media research should pay attention to social-historical contexts, power structures, institutions, and collective action. Unquestionably, sociology should contribute to bringing social theory into communication/ media studies (Hesmondhalgh and Toynbee 2008), expanding theoretical sources, questions, and debates. It's not obvious, however, how a sociology-driven "paradigm shift" would happen across the vast, unwieldy world of communication and media research. Why would communication/media scholars pay attention to sociologists? What sociological questions and arguments would they find intriguing and useful? As long as sociological ideas are weakly institutionalized in the academic infrastructure of communication/media departments, conferences, and journals, analytical boundaries may not change. Sociologists may be increasingly interested in technology and digital media, for example, yet it is not obvious that this interest would have significant ripple effects across the wider, fragmented landscape.

The situation is different in cultural studies, journalism studies, and technology studies where sociology continues to have a strong presence. Here the debate is not about making sociology relevant but, rather, defining what sociological questions are important. For example, options are many for understanding "the social" in technology and digital media, as Kirkpatrick and Ling suggest. Numerous sociological questions remain important, such as the possibility of individual autonomy in the hyper-connected micro-worlds of mediated relations, the power of (social) networks, the "normalization" of digitally mediated social interaction, the transformations of mediated self-identities, and the transformation of "media audiences" in digital media environments (also see Ruddock 2008). Likewise, Miller demonstrates that sociological insights undergird studies of the political economy of the media, stardom, and the environment. Recent research about newsrooms and professionalism amid massive changes in the news industries also attests to sociology's good health in journalism studies (Anderson 2012b; Boczkowski 2010; Ryfe 2012; Usher 2010; Waisbord 2013).

Media sociology remains an archipelago in the academic world, fragmented in different preoccupations and analytical frameworks. There are neither overarching questions to provide a common roof nor encompassing arguments to bring collective attention around common concerns. Sociologists gravitate toward specific lines of inquiry and have more intellectual affinity with fellow media/communication scholars in specific areas of research than with sociology writ large. Empirical interests and debates across communication and media studies, rather than sociological theory, provide analytical foci. This should not be surprising. Given its disciplinary origins and thematic concerns, media sociology is fated to eternal balkanization. If sociology lacks integrated paradigms and offers an eclectic research agenda (Turner and Turner 1990), why should media sociology be different? If communication/media studies don't have a single empirical problem or even analytical subject (see Pfau 2008), why would media sociology have common questions? Both "the media" (industry/technology/processes/practices) and "communication" remain fuzzy and constantly changing subjects of study (Crowley and Heyer 2013).

What if media sociology is not an "epistemic community" with common topics, findings/arguments, and methodologies? Should this be a matter of concern? I don't know. Prioritizing theoretical problems instead of empirical problems may help to bring together arguments and findings around similar preoccupations and mitigate centripetal tendencies driven by the allure of specific communication dynamics and media technologies, institutions, and processes. Yet the chapters show that, despite institutional and analytical dispersion, media sociology remains a rich trove of arguments and questions. I'm unsure whether media sociology would be in a stronger position or more relevant if it coalesced around common theoretical interests and research questions. Nor do I think that this could be possible for the reasons previously mentioned. It would be quixotic to try to develop a holistic media sociology anchored in a common research or analytical corpus amidst the ever-expanding universe of sociology and communication/media studies. The constant push for empirical divisions undermines the prospects for systematic, boundary-crossing media sociology. Long-standing, specialized boundaries anchored in technologies/industries (television, film, radio studies, "social" media), occupations (journalism), and social issues (race, gender, ethnicity, environment, sexuality, health) make general theories difficult. Clustering media sociology in terms of media industries, texts, and audiences, the conventional trinity of media studies, may be appealin,g given standard specializations in communication/media organizations and journals, but it would contradict sociology's insistence that the dynamism of social forces blurs neat analytical compartments, as Jacobs and Orgad remind us in their chapters.

Amid a field fractured in thematic specializations, media sociologists should find common ties and spaces for debate. We should also continue to cultivate and promote a sociological sensibility that grounds the study of communication/media phenomena in macro and micro social forces and processes, and finds communication processes and media institutions central to the analysis of critical social phenomena and problems. These are the continuing contributions of media sociology. Insisting on how communication and media are intertwined with social structures, collective action, and social power remains as important as ever. Hopefully, the ideas presented in this book will contribute to raising new questions, identifying research directions, and informing debates about why sociology matters for the study of communication and media.

Note

1 Here I use "communication studies" and "media studies" indistinctively, although I'm aware that each one can be correctly considered a separate field of study with overlapping areas of inquiry. For analytical purposes, I consider them together, given that the debate on media sociology has referred to communication/media scholarship and academic affiliations in units with both names. By "media sociology," then, I don't narrowly identify with "the media" but include communication and mediation processes. Thanks to Shani Orgad for reminding me about this issue.

PART I
Media, Institutions, and Politics

1

Strategy Follows Structure: A Media Sociology Manifesto

Rodney Benson

Sometimes the best sociology comes from non-sociologists. I was reminded of this truism the other day when I came across an article about John Bogle, the founder of Vanguard. Asked to explain why his company had substantially lower fees than other mutual fund companies, he pointed to its nonprofit ownership model that prevented profits being siphoned away to pay investors or shareholders. In short, Bogle concluded, "strategy follows structure."[1] If contemporary media sociology is in need of a new *raison d'être*, I cannot think of a better one.

Across the vast landscape of media studies, the trends in recent years have been for work that highlights contingency (to the point of voluntarism), complexity (verging toward obscurantism), and culture (ignoring institutionalized power). I speak here of claims, implicit or explicit, in certain strains of theories of networks or actor-networks, post-structuralism, and/or cultural sociology (as opposed to the sociology of culture), which is not to say that these diverse schools agree among themselves! While each of these approaches has its virtues, to affirm that strategy follows structure suggests a different understanding of the social world, a different research agenda, and a different way of linking theory, research, and practice. I do not claim that a critical, structural, "variation-oriented" media sociology should be the only kind of media sociology or the only kind of media studies on offer, but I do argue that it can contribute important insights that none of these other approaches are likely to contribute.[2]

To return to our non-sociologist but sociologically minded thinker John Bogle, I see four distinct propositions embedded in his claim that "strategy follows structure" worth underlining: First, there is such a thing as structure and it has an important social component.

Second, both structures and strategies are multiple (in Vanguard's case, there are of course alternatives to nonprofit ownership): this claim sets this approach apart from totalizing or holistic structural theories. Third, structure is pervasive and primary (generating strategies, rather than the inverse). And fourth, perhaps more controversially, some structural arrangements are normatively preferable to others (e.g. an egalitarian or social justice ethos inherent in the effort to keep fees low for non-elite investors). Let us examine each of these claims in turn before turning to some concrete examples of structural media sociology and a discussion of how structural media sociology counters or complements other approaches to media research and theorizing.

The elements of structure

At the most fundamental level, to speak of the structural is to emphasize the patterned character of human action and to thus create categories that group together various patterns. This move is fundamental to the sociological imagination. While each case is unique, it also shares certain properties with other cases, making generalization possible.

In creating categories, structural analysis inevitably selects and simplifies, opening itself up to charges of reductionism. But any attempt to model social reality involves simplification. Even Geertzian thick description makes choices about what to describe and what to leave out. Structural analysis at its best is simply more transparent about these choices. It encourages a constructive dialogue about which factors – or facets of a complex reality – should be incorporated if the model is to advance understanding and insight. Evidence thus consists of cases that are found to fit into this or that constructed category. Is this a kind of "violent" suppression of the particularity of any given case (an individual or particular social grouping)? In a sense, it is. But as Walter Lippmann long ago showed in *Public Opinion* (1922), simplifying categories – or stereotypes – are produced organically at all levels of society. A reflexive structural sociology has the potential, at least, of minimizing the symbolic violence.

Given that one should be skeptical of all categories, the key question is what to do next. One response, the luxury of the deconstructionist, is to only critique. This kind of work keeps empirical researchers on their toes. In the long run, it can lay the groundwork for new political projects responsive to societal transformations; in the short run, by its refusal to engage with the "system," it can leave the political field open to domination by the most conservative forces. Critical structural sociology, even at its most politically radical, mobilizes critique to (always tentatively) construct new categories that can then be mobilized – both to generate new insights, through the crucible of empirical testing, and to deploy them in real political struggles to combat injustice and discrimination of whatever sort.

Structure, however, generally refers to something more than persistent patterns. It also suggests the importance, if not indeed the primacy, of the social. The cultural turn was a wrong turn to the extent that it acted as if social structure no longer existed. Even if all social reality is discursively constructed, the concept of social structure calls attention to inequalities in the distribution of resources, material as well as symbolic. By diverting attention from such inequalities, the cultural turn is complicit with neoliberalism, as even the respected cultural theorist William H. Sewell, Jr (2005) has conceded. Cultural sociology, as articulated by Jeffrey Alexander (2007), acknowledges the existence of social structure but insists on "analytically" separating it from culture. Unfortunately, the effect is the same: social structure is effectively ignored.[3] A structural approach to media sociology should neither dismiss nor privilege culture, but should seek to understand the complex (but not unpredictable) interrelations between the discursive and the social; there is also virtue in abandoning altogether the structure–culture binary, given that all human activity is both socially patterned and culturally meaningful (see also Gans 2012).

If the mere existence (and persistence) of social structural constraints is thus a first premise of structural media sociology, the second is that these constraints should not be understood in a holistic, all-or-nothing fashion. Fundamental to most sociological approaches is the search for and explanation of variation. Across the social sciences and humanities, field theory – incorporating its many permutations (see e.g. Bourdieu 1984, 1993; Fligstein and McAdam 2012; Lewin 1951; Martin 2003) – has arguably become the dominant model of structural variation. Further developed through a range of national and international comparative case studies (e.g. Benson 2009, 2013; Benson and Neveu 2005; Fourcade 2009; Kuipers 2011; Medvetz 2012), this institutional framework conceptualizes the social world as a set of hierarchically organized, semiautonomous more or less specialized spheres of action, each with their distinct histories and rules of the game. How do these social spheres or fields differ in their functioning, ideals, practices, and stakes? How did they come into being and how have they changed over time? Which tend to be dominant?

Field theory offers a marked advance in analytical sophistication and explanatory power over the binary system/nonsystem model typical of work influenced by directly or indirectly by Weber's "rationalization" thesis. In Foucault (1995), disciplinary regimes may change over time but in a given era one reigns supreme and structures all social action, except at the very margins; in Adorno (2001), there is virtually no escape from the culture industry or the administered world.[4] Under certain conditions, of course, institutional forces may produce homogenization (DiMaggio and Powell 1983), but there are always countervailing forces of differentiation (see e.g. Boczkowski 2010 for a compelling analysis of both processes in online news production). In field analyses, homogenization is a variable, not a destiny.

In his early characterizations of the "system," Habermas (1987b) seemed to be following in the totalizing tendencies of the Frankfurt School, but he has subsequently offered a more variegated rendering of the multiple institutional layers (organized civil society, academia and think tanks, media, legislative bodies, etc.) that lie between the peripheral lifeworld and the executive core of liberal democratic national systems (see Habermas 1996). Manuel Castells's detailed empirical modeling of the flows of "network society" acknowledges variations aplenty but fails to draw them together into an explanatory theory. Just to cite one example, Castells (2007: 244) argues that distrust in government is on the rise across the western world, yet notes in passing that the Scandinavian countries are an exception to this pattern. Always emphasizing fluidity and contingency, this ever-on-the-move sociology of flows doesn't stop long enough to wonder why: a sociology of structural variation would see in this anomaly precisely the kind of data that could refine its explanations.

Structural media sociology's third premise is that structures are pervasive and primary. Why not say structure follows strategy? Structures have to be structured before they can become structuring, do they not?[5] Absolutely, but structuring moments build on pre-existing structures, or as Marx (1994) put it far more eloquently: "Men make their own history, but they do not make it as they please; they do not make it under self-selected circumstances, but under circumstances existing already, given and transmitted from the past." We start with a set of structures, simultaneously cultural and social, and we innovate by making new combinations. The capacity to act, and in certain ways rather than others, is structurally produced.[6]

At the individual level, the capacity to choose among strategies is predicated on a plurality of institutional structures, each with its own distinct logic. Even though each of us may be predisposed to act in a certain way given our family background, education, and occupation (in sum, our habitus), the persistence of some degree of institutional pluralism keeps open the possibility of constructing alternative subjectivities. This possibility is captured in Swidler's (1986) concept of culture as "toolkit" or Lamont and Thévenot's (2000) "cultural repertoires."

At the macro-societal level, widespread cultural innovation or transformation is more difficult to achieve. At moments of economic, social, political, military, even climactic turmoil – in other words, "critical junctures" (Thelen 1999) – there are increased possibilities of creating new institutions (and thus new subjectivities). At best, after the dust settles, what seem to be revolutions of one sort or another usually produce only limited change. A revolution would mean a dramatic deviation from a pre-established course, which is indeed difficult to achieve. "Path dependency" (Thelen 1999; Sewell 2005) is shorthand for all the factors that contribute to inertia: because it is too costly to retool, because of entrenched interests, because after a period of time it simply seems natural and the possibility of things being otherwise becomes literally unimaginable, and so on.

For all these reasons, investigation of the causes and effects of variable social structural arrangements lies close to the heart of the sociological imagination, and by extension, to what is distinctive about a sociological approach to media studies. I would add, however, a fourth and final element of such a research program that perhaps sits less easily with sociological orthodoxy: the need to acknowledge the normative element present in all research. To insist that strategies follow structures is to imply that some structures might in fact be preferable to others. The ongoing furor in some quarters over Habermas's attempts to construct a universal discourse ethics shows clearly the lack of normative consensus. But that should not preclude the attempt to discuss normative questions, far from it: all research, sociological or not, ought to make clear the specific political and ethical presuppositions implicit in the questions it asks.

Normative concerns inevitably guide one's choice of research questions and obviously underpin some of the most frequently studied aspects of media performance. Why do we study sensationalism, diversity, inclusion, and critique, or lack thereof, if we did not think that these somehow contribute to or detract from the good society, however defined? Media sociologists ought to set an example to other sociologists – as well as non-sociologists – by always clarifying "what's at stake." For Habermas (2006), what's at stake is the institutional structuring of an ideal public sphere or spheres, understood in relation to the imperatives of noncoercive, open-ended deliberation. Castells (2012) is less clear but at bottom he seems to be a participatory democrat, concerned with grassroots inclusion and mobilization against oppressive systems of power, whether economic or political. Actor-network theorists' reticence toward making any claims about social power seems puzzling until one understands their overriding concern with the potentially oppressive effects of expert-produced systems of knowledge and their concomitant insistence on the ground-up production of social solidarity.[7] Alexander's (2007) cultural sociology, including his strong injunctions against any form of social reductionism, seems to be mostly motivated by a concern to promote noninstrumentalist forms of civil solidarity.

Specifying what's at stake, however, does not necessarily require the sociologist to take a position. What matters is that the findings are situated in relation to transparent accounts of their implications. This is precisely the approach taken by Myra Marx Ferree, William Gamson, Jürgen Gerhards, and Dieter Rucht (2002) in their comparative study of German and US news discourse about abortion: rather than trying to make a global judgment of the democratic deficits or virtues of either media system, they situate their comparative findings in relation to four distinct democratic traditions.

The kind of normatively transparent, structural variation-focused sociology I have outlined so far could be enacted via a variety of media-related case studies, samples, and methods. One way or the other, however, it must be comparative: variation in both the independent and dependent variables must be incorporated into the research design. Cross-national research is useful to the extent that it provides additional cases and can help test the generalizability of single nation-bound findings; it is absolutely necessary if one is trying to test for the effects of variation in nation-state system-level characteristics, such as national media policies or journalistic professional logics.

Searching for consequential structural variation in media

The first thing to do is banish all references to "the media." The word is plural. There is no single media logic. In addition of course to various technological mediums, there are: media systems (subnational, national, and transnational), media organizations, and media producers and audiences (these latter sometimes interchangeable). These correspond, in turn, to fields of power, particular organizational fields, and the social space of classes. In *Shaping Immigration News* (Benson 2013), my study of US and French newspaper and television news coverage of immigration over the past four decades, I refer to these three elements of field structure as position, logic, and structure. Each of these facets of structural power shapes media production and reception in distinct ways.

Fields of power

Even if globalization is breaking down national boundaries, the nation-state still retains its primary structuring power (Morris and Waisbord 2001). This power is not unitary, however, but is constituted of oppositions. In secular democratic nation-states, an important structuring opposition is that between the commercial and the noncommercial, that is, between the logic of the consumer/client versus that of the citizen. As even Herbert Marcuse (1998 [1941]: 58) once acknowledged, in an otherwise sweeping denunciation of bureaucracy, there *can* be a real difference between private and public: "In the democratic countries, the growth of the private bureaucracy can be balanced by the strengthening of the public bureaucracy. . . . The power of the public bureaucracy can be the weapon which protects the people from the encroachment of special interests upon the general welfare." Marcuse added one caveat: the public bureaucracy "can be a lever of democratization . . . as long as the will of the people can effectively assert itself." (This passage is a fine example of structural sociology of media: Marcuse affirms that structure consists of institutional forms, that these forms vary, that variations in these forms produce different outcomes, and that these different outcomes are normatively consequential.)

Indeed, the overwhelming verdict of systematic discourse analyses is that noncommercial, government-subsidized media, including newspapers in many countries, are more critical, ideologically pluralist, and engaged with historical context and policy substance than purely commercial media (Aalberg and Curran 2011; Benson and Powers 2011; Cushion 2012).

Of course, it is not always the case that publicly funded media serve democratic ends; in many countries, what are called "public" media are in fact government propaganda agencies. Yet, commercial media also often serve, wittingly or unwittingly, as propaganda mouthpieces for governments. Other commercial media effectively promote ideologies – party-based, religious, consumerist – without need of any direct link to government. The question, then, is not specific to government but to all institutional forms. What kinds of ownership, funding, organizational, and professional institutional arrangements promote more or less of various democratic (or other normative) discursive or social outcomes?

Weber's notion of "rational-legal" authority, as elaborated by Hallin and Mancini (2004: 192–3), points to a response. Bureaucratic systems, whether public or private, can be designed in ways that are self-limiting. Where there is effective rule of law, supported by custom as well as coercion, bureaucracies can in fact achieve a certain degree of accountability and autonomy. This is the conclusion of my recent co-authored study of public media regulations in fourteen leading democracies (Benson and Powers 2011).[8] Countries with the highest-quality public media systems have regulatory and funding buffers to prevent partisan political control; they also have mechanisms to ensure democratic accountability and to encourage citizen involvement. Concretely, we found that the best public media systems have certain structural features in common: adequate public as opposed to commercial funding, multi-year funding cycles, autonomous oversight boards, and citizen engagement. A few concrete examples from our study will help illustrate these points.

In most Western European democracies, a "license fee" levied on all owners of television (and increasingly other media devices) funds public media systems. This system provides a direct link between public media broadcasters and their publics and avoids problems associated with funding derived from general government funds. In addition to establishing a buffer against dramatic changes in governmental funding, the license fee also has historically had "a social dimension," in that "by contributing to their national public broadcaster, citizens felt that it was more accountable to them than to the politicians" (Papathanassopoulos 2007: 156).

In the American context, public broadcasters have argued that direct charitable contributions from local citizens to local stations serve a similar role. Philanthropy, however, is not an exact substitute for universal public funding. First, it introduces a strong upper-middle-class influence over public media: this may encourage certain kinds of quality programs that might not otherwise be produced (see discussion in section on "social location" below), but it also creates incentives to ignore the needs and interests of noncontributing citizens. Second, the amount of funding that can be generated by philanthropy is dramatically less than that which can be provided by a universal license fee or direct government funding. Even when individual donations and corporate sponsorships are added to the mix, US per capita funding of public media (PBS, NPR, and their local affiliates) is far below that of other leading democratic nation-states: just US$9, compared to a range of US$40–$160 in the other countries in the study (Benson and Powers 2011: 61).

Total funding is important, but no less important for ensuring the viability and autonomy of public media are procedures designed to ensure their autonomy. In Australia, Denmark, Germany, and the United Kingdom, funding is established for multi-year periods, which lessens the capacity of governments to directly link funding to either approval or disapproval of programming. Charters or other media laws or regulations can restrict the capacity of governments to influence programming in a partisan direction. For example, the Swedish public broadcaster, SVT, is governed by a three-year charter and is owned by an independent foundation, specifically designed to insulate SVT from both state and market pressures. Administrative boards can also serve as a buffer between public broadcasters and the government in power. Their autonomy from political pressure may be bolstered by a variety of means: through staggered terms, limiting the capacity of a new government to immediately control all appointments; through dispersal of authority to make appointments; and through multiple layers of "external" and "internal" oversight, creating an "arms-length" relationship between the public broadcaster and partisan political interference or meddling.

Subsidies to newspapers in countries such as Finland, France, Norway, and Sweden are generally designed to be content neutral, to prevent closing of newspapers that will lead to local monopolies, and to promote pluralism of opinion not provided otherwise by market forces. According to the classic liberal formulation, commercial newspapers, because they are supposedly free of government control, will report on politics in a sustained and critical way. Some commercial media do, but many commercial media outlets offer little or no criticism of government or ignore politics altogether in order to focus on more audience-pleasing human interest, entertainment, and crime stories. In contrast, newspapers that are publicly supported and have a mandate to provide independent, critical coverage more often than not achieve this mandate (Benson and Powers 2011).

Finally, institutional structures have been set in place in many countries to promote democratic accountability of public media. Legal and administrative charters create mandates to provide diverse, high-quality programming and inclusion of a wide range of voices and viewpoints. Funding structures and oversight organizations in Denmark, Germany, and the Netherlands have attempted to ensure that public media are accountable to these public mandates and that public media listen to citizens and involve them in decision making. As the recent BBC scandals have shown, these ideals are not always achieved but, over time, public service media have shown that they offer a diversity and quality of content not supplied by commercial media alone.

It may be true that the license fee or other European-style regulatory reforms are for the moment politically unachievable in the United States; this is just another way of noting that the American institutional "path" long ago took a different direction to that of Western Europe and that regulatory, economic, and cultural inertia make it difficult to change course now. But this also shows the crucial importance of institutionalization: legislative or regulatory victories, no matter how quixotic such efforts may seem, are eminently worth trying because they are likely to have long-lasting effects.[9]

Only through international comparative research can one begin to see media systems as a whole. Through this lens, the distinctiveness of the US system – its extreme hyper-commercialism and weak public sector – is put in stark relief. Without this context in mind, American media research has tended to pose research questions that take the market model for granted, rather than to critically interrogate it in a way that might suggest serious alternatives. For example, Sarah Sobieraj's (2011) study of social activism and the media considerably updates Todd Gitlin's (1980) classic study, showing that many of the commercial and political logics at work in the 1960s still structure news choices in the 2000s. Activists face the same kinds of catch-22s: damned if they do (try to get their message out through the media, in which case it will be stripped of all substantive content), damned if they don't (give up on trying, in which case the message also remains unheard). Sobieraj finds that activists mostly forgo a third possibility: making full use of opportunities to reach publics outside the mainstream media. But there is a fourth possibility that she doesn't take much time to consider: why don't activists try to reform the media system in a way that would make it more receptive to ideas from the margins?[10] Again, given the lack of substantial institutional variation in the US system (at least until recently), this is an understandable omission: cross-national comparative research can make visible what heretofore was invisible, namely, that the media system really could be organized in a different way. For example, my comparative French–US research shows that French news media, including television news as well as national newspapers, are less likely than American media to reduce civil activism to personalized identity quests and more likely to acknowledge its organized collective character and to give space and time to its substantive arguments (Benson 2013). These different forms of journalisms are not accidents but are rather the effects of institutional choices.

It must be emphasized that the differences between the United States and Western Europe are of degree rather than of fundamental kind. Cultural repertoires of civic solidarity and egalitarianism are available for use in American society just as market repertoires circulate in the Western European social democracies. The difference, as Michèle Lamont and Laurent Thévenot (2000) have argued, is that the market and civic solidarity cultural repertoires occupy different hierarchical positions on the two sides of the Atlantic: market logics dominate (but are contested) in America while civic solidarity logics dominate (but are contested) in continental Western Europe. What Lamont and Thévenot do not emphasize, however, is the extent to which national cultural hierarchies are anchored institutionally and materially. Civic solidarity is stronger in Western Europe because of social democratic government policies across a range of spheres of private and public life, including media policies. The particular ideological and formal characteristics of American and various European journalistic practices can thus best be understood as adaptations, accommodations, and forms of (limited) resistance to their national fields of power. In general, media sociology must situate its analyses in relation to fields of power in order to offer any real insight on the (variable) structural forces underlying distinct logics of practice.

Field and organizational logics

Within fields of power (still mostly national), there remains, at least in principle, some degree of variation across particular fields: artistic, scientific, religious, and civic/associational. In the realm of US media studies, investigations of field-based differences have been hampered in part because of the near-total dominance of commercial media. Scholars have tried to identify links between various qualities of news discourse and structural features such as advertising funding (Baker 1995) or publicly traded corporate ownership (Cranberg, Bezanson, and Soloski 2001). The results are tentative to the extent that for the most part these economic structural features have in recent years marked virtually all of the major US media outlets.[11]

As economic and job losses mounted in the US newspaper indus-try during the 2000s – advertising has fallen by half (Pew Foundation 2012) and journalistic jobs have decreased by one-third over the past decade (Downie, Jr and Schudson 2009) – American professional and academic attention finally turned to the question of alternative ownership and funding models, both international and domestic. Santhanam and Rosenstiel (2011) set out to find out why US jour-nalism seemed to be suffering more from the economic crisis than European journalism. The authors came up with three major conclu-sions. First, the publicly traded and private equity ownership forms that are dominant in the United States create higher profit pressures than in other countries and hence "force" owners to lay off workers in order to maintain these high profits. Second, because US news media are so dependent on advertising – as opposed to reader subscriptions and public subsidies, which provide a greater proportion of revenues in Europe – the drop in revenues was more pronounced in the United States when advertising dried up. And third, due to US government policies that allow or encourage debt-driven mergers and acquisi-tions, many US media companies were in a far more fragile economic position than their European peers when the financial crisis hit in 2008.

Even as the US media system remains resolutely commercial compared to its Western European counterparts (Kleis Nielsen 2012), the relatively strong philanthropic sector has contributed to an unprecedented experimentation in new ownership and funding models for journalism. Few of these nonprofit outlets are big opera-tions. Their staffs range from a half-dozen to fifty. Their budgets range from US$1 million to US$10 million.[12] In contrast to the old "legacy" media which relied on business advertising for 70–80 percent of revenues, however, the nonprofit news outlets seek funds from a variety of sources – small and large individual donors, busi-ness sponsorships, local and national foundations. This natural experiment allows sociologists to study how variable forms of media ownership matter in ways that were not possible previously.

Research on field-based variations in media ownership is only begin-ning. For instance, media outlets owned by religious organizations – such as the *Christian Science Monitor* in the United States or the Catholic newspaper *La Croix* in France – might be expected to have a different orientation toward the news due to their religious and ethical commitments. Indeed, as the *Christian Science Monitor* man-aging editor remarked about the Christian Scientist church's attitude about the *Monitor*: "They feel, as we do, that the charter of the paper was to injure no man and bless all mankind through the practice of journalism with integrity . . . There is a charter to basically do good at some civic level."[13] Church financial support for the newspaper makes achievement of this mission possible. In my study of immigration news (Benson 2013), I found the *Christian Science Monitor* to be more ideologically diverse, comprehensive, and critical in its coverage than other US newspapers. Likewise, small media startups linked to the artistic field might be expected to be more experimental and less commercial in their orientation. This seems to be the case with the San Francisco *Public Press*, owned and funded by a northern California nonprofit arts association. The *Public Press* seeks to become the "*Wall Street Journal* for Working People." Because it is free of advertising funding, it has been able to publish investigative articles on Macy's department store and other major companies – the kind of critical business coverage that the business advertising-dependent *San Francisco Examiner* rarely if ever does.[14]

Going beyond traditional news organizations, Matthew Powers (2013) shows how variable forms of funding and organizational structure shape distinct logics of practice at the human rights NGOs that are increasingly becoming major sources and even producers of international news. Powers identifies three key structural variations inside NGOs: whether a human rights NGO has long-term or project-based funding; whether it seeks to influence broad publics or policy makers; and whether research or publicity departments dominate inside the organization. These factors not only affect NGO practices: ultimately, they narrow or broaden the public discourse, they help determine which issues or areas of the world will be given attention, and they influence the kinds of public or private solutions that will be considered viable. This research shows the need for media sociology to take into account variation in other social spaces that interact with the media to produce the news (as well as other forms of cultural expression). Countering the often unblinking praise accorded to civil society as a whole, Powers also demonstrates that different corners of civil society are more or less effective than others in meeting various democratic expectations. He thus provides an important reminder that variation needs to be taken into account in normative as well as in descriptive/explanatory analysis.

At the same time, it is important to stress that field-based logics of ownership and funding do not act alone in shaping news. They intersect with both the larger field of power (which in the US case is dominated by market logics) and with the pre-existing commercial and professional logic of the journalistic field. For example, despite

the *Christian Science Monitor*'s self-conscious efforts to offer a different kind of quality journalism, the newspaper has increasingly felt
constrained to maximize hits to its website, "monetize" its content,
and in general "find a business model that works."[15] Many of the
new nonprofit news organizations emphasize professional journalistic
values consistent with long-standing conventions of mainstream
news (the main difference being that they may be more likely to
put their ideals in practice than their commercially funded peers).
Cross-national comparative research can help tease out this complex
interplay between the logics of organizations, fields, and the larger
field of power. Within a given macro-field of power, there may be
substantial variation across the various mezzo-level fields, but the
dominant fields in any given national field of power set the tone.
Thus, *Le Figaro*, while highly commercial in the French context, is
distinct from commercial US newspapers because it is shaped by a
French national field of power far less commercialized than its US
counterpart (Benson 2013).

Social location

Within national fields of power and particular fields, particular media
outlets may still vary substantially due to their specific social location.
Different media tend to be produced for different class fractions, a
tendency that is only accentuating in this era of media fragmentation
(Williams and Delli Carpini 2011). For this reason, the sociology of
production and reception are intricately linked, and discursive "dispositions" are likely to parallel the structural "positions" of media
outlets and their audiences. Social location is likely to trump the
power even of the media mogul: at minimum, his or her success will
be predicated on being able to efficiently locate and expand an audience by pandering to its preconceptions.

In my research on immigration news (see Benson 2009, 2013), the
financial newspapers *Les Echos* and the *Wall Street Journal* were the
most likely to emphasize the "good worker" frame, that is, the claim
that immigrant workers were good for the economy and did work that
domestic workers would not do. This frame clearly accords with the
worldview of most of their business sector readership. Newspapers
with the highest proportions of lesser-educated, lower-income readers
such as the *Daily News*, the *New York Post*, and *Le Parisien* tended to
focus most on crime and human interest and put ordinary citizens,
rather than elites, at the center of their stories. Going beyond specific
frames and sources, I also found that media outlets whose audiences

had the highest concentration of cultural capital (as measured by education and occupation) tended to offer the most ideologically diverse news: *Libération* in France and the *Christian Science Monitor* in the United States.

Research that closely analyzes social class-based differences in the production and reception of news or other cultural forms remains all too rare. The need for this kind of structural analysis, however, is only going to increase. How the internet is transforming or not transforming social life can only be adequately understood in relation to such class dynamics. Euphemistically called lifestyle differences, such distinctions are at the heart of corporate marketing on the Web (Turow 2011).

Media sociology's distinctive contributions

If my analysis is correct, theoretical strategies ought to follow from structures too. Media studies departments are structurally compromised: their revenues mostly come from students who want to work in corporate advertising, public relations, entertainment, or journalism. This does not mean these students only want or will get a vocational education. It does mean that certain kinds of critical theory go over better than others: celebrations of "active audiences" and the liberating powers of new technologies are perennial favorites; theories whose critical components dissolve in their own obtuse abstractions threaten no one. A critical media sociology of structural variation is indeed structurally disadvantaged in this environment: its lucid questions hit too close to home. Early sociological interest in media notwithstanding (Katz and Pooley 2008), it's not as if there ever was a golden age either in sociology, political science, or anthropology for a critical institutional analysis of media, especially for studies focused on the United States. Rather than leading to resignation, however, such inherent difficulties only ought to strengthen our resolve to secure any institutional foothold that is possible for structural media sociology inside (as well as outside) the academy. Taking a page from cultural sociology, the time is overdue for structural media sociology to develop and diffuse its own "strong program."

In his book *The Media and Modernity*, John Thompson (1995) perceptively captured three major threads of media and communication research – a critical institutional tradition he primarily associates with the Frankfurt School and Habermas (but would incorporate in principle Bourdieu and other structural theorists), a hermeneutic/

cultural tradition, and a media-technologies or medium-theory approach inspired by Marshall McLuhan. Interest in media as technology has sparked the creation of an official American Sociological Association section in communication and information technologies. The hermeneutic tradition is well represented in the sociology of culture's culturalist turn, while the production of culture focused on the arts and music and inspired and mentored by Richard Peterson is enjoying a renaissance (Peterson and Anand 2004) in both cultural and economic sociology.

What is left for media sociology? Clearly, there is room for expansion in the critical institutional component of Thompson's tripartite model. Based on my casual observations of ASA conference catalogues and my experience serving as chair of the conference media sociology sessions one year, I would say that media sociology has become the primary home base and self-definition for sociologists studying news, social movement/media relations, social problems constructionism, and political communication more broadly, or to put it another way, organized communication practices in relation to media organizations (both mainstream and marginal). Media sociology can and must draw from – as well as contribute to – theoretical innovations in the broader sociology of culture and organizations. But whereas these other traditions can sometimes come off as abstract and disengaged, media sociology is almost always political, in the broad sense of the term. Media sociology ought to be – it isn't quite yet – the place where institutional, hermeneutical, and technological schools of media studies can engage in debate and mutual critique: think Bourdieu meets Alexander meets Latour. In other words, media sociology ought to privilege critical institutional analysis of media (given its current lack of representation elsewhere), but it should also remain in dialogue with other approaches.

To remain relevant, media sociology also needs to pay more attention to a range of popular cultural genres beyond news (see e.g. Grindstaff 2002; Lopes 2009). Sociologists ought to pay heed to political scientists Bruce Williams and Michael Delli Carpini (2011), who break down the artificial barriers between news, advocacy, and entertainment and analyze all of these genres in relation to their political usefulness and democratic relevance. Similarly, media sociology should not cede the question of innovation to organizational and economic sociology. In their research on "creative labour," David Hesmondhalgh and Sarah Baker (2011) draw on these approaches while also asking questions about domination and emancipation rarely uttered in these subfields. Yet they also avoid the totalizing tendency so common in critical theory in order to explore the variable structural factors that make creative autonomy more or less achievable.

At the same time, media sociology should take advantage of its position between sociology and humanities-oriented media studies to serve as an interlocutor, or even translator, between the two. Sociologists in interdisciplinary media studies departments have the rare opportunity to engage with theoretical and methodological approaches often effectively banned from even the most intellectually adventurous sociology departments – in some cases, to their detriment. Just to take one important example, American sociology is still remarkably western-centric, with Western Europe usually marking the outer limits of its international aspirations. As media sociology moves "beyond the western world" (Hallin and Mancini 2012), postcolonial theories (Shome and Hegde 2002b) can help comparative researchers be more reflexive about the fit of their ontological categories, as well as their broader epistemological and political preconceptions.

For its part, media sociology can provide some welcome clarity and rigor to the vague or overblown claims that often circulate in media studies. For example, what does it mean to say that global media flows are becoming increasingly transnational? In fact, most transnational media still operate in and through national fields. They may in some cases also constitute a transnational field (Kuipers 2011): in such cases, power dynamics are at least partially linked to the hierarchical relations among the nation-states involved. This is not to say that there do not exist transnational media, either large-scale transnational media or dispersed diasporic media. But what seems at first glance to be a chaotic, contingent, fluid process may in fact display patterned activity that can be linked to systematic structures of power at the subnational, national, and global regional levels (Couldry and Hepp 2012; Straubhaar 2007).

In his masterful social history of the telephone – whose introductory chapter offers one of the best critical overviews of social theories of technology – Claude Fischer suggests a tone of respectful dialogue with the more speculative branches of media studies while making clear the importance of empirically verifiable claims for sociological investigation:

Some writers, such as Kern, Meyerowitz, and Ronnell, have speculated about the implication of the telephone at deeper levels of the American psyche and of American culture than I have treated here. Ronnell has

suggested, for example, that the "ringing [of a telephone] corresponds
to a deeper, more primal voice within us, perhaps a parental voice . . .
We cannot resist the command." They may be right, but it is a challenge to find reliable, relevant evidence. Thus, these sorts of arguments
are difficult, if not impossible, to evaluate empirically. (Fischer 1992)

Media studies often imagines itself on the cutting edge. Sociology
can help bring it back from the abyss. Against the ever-renewed fervor
about how this or that new technology is going to change the world,
the sociological impulse is ever skeptical. How many people are using
this new gizmo? Who are they: what is their economic, educational,
and professional background? And what are they doing, exactly?
More often than not, it turns out that the new technology that is
supposedly changing the world is not only not changing the world
but is mostly reinforcing and extending pre-existing systems of power
(Curran, Fenton, and Freedman 2012). With Raymond Williams
(2003 [1974]) blasting away, Marshall McLuhan's formalist probes
about the inherent logics of media technologies are brought crashing
back to earth. When I teach McLuhan and Williams back-to-back,
most students think Williams won the "debate" but their heart still
belongs to McLuhan. It must be conceded that there is something in
McLuhan's often-eccentric diagnoses that still rings true.

Obviously, there are limits to the sociological understanding:
there are other forms of understanding and insight that should be
respectfully attended to. In his poetic analysis of the unique aesthetic
qualities of television itself as a medium, not as the purveyor of any
particular content, Raymond Williams seems to cede some ground
to McLuhan and to gracefully acknowledge the limits of scientific
analysis: "when, in the past, I have tried to describe and explain
this, I have found it significant that the only people who ever agreed
with me were painters." Maybe there is hope after all for a dialogue
between the ever-warring artistic and scientific fields.

There are also wars aplenty inside sociology. This chapter is a call
not simply for more sociological attention to media, but for a particular
kind of comparative sociological attention. George Steinmetz's (2004)
conception of "critical realism" comes closest to what I have in mind:
a theoretically driven, comparative research program that tries to steer
a path between large-scale quantitative research oblivious to context
and the small-scale qualitative research that insists that all cases are
ultimately incommensurable. As Steinmetz (ibid.: 394) rightly insists,
"the production of sociological knowledge involves movement among
case studies, comparisons among case studies, and theory."

While acknowledging complexity and contingency, this sociology searches for the patterns that help explain elements of social order. It continues to insist on the stark reality of the social, even if it is discursively constructed. And it engages politically not only in the critique of categories but also in their everyday use in relations of power. At every level, there is an attempt to explore how structures of power enable and constrain strategies of action. A media sociology that could accomplish all this would contribute mightily to both sociology and media studies. It might even be worthy of a manifesto.

Notes

1 Jeff Sommer, "A Mutual Fund Master, Too Worried to Rest," *New York Times*, August 11, 2012, available at: http://www.nytimes.com/2012/08/12/business/john-bogle-vanguards-founder-is-too-worried-to-rest.html?pagewanted=all&_r=0, accessed September 2, 2013.

2 I wish to thank Helen Nissenbaum for her helpful comments on an earlier draft of this essay. That at least some corners of cultural theorizing find sociology threatening or at least off-putting is evident in the online editorial published by the literary-arts journal *n+1* entitled "Too much sociology." See http://nplusonemag.com/too-much-sociology, posted April 8, 2013 and accessed September 2, 2013.

3 In *The Civil Sphere* (2007), Alexander has almost nothing to say about social class. The omission may not be innate to the "strong program" in cultural sociology but does seem to be typical of studies influenced by this approach.

4 Pessimistic theories of all-encompassing power are predictably attractive to each new generation of graduate students, and certainly this was the case with my own at Berkeley sociology in the early 1990s (going to graduate school, after all, constitutes a form of rejection of the system), as well as to radical theorists who eschew "empiricism" but effectively support their arguments with empirical evidence, just not systematic. It must be admitted, however, that variation is not only an empirical question. Holistic theorists may ignore variation because they think it is politically insignificant (e.g. variations within neoliberal capitalism do not take away from the fact that it remains neoliberal capitalism!). Research on the social effects of institutional variation has an elective affinity with projects of reform rather than quietism or revolution (the only choices that follow from totalizing models), albeit possibly quite radical reform.

5 I thank Patrick Carr of the Rutgers Department of Sociology for reminding me of the need to address both aspects of Anthony Giddens's structuration process, the structuring as well as the structured (see Sewell 2005: ch. 4).

6 Most sociologists see structures, of whatever variety, as extensive and

durable. Actor-network theory sees them as fragile, ephemeral, and atypical, "patches of order in a sea of disorder" in the words of philosopher Michel Serres (Law 2009: 144). Perhaps structuralists and anti-(post-)structuralists alike tend to find what they are looking for. Gil Eyal (2010), however, has usefully suggested one possible empirical accommodation between the two models: that weak actor-networks are the "spaces between" strongly institutionalized fields.

7 For example, Latour (2005: 37) elaborates a conception of politics on a global scale that is more open-ended than that defended by Habermas. He writes that, through "those makeshift assemblages we call markets, technologies, science, ecological crises, wars and terrorist networks," we are already "connected" – "it's simply that our usual definitions of politics have not caught up yet with the masses of linkages already established."

8 Drawing on diverse primary documents as well as direct consultations with scholars and policy makers in each country, we examined public service media policy and regulation in Australia, Belgium, Canada, Denmark, Finland, France, Germany, Ireland, Japan, Netherlands, New Zealand, Norway, Sweden, and the United Kingdom.

9 In all capitalist societies, social democratic victories (universal retirement income and health care for the elderly, disability support, etc.) were won over and against the "path dependency" of laissez-faire. Once institutionalized, however, neoliberal political forces have had a hard time repealing them: witness the ongoing difficulties of Republicans in the United States to privatize Medicare and Social Security. The same principle holds for media policy. The success or failure of efforts to maintain or expand the "public" component of the internet, against commercial encroachment, will have long-lasting effects (see Benkler 2006).

10 Sobieraj (2011: 164) at least notes in passing that "associations would be well served to work toward media reform (we all would)." This is admittedly not the focus of her study, which makes many other notable contributions. The problem is that the structure of the media system is so rarely the focus in any US media or cultural sociology.

11 Cranberg, Bezanson, and Soloski (2001) call attention to a particular shift in US securities law that allowed greater communication between institutional investors and company managers. This is a significant change because institutional investors have concentrated economic power and are arguably more oriented toward short-term profit maximization than other investors. Cranberg et al. argue that this legal change, combined with an increase in institutional investor holdings in newspaper companies (on average about 90 percent by the early 2000s; see Soloski 2005), has been a key factor in motivating cuts in newsroom personnel, the quickest way to increase profit margins. In this case, the authors' conclusions are based largely on temporal rather than spatial variation: it does not analyze cases substantially "less" dominated by

institutional investor stock ownership for the simple reason that few such cases existed in the United States at the time of the study.

12 See recent reports on the new nonprofit news published by the Knight Foundation, Pew, and the Oxford-Reuters Institute for the Study of Journalism.

13 Marshall Ingwerson interview with author, Boston, May 2011. These interviews are part of a research project on media ownership that I am conducting with Julie Sedel of the University of Strasbourg in France and Mattias Hesserus of the University of Gotteburg, Sweden. The project received initial funding from the Swedish Ax:son Johnson Foundation.

14 Michael Stoll interview with author, Boston, April 2011.

15 Author interview with Ingwerson, op. cit.

2

Linking Media Sociology to Political Development in Trans-Legislative Democracies

Michael Schudson

Media sociology has contributed much to understanding what the news media do and what forces impinge on the production of news. At the same time, while sociological studies of news production have usually asked, explicitly or implicitly, how well the press provides the information citizens need to make democracy work, they have rarely explored what democratic theory tells us about the role of the press in democratic societies. Notwithstanding the sophistication of media sociology about how news organizations work, it has usually been abstracted from the changing character of democracies within which journalism operates. Not only the specific processes of democracy change but even its objectives. Changes in governance since 1945 have substantially altered basic mechanisms and even ideals of democracy, but this has barely registered on civic education, journalistic consciousness, or sociological awareness. At least four important changes should have – and still should – provide a framework for reconsidering the political functions of the news media in contemporary democracies:

1 the rise of the administrative state: a move from legislative to executive power as the focal point of governance (and accordingly from legislative craftsmanship to administrative implementation);
2 the expansion of active citizenship from occasional, election-centered participation to holding government accountable year-round through social movements and street-centered political pressure, expansion of nongovernmental organizations that monitor government, development of consultative and advisory roles for citizens with government, and institutionalization of routes to political action through the courts;

3 an expansion not only of outside monitorial functions but internal ones, with both executive and legislative branches of government taking on a vastly expanded capacity to gather (and publish) data, reports, and assessments of their own (or each other's) activities;
4 the partial displacement of nationalism by globalism as a context for problem-solving and politically relevant models and comparisons.

If media sociology were to take these changes seriously – as a number of political scientists and political theorists have been doing for the past decade – would it look different? Would it address journalism's role in an original way? This chapter raises the question, seeking to call to the attention of media sociologists important work in political science, political history, political theory, and political sociology that implicitly suggest that a revised portrait of the democratic role of media is in order not because the media have changed – though, of course, they have – but because fundamental structures of democracy have changed. This chapter, then, is less an analysis of what media sociology has achieved than a plea for sociologists and communication scholars who study news organizations sociologically to set their work in a broader context. Media sociology, from its 1970s revival, has hitched itself to democratic values, analyzing media institutions to understand why their products have generally proved less adequate for informing citizens than scholars wish they were. But just what kind of news the media should provide citizens in a modern democracy depends on what a modern democracy *is* – and this is where I think media sociology needs a substantial face-lift. This essay, then, is not a review of the media sociology literature but a call to reconsider that literature in light of the new understandings of normative and empirical presuppositions about democracy within which it has been framed.

General characterizations of democratic transformation

In the long stretch of history from ancient Athenian democracy to the twenty-first century, popular government has shifted from what political theorist and historian John Keane has called "assembly" government to "representative" or "republican" government to "monitory" democracy. In what became the United States, "assembly government" was largely limited to local government in New England; the town-meeting model never became the template for US state or federal government. At the federal government, representation was the primary governmental form, even though in the beginning the general public voted directly only for representatives in the House of Representatives. The Senate was elected by state legislatures, and the president was elected by the Electoral College and only indirectly by popular vote. In the "early republic," as historians call the period from 1789 to roughly the 1830s, the government was an elitist republican government or what historian Morton Keller calls a "deferential-republican" government. In that system, ordinary citizens were not expected to "be informed," propertied white male voters had an obligation of periodic service – notably in the militia – and more esteemed and affluent members of the community were expected to serve periodically in public office.

In the democratic republic that followed – from about 1840 to 1945, politics became less a simple reflection of local social hierarchies and more the product of formal organizations, notably political parties, with the franchise extended to all adult white males. The political culture at the same time became more individualist, with information growing relatively more central, kinship and social connection relatively less so. Picture a transition from the settled, rural lives of a Jane Austen novel to the urban dangers, adventure, and opportunity of the young protagonists of Charles Dickens. The whole political atmosphere grew more democratic and more complex, with parties organizing lengthy and entertaining campaigns, with pluralist opportunity for protest, dissent, and demonstration, and civil society participation growing rapidly and well beyond parties into movements like abolitionism, temperance, and sabbatarianism.

In the post-1945 period, there has been a politicization of everyday life, a sprawl of rights-consciousness, new availability of low-cost, civic engagement from 10K runs for breast cancer research, benefit concerts and blogging to more traditional forms like petitions. Keane (2008) refers to the post-1945 era as the rise of "monitory democracy." In this era, representative institutions constituted through elections are not superseded but they are powerfully supplemented in ways notable enough to qualify as a new species of democratic governance; Keane's term – "monitory democracy" – is in my judgment the best to date and Keane's elaboration of what it means the most provocative.

It is not the only designation that has been advanced. In an impressive comparative study, *Democracy Transformed? Expanding Political Opportunities in Advanced Industrial Democracies*, political scientists Bruce Cain, Russell Dalton, Susan Scarrow and their colleagues discuss the changes of recent decades as the move to "advocacy democracy" (Dalton, Scarrow, and Cain 2003: 10). "Advocacy democracy" identifies some of the motivations for the public activity of interest groups, but significant parts of the "monitory" mechanisms of the present are not about advocacy at all, except in a sense the advocacy of democratic self-governance itself. Such activity would include: establishment, improvement, and public availability of government databases; emergence and widespread publicity of commercial and noncommercial opinion polling; establishment and growth of publicly monitored internal government audits and inspections (in the United States, notably the Inspectors General Act of 1978 and its subsequent expansion); growth of budgets and staffs for the development of more expert legislative oversight of executive agencies; development of new modes of citizen participation in government advisory committees; creation of governmental mechanisms, like the Freedom of Information Act, to assist individuals and private organizations to uncover information that government agencies by habit or subterfuge have kept from the public; judicial expansion of "standing" for groups to represent in litigation the interests of a public adversely affected by particular governmental decisions; growth of various administrative procedures, like those requiring environmental impact statements, for public comment and review. All these developments encourage public monitoring of government power; many ease the way for "advocacy" but are not designed specifically *for* the sake of advocacy. "Monitory democracy" directs attention to the variety of new ways that power, particularly government power, is monitored by institutions in and out of government, arriving at a set of institutional mechanisms and newly accessible routes to what Keane calls "the continuous public chastening of those who exercise power" (2008: 817). The contrast to representative democracy lies particularly in the term "continuous." Elections offer the occasional public chastening – and monitory democracy could not function without them – but monitory democracy extends the repertoire of mechanisms of oversight that operate day in and day out.

Other efforts to name the character of democracy in the late twentieth and early twenty-first centuries include French political theorist Bernard Manin's suggestion of "audience democracy" to indicate the growing role since 1945 for citizens in general and a shift away from a primarily parliamentary democratic style. In Manin's account, the eighteenth century saw the birth of "parliamentary democracy" where voters were to select a "person of trust" to represent them – a local notable who would vote on his own conscience, based on his understanding of the public good. This was supplanted in the nineteenth century by "party democracy" where elected representatives were members of parties expected to maintain loyalty to the priorities of their party platforms. After 1945, party democracies gave way to "audience democracy" where candidates were freed from party discipline and increasingly expected to respond individually to public opinion and a diverse array of interest groups, experts, and others (Manin 1997).

US historian Morton Keller speaks of "America's three regimes" – a "deferential-republican regime" that endured from the 1600s into the early 1800s; a "party-democratic regime" that lasted from about the 1830s until the New Deal; and a "populist-bureaucratic regime" that has been the framework of American politics from the New Deal to the present. According to Keller, what makes it "populist" is that politics has shifted from a politics of how to "constrain" federal government's power to a politics of how to "use" that power. In the party-democratic period, voting was conceived as protecting citizens' liberty from the government. In the populist-bureaucratic era, voting has become "an instrument to induce government to respond to the popular will as that will is expressed through public opinion polls, the media, and advocacy groups, as well as through the more traditional medium of the parties." In tandem with populism's displacement of parties as the lords of the public policy agenda, bureaucrats (and along with them judges) have "sought to displace politicians as the primary dispensers of public power" (Keller 2007: 202).

None of these efforts to give a name to the political structure of the present era has so far taken hold. All of them, however, basically identify the same set of political changes; there is a scholarly consensus across several disciplines that there has been a substantial political transformation and about what its essential elements have been. In all these discussions, the conventional view of both journalists and scholars studying news, viz. that journalism should inform citizens so they can vote in elections in an informed way, is clearly rejected as far too limited a model of how citizens participate in democracies today.

I want to offer a term of my own. It requires, however, modifying the name of the democratic system it replaces – what has most commonly been called "representative democracy." Retrospectively, that term places at its center just one type of representation, namely of voters in the legislature through elections. After 1945, democracies added new mechanisms of representation. Democracies today are not "post-representative" – democracies are more representative than ever. They are not even post-legislative, but they might reasonably be called "trans-legislative," dependent still on legislatures but cinching them into a system where they operate with respect to competing and constraining representative forms.

In trans-legislative democracy, what should we expect or want news media to do? We expect from the media "accountability journalism," the watchdogging of government and other powerful institutions; we expect the media to offer a model of reasoned discourse about public affairs; we expect the media to be model citizens of the "If you see something, say something" breed (to quote the brilliantly concise civic admonition posted for New York City subway riders); and we expect the media to provide a representation of and a tolerance for various legitimate viewpoints (what counts as "legitimate" is, of course, contentious). These, at least, are the demands I hear most often. These matters are more a part of the common public discourse than in the nineteenth century when newspapers were understood to be the voice of parties, political factions, and distinct groups and not professional journalists speaking to, and in a way for, the general public.

It is possible that the media's task in a trans-legislative democracy is little altered from what it was: inform citizens so they can vote intelligently. The argument I want to explore, however, is that changes contributing to the move beyond legislative democracy suggest new, as yet unacknowledged, democratic roles for news organizations. A media sociology appropriate to our day must conceive itself in relation to democratic norms that are not confined to electing representatives.

Four changes toward trans-legislative democracy

Rise of the administrative state

In the United States, the administrative state began to emerge at the end of the nineteenth century in the Progressive Era, but became central to the operation of federal government only with the New Deal reforms of the 1930s. Before 1933, there were only two important federal regulatory agencies: the Interstate Commerce Commission and the Federal Trade Commission (McCraw 1984: 210). Thereafter, the regulatory agency appeared as a powerful, new, and hybrid form in the world of government. James Landis, himself a chief architect of New Deal regulatory agencies, emphasized (and defended) their "quasi-legislative, quasi-executive, quasi-judicial" character (McCraw 1984: 213) The Administrative Procedures Act of 1946, as Judge Richard Posner put it, "signified the acceptance of the administrative state as a legitimate component of the federal lawmaking system, but imposed upon it procedural constraints that have made the administrative process a good deal like the judicial" (Posner 1997: 954).

Policy initiatives of the 1960s and 1970s were also transformative. The federal budget, in constant dollars, doubled between 1960 and the late 1970s after a "wave of federal initiatives in health, man-power, income maintenance, transportation, and urban affairs," as well as "consumer protection, the environment, cancer prevention, and energy" (Heclo 1978: 89).

Little in these momentous developments altered civic education or, for that matter, journalism. For journalism, covering elections, the presidency, and Congress seemed a full plate as each grew in complexity. Presidential primaries and the "permanent campaign" replaced party conventions for nominations, and the president's weight grew as government expanded and as foreign policy became a permanently large feature of presidential responsibility in a leading world power. Congressional operation, from the 1960s on, became more publicly visible and more internally democratic, less controlled by custom and seniority, more a platform for newer and younger members – and therefore an altogether more difficult story to report. The bureaucracy, in contrast, was something of a black box, still understood to be concerned with the mechanics of implementing laws originating in Congress and the White House. Of course, agen-cies operated with a degree of discretion, but, in the conceptual model of democracy that Americans still work with, administrative discretion is noise in the system more than it is government by design.

That conceptual model does not prevail in more specialized literature. An entire academic field, public administration, is primar-ily concerned with the legitimacy and effectiveness of government bureaucracies or, in the more exalted terminology of British civil service tradition, "public service." A key concern is the relationship of democracy and public administration and what has been presented as a central paradox: how can a form of government dedicated to public participation delegate so much of its daily operation and deci-sion making to a professionalized, generally unelected, and publicly almost entirely unknown, body of officials (Box 2007)?

From occasional to year-round political participation

Americans go to the polls more frequently, and vote for more offices when they get there, than in other democracies. Even so, this is an

activity of one or a few days per year; it rarely excites much attention, or turnout, except once every other year when national offices
are contested. But political participation has grown in nonelectoral
domains.

First, there has been a proliferation of opportunities for expressive
politics. Public opinion polling was originally imagined (by George
Gallup) as an alternative to political parties for identifying people's
political attitudes and preferences (Gallup and Rae 1940; Schudson
1998). Your agreement or otherwise with this description depends
on whether you think there is some underlying political essence
that polling taps – a dubious proposition, in my view. But certainly
polling offers a more continuous and granular account of where
people stand at a given moment on a range of public questions than
do elections or the opinions of political party leaders speaking on
behalf of "the people." Politicians have become highly cognizant of
polling and, at least to some degree, responsive to it. Other arenas
for political expression have also grown – not only in online communication but, well before the Web, in improvements in cheap, easily
operated printing technologies (the mimeograph machine, photo-
copier, commercial development of photocopy stores), in direct mail
solicitations (for campaign contributions or for membership in voluntary organizations), and in inexpensive, long-distance telephone
calling.

Second, social movements have become more easily mounted
and they do not wait for elections. Sociology has been perhaps too
successful in making the term "social movement" appear to be a
common feature of human social life, something that seems to have
been always with us, but historical sociologists – notably Charles
Tilly – have portrayed social movements as relatively modern. Social
movements were rare before the 1800s, but democratization and
democracies have encouraged them, and various mechanisms have
made them easier than ever to instigate (Tilly 2004). Only in the
early nineteenth century did social movements become "a distinctive,
connected, recognized and widely available form of public politics"
(Tilly 2004: 29). Defining this more fully, Tilly writes that the social
movement emerges when people make collective claims on authorities and "frequently form special-purpose associations or named
coalitions, hold public meetings, communicate their programs to
available media, stage processions, rallies, or demonstrations, and
through all these activities make concerted public displays of worthi-
ness, unity, numbers, and commitment" (Tilly 2004: 29). The social
movement "has arrived on its own terms," Tilly declares, when

these things regularly take place "outside of electoral campaigns and management-labor struggles" (Tilly 2004: 29).

In the past half-century, rapid and relatively inexpensive means of communication and transportation have made populous demonstrations still easier to stage. Telephones, direct mail advertising, cheap and widely distributed printing, broadcasting, and, in recent years, the internet and social media facilitate the formal and informal communications by which social movement mobilization thrives. Today, advanced industrial societies are "social movement societies" where social protest has become "a perpetual element" of politics rather than sporadic, where movement activity is so well organized that it must be regarded as an instrument within conventional politics (Meyer and Tarrow 1998: 4).

Third, organized interest groups have grown more numerous, powerful and focused on directly influencing government. For the United States, scholars see this dating back to the late nineteenth century (Clemens 1997) but note rapid proliferation from the 1960s on of private organizations seeking to exert influence on Washington policy makers. No reliable estimate exists of the changing number of organizations seeking to influence Washington policy, but in many sub-domains of public policy growth has been dramatic – as with groups speaking for the elderly in the 1960s, groups associated with the women's movement and environmental organizations in the 1970s, and citizens' groups of all sorts (as opposed to venerable, occupation-based groups) from the 1960s onward (Walker 1983: 394–5; see also Heclo 1978: 97; Loomis and Cigler 1998). While some scholars have mourned the long-term decline of voter turnout and participation in face-to-face, chapter-based federated voluntary organizations like traditional men's clubs, women's organizations, and parent–teacher associations (Putnam 1998; Skocpol 1999), others have observed a veritable "participation revolution" (Loomis and Cigler 1998: 10).

Why was there growth of politically engaged voluntary organizations after 1960? Political scientist Jack Walker offers a concise, four-part answer. First, long-term growth in educational attainment provided "a large pool of potential recruits for citizen movements" – and he might have added that this "long-term" growth got a great boost with the GI bill that helped make college attendance much more widespread after World War II than it had been for earlier generations. Second, improved communications made it easier for central offices in Washington to recruit members (initially through direct mail and WATTS long-distance calling) and to mobilize members for letter-writing campaigns and other active political expression. Third, the civil rights movement and the movements that learned from its tactics and its successes raised general awareness of shortcomings in American society, prompted a broad desire for social change, and bred a sense of crisis that stimulated a desire to be involved. Finally, with government programs expanding, particularly in legislation enacted during Johnson's presidency, government agencies themselves, along with reform-minded private foundations, promoted formation of voluntary associations among people who benefited from new social programs and among professionals and others who provided the new services, not to mention among business groups that felt threatened by new environmental, occupational health and safety, and other legislation (Walker 1983: 397; see also Loomis and Cigler 1998: 20).

Fourth, there has been a judicialization of politics, particularly in the United States, that has made the courtroom and not just the polling place a potential arena of effective individual political influence. Between 1850 and 1935, the US Supreme Court heard just sixteen cases concerning discrimination on the basis of race, religion, national origin, or sex; the person alleging discrimination prevailed in nine of the cases. From 1936 to 1945, there were seventeen more cases and the party alleging discrimination won twelve times. From 1946 to 1964, there were 106 discrimination cases, and the party seeking redress against discrimination won 90 times (Burstein 1985: 17). In a different version of this count, in 1935 the court took up civil rights or civil liberties in two of the 160 cases it decided; in 1989, it did so in 66 out of 132 cases decided (Leuchtenburg 1995: 235).

Greater use of the legal system for political ends rapidly increased in the 1960s. At the same time, the individual use of the legal system for personal ends has been discouraged by a strong political attack on "trial lawyers" and what critics argue are outrageous judgments to individuals who sue large corporations for damages allegedly caused by the corporation's negligence. Persuasive survey research finds that, in fact, Americans are rarely eager to solve their problems in the courtroom and "victims of injury are reluctant to sue, not over-eager." Several legal scholars have argued, based on this research, that, in the words of legal scholar Richard Abel, "our enthusiasm for participation in politics, the market, cultural life, and social services should extend to participation in the legal system. Litigation is an important form of political activity" (Abel 1987: 450). For Abel, "To assert a legal claim is to perform a vital civic obligation" (1987: 454).

Often, these individual assertions of legal claims are sponsored – i.e. organizations like the American Civil Liberties Union (ACLU), the National Association for the Advancement of Colored People (NAACP) and conservative public interest legal organizations have actively prospected for plaintiffs in lawsuits designed to advance political agendas.

The move from the parties and the press to a much more widely distributed array of civil society monitors is what Catalina Smulovitz and Enrique Peruzzotti have called "societal account-ability" (Smulovitz and Peruzzotti 2000). They argue that, in the formal governmental structure of democracies, there has long been recognition of a "horizontal" and a "vertical" dimension of account-ability. The vertical dimension is the institution of elections that holds elected officials accountable to the voting public; the horizontal dimension includes the various mechanisms that hold one branch of government responsible to other branches through a system of "checks and balances." They insist, however, that there is a vital third system of accountability in which civic associations, NGOs, social movements, ombudsmen, and the news media are the chief players. In societal accountability, organizations exercise control over government officials by exposing wrongdoing, activating horizontal accountability mechanisms, and by providing ammunition that can also be used in the vertical accountability system of elections.

The development of internal audits and their public report

In the military, there have been "inspectors general" (IGs) going back to George Washington's day, but not until the post-Watergate era did the Ethics in Government Act of 1978 establish a systematic plan that every Cabinet-level agency and most other major federal agencies (including the FBI, the CIA, and the Defense Department) should each have its own IG office empowered to audit the depart-ment on an ongoing basis. The IGs, through semiannual reports on the agency each is empowered to monitor, make public an assess-ment of waste, fraud, and abuse of public trust in the agency. In fiscal 2008, IGs collectively made recommendations to save over US$14 billion, conducted investigations that identified more than US$4 billion IGs were able to recover, produced more than 6,000 indict-ments, more than 6,000 successful prosecutions, and nearly 5,000 suspensions and disbarments (Council of the Inspectors General on Integrity and Efficiency 2009).

The Congress as a whole is a watchdog on the executive. Its

capacity to monitor the executive has not kept pace with the rapid expansion of the executive's administrative tasks, but has nonetheless advanced noticeably. In 1947, there were about 1,400 staff assistants to members of the House and 600 in the Senate. In the early 1960s, the comparable figures were 3,000 and 1,500 – by 1977, the number of personal staff members had doubled in each branch of the Congress (Patterson 1978: 165). Discussions of "civil society" or "the public sphere" ordinarily place that society or sphere entirely outside government, but this is an error. Civil society overlaps with government in that political parties – private associations contesting for government leadership – in practice take on legislative and executive power when they control the legislative or executive branch of government. And the actions of Congress as an investigative agency (with subpoena power) holding the executive accountable, and as a debating society airing criticism of executive behavior, are major features of what Congress does. These Congressional operations are not primarily about law making but about communicating and constituting a public agenda and a public tone.

The impact of globalization

Vast areas of the world have been part of a global society for hundreds of years, especially since the expansion of the European powers from the 1500s onward, notably Britain, the Netherlands, France, Spain and Portugal. Through colonialism, the world was both integrated and divided – politically and economically. What did not happen, however, was a moral or normative integration. In that regard, World War II provided a "decisive break." In particular, it was only after the war that "human rights became, for the first time, a recognized international issue-area" (Donnelly 1986: 614–15).

Uncodified transnational norms are meaningful but generally vulnerable to violations by powerful states; they are better enforced when powerful states find common cause against violations by weaker states. But, nonetheless, the norms articulated in 1948 in the United Nations Declaration of Universal Human Rights, brought to life by anticolonial movements in South Asia and Africa and persisting in the work of transnational organizations fighting racial and sex discrimination, have been the heart of an emergent, makeshift global society (Keck and Sikkink 1998). This led to a moment – now an almost comic historical footnote – when Justice Antonin Scalia at the US Supreme Court, in several widely noted opinions (particularly in his dissent in *Lawrence v. Texas* 2003, on the constitutionality of same-sex sodomy laws), excoriated his colleagues who mentioned rulings in foreign courts on the same or similar issues. Justice Scalia was certainly correct that the views of courts in other countries had no precedential force in American law, but he was wrong to imply that reference to foreign legal opinion was new or unusual for US courts. Inspired by Justice Scalia, a number of Congressional resolutions condemned or sought to ban citations of foreign law – and Justice Scalia himself balked at such legislative interference with Court prerogatives. But the episode illustrated sensitivity in American political culture about acknowledging transnational moral (if not legal) norms (Seipp 2006).

Obviously, there has been a dramatic growth of global communications in the past two decades. Not only have new technologies enabled quick, efficient news transmission to US news outlets from far away, but also far-away news organizations, bloggers and citizen journalists can now make their voices heard by US and other audiences around the world. Before 2000, very dedicated Americans could listen to the BBC on short-wave radio or subscribe to *The Economist* or *The Guardian*. But now this is simple and cheap for anyone with internet access. And, even without the internet, BBC News is available daily on many national public radio and public television affiliates. There has been a globalization of the world's journalisms.

Where the media – and media sociology – fit in

Whatever goes on in newsrooms today, it happens in a context different from the world Robert Park discussed in the 1920s, or Leo Rosten in the 1930s, or David Manning White and Warren Breed in "gatekeeping" studies in the 1950s, or even the works of the 1970s by Mark Fishman, Herbert Gans, Todd Gitlin, Gaye Tuchman, Marilyn Lester, Harvey Molotch and others that are still mined for insights about the media. On the contemporary stage of democracy, news media share their "accountability" portfolio with other substantial entities – and, at the same time, conceive their democratic mission in a way that is more expansive than even "accountability" suggests. I cannot expound at length here about journalism's role in democracy but, to simplify quickly, I think it is fair to say that journalism's function in a democracy operates in three different ways. First, journalism plays an institutional role with respect to government. It is a watchdog on government. But it is a watchdog whose primary audience is the government itself. It is a theater in which intra-governmental conflicts play out on a public stage. And it is all these things, whether it has a big audience out in the provinces or a small audience. It could be all these things even if nobody in Peoria is following the news so long as people in Washington *believe* they are following the news. It inspires in public officials a fear of public embarrassment, public discrediting, public controversy, or, for those elected into office, fear of losing an election. The media may be valuable not because they are nice or behave as honorably as Eagle Scouts (Schudson 2008: 50–62). Their value is that they make powerful people tremble. In this role, news is more likely to alert one branch of government to signs of wrongdoing in another, or one party's leaders to mischief in the other, than to lead citizens generally to action.

Second, journalism is not only about inspiring fear of publicity in government leaders but also about encouraging thinking, reflection, debate, and engagement among highly attentive publics – often, but not always, elites. The media are a forum for debate and criticism among highly involved and highly attentive elites. This may be the democratic function that comes closest to the Habermasian ideal of a public sphere.

Finally, journalism educates the citizenry at large and on matters of democratic culture as much as on democratic governance. News informs citizens of what their representatives are up to, yes, and what dangers and opportunities loom on the horizon for the republic, but also about who their fellow citizens are and how, for better and for worse, they act, think, and believe. In journalism's watchdog role, the general public normally takes a back seat. Journalism's "watchdog" power places the media among the checks and balances on power, and it is here that it serves as a "fourth branch of government." In journalism's impact on attentive minorities, it is the common ground of a public sphere, even if one that reaches the masses of citizens only as translated and retranslated, if at all. In its broad educational role, journalism puts the public in the front seat and democracy lives not in a government that is prevented by publicity from doing wrong but in a citizenry that is enabled by information to participate in governing itself.

Journalism plays a vital role in making a better, more democratic society in its educational role, even when the education it offers is not about government. Philosopher Joseph Raz writes about how important it is for the media to write about and thereby legitimate the various styles of life in society, giving them "the stamp of public acceptability" (Raz 1994: 140). These various "soft" topics, what was once disparaged at the *Washington Post* as the SMERSH topics of "science, medicine, education, religion, and all that shit," not to mention diet and restaurants and cars and sports and celebrities, can become distractions from public life; but they can also be doorways from private affairs to public life. We need no journalist to tell us we have neighbors living next door, but we may often need the stamp of media attention to humanize neighbors we barely know and to remind us that they live in a public world that they share with us.

Have the changes toward monitory democracy or trans-legislative democracy over the past seventy years, charted here, offered direction, or even pause, for how journalists conceive of their democratic role or how sociologists envision media sociology? They should.

Journalism is simultaneously what Matt McCubbins and Thomas Schwartz have called "police patrol" and "fire alarm" mechanisms for monitoring government and other powerful institutions (McCubbins and Schwartz were discussing modes of Congressional oversight of the executive – McCubbins and Schwartz 1984). When reporters are assigned to different beats to cover what editors judge to be the important aspects of public life, news organizations operate like police patrols. When disgruntled citizens, leaking bureaucrats, attentive friends and relatives of journalists, partisan and nonpartisan bloggers and others contact news organizations to grouse about something, they treat the network of news organizations as a system of fire-alarm boxes. The person who trips the fire-alarm box may save a house, a neighborhood, or a city; in the news network, that person may solve a crime, topple a corrupt official, a bank, or a government.

Governments have instituted their own police patrols and fire alarms but this is not widely understood. The media cover the reports of the offices of the IGs fairly often – but almost never mention what an IG *is*. What does an IG do? How does an IG come to his or her job? How long is a term of office – if there even is a term of office? What are IGs' powers? To whom does an IG report? Are IGs' reports public? I have read at least two dozen *New York Times* news stories over the past several years whose news comes directly from IG reports, always properly credited, but in no case has the nature of the IG's office ever been explained, let alone the relatively recent origin of the office been mentioned. What an IG does is taken to be just as self-evident as what a senator is, or what the vice president, Speaker of the House or Cabinet secretaries do. Yet all these other stations in the political firmament have existed since the 1790s, while the IG's office is only a post-Watergate reform of 1978. Journalists do not inform readers about this, nor to the best of my knowledge have media sociologists ever written more than two pages about these and other internal auditors and investigators of government. (I will claim credit for the two pages – see Schudson 2010: 104–5.)

But if accountability journalism depends in part on self-accountability in government, why is that not a topic for sociology? If hundreds of notable journalistic breakthroughs depend on the Freedom of Information Act (FOIA), why is the FOIA process not a subject of sociological concern? If training of FOIA officers in government is provided through an ironically-named voluntary organization, "ASAP" – the American Society of Access Professionals – and if ASAP membership includes not only government bureaucrats but also journalists and others who are interested in improving the operation of FOIA, why is there no study of this collegiality among reporters, activists, and the government officials who are commonly believed to be defending the confidentiality of government information *against* these very reporters and activists?

If media sociology is to be relevant to the study of democracy, it should address democracy as it actually functions. Instead, it has ignored fundamental changes shaping democracy today to focus on the newsroom's changing technologies and work relations. Newsrooms remain vital, but there is much other work that might be undertaken. We could use serious study of the role of the FOIA (federal) and state freedom-of-information policies and practices in daily journalism. How often, under what circumstances, with what assistance or training (from the news organization's legal staff, independent legal clinics, journalism associations like the Reporters Committee for Freedom of the Press, or journalism schools), and with what results do reporters file FOIA requests? How valuable has freedom-of-information legislation proved for journalism? How much of a barrier to journalistic investigation do the complexities, delays, expenses, and inefficiencies of the operation of these laws prove to be? What are the relations of reporters to inspectors-general? When IGs submit their reports to the Congress, do they also send out press releases? Or notify a select group of reporters? Do reporters routinely keep up with IG offices? Do IGs normally seek out or avoid journalists? And, to follow the fire-alarm box metaphor, how are citizens to know what the variety of alarm boxes are, where they are located, and how to raise the alarm?

Meanwhile, how should media sociology incorporate non-news organizations that have assumed news reporting and news commentary roles? The growing role of civil society organizations includes groups like Human Rights Watch and others doing serious news reporting themselves. They take an advocacy position, to be sure, but sometimes they are much closer to conflicts in dangerous places than are professional news organizations. How do we judge the work they do? How do we incorporate an understanding of these quasi-news organizations into a broader sociology of news? There are more, and more different kinds, of watchdogs with a shifting set of tools for monitoring government, than we have ever seen before, and still very few studies in the field loosely called "media sociology" that have kept up with these changes in empirical studies or conceptual grasp.

Media sociology has helped understand journalism by focused attention on the operation of news organizations but, meanwhile, the world that news organizations cover has changed in dramatic ways, including the ways in which citizens seek to influence government. The newsroom, and the study of newsrooms, still imagines the voting booth as the ultimate shrine of democratic participation. This is no longer the case. An understanding of the role of the production and circulation of news in democracy has to acknowledge and incorporate this into future work.

3

Back to the Future? The Sociology of News and Journalism from Black and White to the Digital Age

Howard Tumber

Introduction

The development of new communication technologies is altering the way people access information and creating a new dynamic in the production and circulation of news. The emergence of bloggers, startup media companies, citizen journalists, and other innovative news sources and actors are questioning existing notions of news production (Anderson, Bell, and Shirky 2012), how the media agenda emerges, and what types of relations among relevant actors are possible. This chapter revisits the contributions of sociology to the field of news production in the 1970s and 1980s, making a case for supporting this discipline's current importance in understanding twenty-first-century news production. The sociology of news production faces a new opportunity to be at the center of research by providing systematic methodologies and updating theoretical frameworks for critical analysis of new forms of journalism and news production. Similarly to the 1970/1980s, sociology can now provide communication scholars with evidence for the examination of aspects of journalistic practices. Proposals for discovering contemporary interrelations between different actors in the media structure should not overlook the contributions generated by previous sociological work and the useful frameworks it provided for understanding the complexity of news production.

The golden age of media sociology: 1970s and 1980s

The 1950s was the time when formal academic studies in the field began to emerge in the United States (Schudson 1989: 264). Most studies, though, came from outside of sociology (Tumber 2006), focusing on specific cases such as David Manning White's article (1950) on the gatekeeper role of a news editor in Chicago. It was at the beginning of the 1970s that sociologists' work in media studies produced crucial contributions for the development of this field. In the second half of the twentieth century, British media studies was just emerging and, although a lexicon with which to talk about news production existed (Breed 1952, 1955; Cohen 1963; Gieber 1956; White 1950),[1] it was Jeremy Tunstall (1971) who made the most profound and systematic contributions to the sociological study of media production. Prior to his work, mass media research was mainly approached either from a social psychology or a political science perspective (Tumber 2006: 60).

Collections edited by Tunstall (1970) and Denis McQuail (1972)[2] are considered milestones in the area of media studies (Tumber 2000: 3) and several authors consider Tunstall's research pioneering. His studies resulted from a sociological approach to national journalism. *Journalists at Work*, Tunstall's most revealing study, introduced scholars to new topics intimately connected with news production and political influences (Tumber 2000: 7). In the United Kingdom, media studies began to be considered as an independent area of research, largely due to Tunstall's examination of journalists' patterns of behavior and his efforts to develop a journalism literature (Zelizer 2004: 19, 56).

> A significant revelation of the Tunstall study, by contrast with generations of journalistic memoirs which had preceded it (and which continue today), was the extent to which news was not an unpredictable and chaotic universe of events but was the steady and reliable prediction, preparation and routine management of "institutionalized" news, a finding which has been confirmed in a number of succeeding studies. (Tumber 2006: 60)

Tunstall (1971: 6) aimed to create a conceptual framework for analyzing and research hypotheses for developing the field. His work greatly inspired other social researchers. His ideas and the study of news organizations and journalism were continued and developed between the 1970s and 1980s in the United Kingdom and the United

States in the sociological works of Mark Fishman, Peter Golding, Philip Elliot, Phillip Schlesinger and others, in what can be considered a 'golden period in media production studies' (Tumber 1999).

Sociology of media and journalism was characterized by critical study of what other disciplines saw as naturally given. This ethos of denying news objectivity by deconstructing news phenomenon as social constructions (Molotch and Lester 1974; Tuchman 1976: 97) was and still is crucial, producing a significant milestone in the development of news production. Sociology constructed a reservoir of concepts useful to making a coherent narrative and explanation of existing practices in journalism and news organizations (Tumber 2000; Zelizer 2009: 36). The existing conceptual corpus was based on well-established sociological theories such as Gramsci's work on the idea of *hegemony* (Dreier 1982; Gitlin1980: 252; Gouldner 1976: 232), Marxist views of class interests as a key engine of social interactions (Dreier 1982; Miliband 1977), and Weber's understanding of bureaucratic models and mutual affinity among institutions (Fishman 1980). However, it was the innovative analysis and critical revision of classical sociological theories (Dreier 1982) that generated a groundbreaking contribution to the field.

Schudson's (1989: 267–8) sociological analysis of news production and Zelizer's positioning of journalism in the academy (2009: 36) consider that most sociological analysis searched for behavioral patterns in a level of analysis focusing on a collective, macro level rather than looking at specific practices and deviations of norms. A recognized scholarly consensus existed about the role of 1970's and 1980s' sociology in showing connections between news production and channels used by official sources and political elites (Herman and Chomsky 1988; Dreier 1982; Fishman 1980; Murdock 1973), as well as the requirements of news organization to fit into a broader, economic capitalist context (Dreier 1979, 1982; Schudson 1989). The sociology of media could therefore outline general practices, journalists' behaviors, and the macro-level structure of news production.

Several scholars continue to recognize the great importance of the 1970s' and 1980s' work to explain the social phenomena of news production (Benson 2004; Gamson 2004; Nielsen 2012; Tumber 2006). However, other critiques state that this corpus of ideas and theories was useful for understanding journalism and news production in postwar, western societies but is insufficient to explain clearly how media create news in the twenty-first century. From this perspective, sociology is useful in presenting a professionalized image of journalism in mainstream media organizations, but leaves out new journalistic practices departing traditional mainstream hierarchical media organizations (Anderson, Bell and Shirky 2012; Zelizer 2009).

Some critiques of sociological explanations of news production are linked to the complexity involved in interpreting the cultural symbols and values required for communication. On the one hand, sociologists need to acknowledge the general context in which journalists and editors are embedded and that selection and narration of stories is only possible within specific cultural contexts that "intuitively" indicate what a good story may be (Gans 1979). Description of this broader context is part of a sociological understanding of the complexity in which journalisms and news organizations need to operate to interact with audiences and institutions and to communicate meaningful content. Gans's (1979) study revealed that much of what journalists see as natural resulted from culturally constructed values in specific national contexts. As Schudson (1989) and Benson (2004) suggest, ignoring local culture when trying to understand news production decontextualizes human actions, resulting in a sociological mistake. On the other hand, explaining journalists' decisions in terms of cultural factors has usually blurred the accountability of sociological methods and their theoretical assertiveness. The "soft" nature of cultural values and ideologies called to explain editors' decisions and journalists' behavior is seen as a complicating factor in the explanation of the news production process (Benson 2004; Gamson 2004).

Some of these critiques appear to overlook the fact that sociologists of news were able to make direct observations of journalists at work and follow connections of news organization with other institutions (Tuchman 1978). This was possible because sociologists already possessed theoretical baggage with which to understand the importance of socialization (Breed 1955) and institutional structures in everyday practices (Golding and Elliott 1979; Tuchman 1978). Different approaches to media studies already existed when the sociology of news was in its golden age. Yet, it was the combination of empirical observations of news structures and media professionals' everyday practices, together with solid conceptualizations of social phenomena that allowed for recognition of sociology as a key discipline in studies of news production.

Novel phenomena produced by different organizations and cultures in news production may not find a full or simple explanation in the observations of 1970s' and 1980s' sociology. Following existing critics, a new set of concepts and empirical work may be needed to explain current trends adequately, e.g. corporatization, media concentration, personalization, and self-broadcasting information produced by digital technologies and forms of interaction such as social websites, blogs and mobile communications. The analysis of UK and US sociology in the 1970s and 1980s nonetheless provides useful insight into current news production practices. To assess those contributions, key authors in this field need to be revisited: Bantz, Breed, Fishman, Baranek and Chan, Cohen and Young, Dreier, Ericson, Gans, Golding and Elliott, Molotch and Lester, Schlesinger, Sigelman, Tuchman and Tunstall. The strength of these authors' work pertaining to the so-called golden age lies in the knowledge gap that sociology was able to fill. Before the 1970s, what constituted a media event and how journalists produced news were aspects overlooked by the literature. These issues were first examined in sociological and political research by Tunstall (1970, 1971) (Tumber 1999, 2000: 3; Zelizer 2009: 33). The contribution made by these memorable pieces of work was not only their academic rigor but their description of journalists' practices in accordance with existing ideas. In other words, there was a "community consensus" built into sociological analysis of how news organizations and journalism might be understood (Zelizer 2009: 31).

This research, conducted during the 1970s and 1980s, focused on dominant news production practices in the United Kingdom and United States and considered newspapers and TV organizations with vertical hierarchical structures (Zelizer 2009: 36). Based on interviews, direct observations of newsrooms, and ethnography, researchers approached news production issues from different angles: cultural viewpoints, anthropological studies and observation of tasks and spatial distribution of teams in newsrooms, structural analysis of news organizations, and analysis of norms and values according to systemic perspectives. These social scientists could explore routinized practices, power relationships, and institutional connections from a critical perspective and in a theoretical framework lacking in other disciplines.

This research usefully explained key aspects of news production: the way in which conflicting interests between actors and goals could exist and dissolve in the routine of news organizations and the journalist socialization process (Bantz 1985; Breed 1955); the limitations of journalistic practice and news requirements imposed by the logic of existing news production structures (Breed 1955; Dreier 1982: 115; Fishman 1980; Golding and Elliott 1979); the existing complexity of the news production given by the coexistence of multiple agencies and layers (Fishman 1980; Golding and Elliott 1979); the impact of market-orientated news organizations and sociocultural ethos on the journalism profession (Bantz 1985; Dreier 1982: 114; Golding and Elliott 1979; Schlesinger 1978); and the coexistence of biases and interests in news organizations with professional news production ethics (Breed 1955; Sigelman 1973).

Examining different approaches and subjects of study, one can see the need for sociologists to cover different facets of the complex phenomena of news production. Some critics of the sociology of media seem to find, in the impossibility of single studies covering the whole spectrum of media production, a pretext for questioning the value of sociological analysis. Instead, the variety of approaches, from structural analysis of the political economy of media production to anthropological studies of the way journalists learn and follow the norms and ideologies of specific news organizations, can be seen as a valuable means of systematizing observations and generating analytical tools. Schudson's analysis (1989) and classification of the sociology of news into three categories recognized the contribution of sociological research to the field, although he emphasized the limitations of these approaches and the artificial divisions between them.

The technical, political, economic, and social landscapes are not the same as they were forty years ago when Tunstall published his observations on news production. Concentration of media corporations, new methods of producing and distributing news – including blogs and social websites – and the globalization of, and increasing connectivity among, people and organizations have brought new dynamics and actors into news production (Castells 2009; Tumber 2006). Studies considered essential for describing news organizations and their hierarchical and bureaucratic structures thirty or forty years ago may yet be relevant to understanding some characteristics of news production in the digital age.

Although the scenario in which journalists and news organizations work has changed, methodical observation and analysis of observed interactions at different levels can be applied to new forms of producing news and provide a framework to observe what changes have occurred in the politics of news construction. The analysis of journalists working with institutional and bureaucratic systems, for example, conducted by Fishman (1980) and Gans (1979) revealed news organizations' reliance on official sources and narratives for detecting news events and accessing information. The systematic analyses of Gitlin (1980) and Fishman (1980) on the prominence of official sources in journalists' coverage revealed the mechanisms by which bureaucracy and political elites reproduced established views about media events. Furthermore, methods used by Ericson, Baranek, and Chan (1989) and Schlesinger and Tumber (1994) to investigate source media relations could be usefully adopted to explore today's news production.

If sociologists in the 1970s and 1980s discovered that work routines for news production were established in a fashion that favored governmental reporting channels, corporate public relationship officers and big media agencies (Dreier 1982; Epstein 1973; Gans 1979; Tuchman 1978), it was because they could approach the media and explore the ways in which journalists worked, and the connections between the media and other organizations interested in shaping public opinion. Instead of suggesting that sociology of news can no longer provide relevant methodological and theoretical frameworks, we can ask to what extent sociologists have investigated the new dynamics and structures of globalized, digitalized media.

Updating definitions: journalism and news production

In what has been called the third age of journalism, from the 1980s onward aspects of professional journalism have been challenged with a blurring of the line between the public and journalists. The widening of professional practice and the incorporation of new channels of communication and interactive communications enable citizens to distribute information. These developments are having a major impact on the role of journalism, with the proliferation of sources involving the public challenging the role of journalists as "experts" in disseminating information. Journalistic culture is being transformed in a manner that alters the public/journalistic distinction (Tumber 2006: 59).

Definition and delimitation of journalism and news is becoming a contested field, due to the plurality of voices involved in producing and studying the news. Development of digital technologies, media globalization, and new fields of communications research and teaching have displaced traditional producers of media research – sociology, political science, and social psychology – creating new disciplines and departments of media, communications, cultural studies, and journalism (Tumber 2006: 65). As Zelizer emphasizes:

> Over the years academics have invoked a variety of prisms through which to consider journalism – among them its craft, its effect, its performance and its technology – they have not yet produced a scholarly

picture of journalism that combines all of these prisms into a coherent reflection of all that journalism is and could be [. . .] The study of journalism remains incomplete, partial and divided, leaving its practitioners uncertain about what it means to think about journalism. (Zelizer 2009: 30)

Different interests involved in journalism and its investigation make it impossible to find a single vision of what is news. Studies of journalism can be found in a wide range of academic research, e.g. communication, literature, business and sociology (Zelizer 2009: 29). Moreover, three main actors involved in media studies – journalists, journalism educators and journalism scholars – differ as to what is the proper field of journalism (Zelizer 2009).

The appearance of new actors, e.g. startups and bloggers, and of novel forms of news reporting, such as digital citizen journalism, have not expedited clarification of the field, but rather have increased complexity in media studies. Via the massive use of social websites such as Facebook and YouTube, news "can reach a huge audience quickly and at no additional cost. The presence of networked video cameras in people's pockets means that an increasing amount of visual reporting comes from citizens," as well as providing new tools for reporting and presenting news (Anderson, Bell, and Shirky 2012: 14).

The new communications environment facilitates the blooming of alternative forms of producing information in which nonprofitable and collaborative logics have found fertile grounds (Anderson, Bell, and Shirky 2012; Benkler 2006). The current news "ecosystem contains new assets, such as an explosion in digital data and computational power. It also contains new opportunities, such as the ability to form low-cost partnerships and consortia, and it contains forces that affect news organizations" (Anderson, Bell, and Shirky 2012: 18). Furthermore, people using social websites and blogs daily publish their own information in real time without the intervention of journalists, and data is gathered today faster and more cheaply than ever (Anderson, Bell, and Shirky 2012: 18). If alternatives to the dominant, vertically organized and usually profit-driven model already existed, they have now gained previously uncontested spaces and are more noticeable (Anderson, Bell, and Shirky 2012).

However, the strengthening of alternative media has not replaced the traditional logics behind news organizations (Nielsen 2012). These new forms coexist with traditional ways of creating news and traditional tendencies towards the centralization of media; profit-driven models are also replicated in the digital space (Benkler 2006; Vaidhyanathan 2011). Several different models for producing news, including diverse types of funding sources and economic goals (profitable v. nonprofitable), broader and specific audiences, political orientations, connexions with the governmental level, interest groups, private companies, political parties and nongovernmental organizations, all contribute to shaping a complex image of the range of practices included under the umbrella of media studies (Anderson, Bell, and Shirky 2012: 5–7).

As a result, discussion of the meaning of journalism is required if we are to understand the analytical approaches taken by the sociology of news and journalism. The definition of journalism, its practices and scope, is a contested issue (Zelizer 2009: 30).

Some authors searching for a framework to analyze new forms of producing news in the digital age suggest the need for multidisciplinary, collaborative efforts to understand a new paradigm (Anderson, Bell, and Shirky 2012; Gans 2011; Zelizer 2009). This option is presented as a synthesizing solution for covering the multiple views on the practices and study of journalism. If this option sounds promising for all stakeholders, it is also true that, in trying to find an inter-field solution, the study might end where the problem starts: "in being everywhere, journalism and its study are in fact nowhere" (Zelizer 2009: 29). As Gans argues, "getting researchers and journalists to work together is a daunting task, especially given the many differences between the two professions" (2011: 11). However, it is important to recognize that in the process of understanding new forms of news production, both journalists and researchers need to collaborate. If the media have changed, academics need to observe the current topics and forms of news production of this new structure.

In contrast to the "multidisciplinarists," sociologists have emphasized the need to redefine the sociological framework for studying news production and journalism. This position starts from recognizing the great potential of sociology for analyzing institutions and actors, proposing a review and update of existing sociological methodologies and knowledge to produce a framework relevant to twenty-first-century media (Benson 2004).

Different academic fields and media practitioners working on journalism studies have defined journalism and good practices according to the consensus built around their own communities, common practices, and interests. However, one of the main problems with existing journalism and media studies is their narrow and isolated approach to journalism practices. The "compartmentalization" of the phenomenon by scholars simply presents an incomplete picture of journalism and does not help to provide useful concepts for the clarification and analysis of the different practices involved in the production of news and its scope (Zelizer 2009: 34). Research community consensus is necessary to enable a new and useful framework. Sociology is well placed to build this consensus, as "what academics think relies upon how they think and with whom, and perhaps nowhere has this been developed more as in the sociology of knowledge" (Zelizer 2009: 30).

By looking at 1970s' and 1980s' media studies, it is relatively easy to see that sociology provided an array of sociological concepts and ideas to explain the world of journalism and news production. In recalling sociological terms such as bureaucracy, hierarchy, reference groups and norms and values created in subcultures, sociologists were able to meaningfully explain the world of news organizations. The needs, goals, and behavior of journalists and news organizations could then be interrogated. The sociological analysis of news production uncovered the complexity of the media phenomena. Consequently, sociology of media was (and is) in a highly recognized position and can provide a model for analyzing news. Sociological work's theoretical and empirical attempts to recognize the relevant variables intervening in news production need to be regained and adjusted to account for changes in the media field.

The first task of sociology is not to take for granted the value or objectivity of new ways of accessing information and producing news. Instead of looking simply at digital media as a source of information, Molotch and Lester's (1974) conceptual and methodological attempt to create a typology of news, for example, could be emulated to provide academic analysis with a framework for understanding the dynamics of news production. Some authors are already getting to grips with this challenging task. By considering the theoretical approach of three key contemporary authors in the sociology of media (Manuel Castells, William Gamson, and Jürgen Habermas), Benson (2004) shows that existing sociological work has been unable to provide a systematic model for understanding current production of political news. In his critique, Benson highlights the imprecise terminology and reductionist approach of some of these studies.

Benson argues that Castells's "model is too broad to provide much theoretical leverage; Castells's concept of 'media space' cannot help explain why some political debates are more or less simplified, personalized, dramatized, or contextualized than others" (Benson 2004: 277). On the other hand, Habermas's analysis of the transformation of the public sphere and the loss of rational-critical space for debate can be considered only a partial view of the phenomenon because his theory "largely revolves around the single variable of commercialization" (Benson 2004: 277). His revision of some classic theoretical models also shows an oversimplification in media studies that consider mass media as flat and common spaces in which different actors establish different interpretations and definitions of political events. These approaches do not account for the power and dynamics of media structures (Benson 2004: 278).

Towards a new approach for the study of news production

Digital technologies add new voices to the media landscape, demolishing old economic barriers to news production and distribution (Benkler 2006; Castells 2009). Similarly, new rules for accessing and publishing information are being applied in news production. However, this does not mean that old-standing institutions, interests, and learnt behaviors are disappearing. There has never been so much diverse and free-access information as it exists today in the digitalized world, but, like the majority of the TV audience who watch a few of hundreds of available channels, most people still regularly access a few well-known websites to get the news. A greater diversity of information may continue growing, but "audience attention spans for the news will continue to be bounded; the audiences with greater interest in the news and longer attention spans will be able to turn to targeted news" (Gans 2011: 8). "Internet is, in fact, exhibiting concentration: Both infrastructure and, more fundamentally, patterns of attention are much less distributed than we thought. As a consequence, the Internet diverges from the mass media much less than we thought in the 1990s and significantly less than we might hope" (Benkler 2006: 214).

In recent decades, "the newsmakers, the advertisers, the startups, and, especially, the people formerly known as the audience have all been given new freedom to communicate, narrowly and broadly, outside the old structures of the broadcast and publishing models [. . .] new tools and techniques, and, more importantly, new assumptions and expectations, and these changes have wrecked the old clarity" (Anderson, Bell, and Shirky 2012: 1).

Anderson, Bell, and Shirky (2012) and Beer and Burrows (2007) have identified a change in role from what was formerly known simply as an audience of consumers to one of users and publishers of information. Similarly, journalists are finding ways to incorporate the new possibilities for accessing information (Anderson, Bell, and Shirky 2012). However, it is incorrect to believe digital technologies have eradicated all previously existing relationships and power behind media structures. Furthermore, it would be dangerously mistaken to believe digital technologies per se are a revolutionary force (Benkler 2006) and that sociological frameworks cannot contribute to accounts of changes in the media.

Benson (2004: 275) argues that research on political journalism requires the application of sociologically systematic models for conceptualizing political news production. He makes a sociological claim to bring the specificities of the media and their structural analysis back to improve understanding. Media structure must be considered as an independent variable "in the process of political meaning making rather than just a convenient indicator of the outcome" (Benson 2004: 276).

For Benson, historical and cultural formations in which media institutions and other social actors interact are considered essential to understand the current structures operating in news production (Benson 2004: 279). However, the notion of culture cannot be used as an explanatory variable of practices and institutional logics. By recalling the existence of a journalist culture, or "national culture," to explain journalists' practices and news organizations' dynamics, the term 'culture' obscures factors intervening in news production. Instead, Benson suggests that three main structural factors – (1) commercial, (2) political, and (3) the inter-organizational field of journalism – should be incorporated in media production analysis (Benson 2004: 280).

Benson identifies four intervening aspects connected with the first of these three factors: "a) concentration of ownership, b) level and intensity of competition, c) profit pressures related to type of ownership and d) type of funding" (Benson 2004: 281).

Regarding political structural factors, Benson's analysis focuses on the state's role. There are four political variables affecting news production: (a) political pressure; (b) censorship; (c) the definition of the political agenda; and (d) the decisions taken to facilitate news production (i.e. financial aids, diffusion of technologies and networks for news coverage). In line with Fishman (1980) and Schlesinger and Tumber (1994), Benson argues that there is a clear continuity in the manner of news production. This is partially structured by news organizations' usage of some sources, especially official ones, over others outside of official channels (Benson 2004: 283). Finally, in Benson's proposal, the inter-organizational field of journalism remains a dimension requiring further exploration for the structural analysis of news production. The idea of consensus created among news production actors is understood as necessary to routinize a set of rules to maintain practices meeting news production participants' collective interests (Benson 2004: 283).

Benson (2004: 285) states that it is impossible to explain news production based on one specific variable or direct casual relations between listed variables and forms of media production. However, sociology can still provide a method and model, such as comparative research in Benson's proposal and Gamson's work (2004), to understand the different types of news production. Benson's sociological efforts suggest that sociology could possibly identify measurable factors for understanding the different types of news production. Sociology can offer a structural model to develop a comprehensive theoretical framework and a systematic approach for drawing relevant conclusions.

A comprehensive approach to the study of twenty-first century media and journalism requires a combined interdisciplinary effort from at least five different perspectives: sociology, history, language studies, political sciences and cultural analysis (Zelizer 2009). Tunstall has suggested that media researchers should continue to adjust and apply theoretical perspectives from neighboring fields such as organizational theory, conflict theory, linguistics, and collective behavior to offer a more complete analysis of the impact and logics of news production (Tumber 2006: 65). These disciplines also need to integrate those currently performing, developing and teaching the craft of journalism. To generate a revaluation of sociological studies on news production, one must consider what existing theoretical and methodological efforts in sociology are still relevant for understanding journalism and media production.

However, the revision of sociological definitions and frameworks for media analysis should also consider existing continuities in the way that news organizations operate and interact with other institutions such as private companies, governments, and lobbies. In the requirement to include the use of new technologies, actors, and the reconfiguration of roles, media researchers should not forget that there are several continuities in the way that news production is funded, influenced, and validated (Nielsen 2012).

When Tunstall began his project, the economic and political climate and media landscape in Britain were very different from today (Tumber 2006: 58). However, many of the observations produced in the 1970s and 1980s are as relevant today as they were forty years ago. Media organizations are changing and facing the need to adapt their method of news production. However, some of their aims are still secured within a social structure and dynamics that can be better understood with the help of the sociological work of Tunstall (1971), Breed (1955) Fishman (1980) and Golding and Elliott (1979) among others. Consider one example: analysis of public service broadcasters in countries such as the United Kingdom suggests they still "exhibit few tendencies towards post-industrial forms of production [and] they are still large, bureaucratic, integrated enterprises" (Nielsen 2012). These organizations play a key role in the media landscape and their characterization requires attention to the relevant analysis of structures, journalist norms, practices, and cultural environment provided by previous sociological studies. To ignore these works would be an academic mistake and a media studies downgrade. Moreover, there are enough reasons to believe that behind the technological changes and new practices, the mainstream news channels most probably will survive whatever the technology. As Schiller remarked, at the beginning of the twenty-first century "Tunstall's original and critical analyses are as useful today as they were courageous and far-seeing twenty years ago" (Tumber 2000: 7).

> Even in digital form, these and other mainstream news media will be owned and operated by large firms, not very different from the handful of newspaper chains and other large firms that have been supplying national news since early in the twentieth century. Whatever the shortcomings of large firms, at least they have funds to pay for as labor-intensive an activity as reporting the news [. . .] the basic news paradigm that has driven the national news delivered to the general audience for about a century will continue relatively unchanged. (Gans 2011: 9)

Tunstall's analysis of news organizations suggested a framework to conceptualize the logic and objectives behind news production. It identified four types of goals: audience revenue, advertising revenue, non-revenue, and mixed goals (Tunstall 1971: 51). "Tunstall's goal bargaining approach emphasised that no type of news gathering is rigidly tied to just one type of goal and that all specialist news-gathering fields include an element of each of the three goals with some fields lacking a predominant goal" (Tumber 2006: 61). In addition, Tunstall showed the problematic of power and influence behind the occupation and communication of media events and the relations between the source of information and the established journalists' practices for producing news. This framework could be applied to different scenarios and media situations for categorizing different types of news production.

It is evident that digital developments (Benkler 2006) have brought changes to ways of producing, disseminating, and sharing news that were not possible in the era of the early twentieth-century mass media. These new possibilities are creating new dynamics and methods for gathering and processing news that Anderson, Bell, and Shirky (2012: 13) calls "post-industrial journalism." The new process of news production and the news organization's adoption of new logics may involve an "increased openness to partnerships; increased reliance on publicly available data; increased use of individuals, crowds and machines to produce raw material; even increased reliance on machines to produce some of the output" (Anderson, Bell, and Shirky 2012: 13). However, these changes do not suppose a break with existing goals of news organizations. An analytical framework and systematic analysis are needed more than ever to understand changes in news production. Many of the logics and functions carried out by different institutions involved in news production may have changed, but others have just readjusted or changed their skin in order to continue with their own goals, standards, and professional norms and codes. Revisiting classic sociological work enables us to account for these changes and perhaps inspires development of comprehensive studies that could separate futurology and informal observations from firm, well-documented social research. Moreover, critical thinking is a valuable tool for analyzing new news production practices. The sociology of the 1970s and 1980s was useful in showing the role of institutions and the politics of journalistic practices in news construction. The sociology of the twenty-first century could indicate whether, in the use of digital media, specific data coding and editorial decisions are far removed from being more objective or an open form of producing news.

Conclusion

As it was thirty years ago, sociology's classical contribution has been to review critically the existing structure and practices which are usually not considered or taken as naturally given. The old sociological critical exercise of questioning journalistic practices and the structures in which these practices take place is as useful today as it was forty years ago. If some digital media advocates claim that the use of *big data* is an innovation, allowing journalists to access a deeper and more exhaustive account of the reality (boyd and Crawford 2011), sociologists should not forget that media, as Molotch and Lester (1974: 111) emphasized, do not reflect the "world out there, but the practices of those having the power to determine the experience of others." The sociology of media must examine more closely how these devices are being constructed and how decisions are made to filter digital information and publish some stories.

The sociology of news can provide more than just a critical view. It can also offer a comprehensive theoretical framework to explain news production. As it did in the 1970s, sociology can now supply systematic evidence for examining aspects of journalists' practices in order to understand continuities, changes, and tensions between news production's different actors. Emergence of new forms of interaction and communication should not prevent researchers from observing existing continuities in the structures of news production and media organizations (Nielsen 2012).

The great efforts of sociologists in the 1970s and 1980s were fruitful for the understanding of existing relations and structures of news production. The different methodologies and theoretical frameworks employed enabled empirical observation and the tracking of actors in the field and innovative interpretations of the interests, logics, and dynamics involved in the social construction of news. If the sociology of the twenty-first century is to generate a similar contribution to the field of media studies, it should start by complete immersion in the new structures and practices used for producing news. Only then will researchers be able to understand fully the new relationships behind digital innovations and existing organizations.

Notes

1 Gieber's (1964) more complete study on several news editors was still focused in the US state of Wisconsin.
2 Tunstall's (1970) *Media Sociology* and McQuail's (1972) *Sociology of Mass Communications* were readers which marked the beginning of a new era in media studies.

PART II
Media Industries and Audiences

4

Agency, Social Interaction, and Audience Studies

Richard Butsch

Sociology is the mother of many disciplines (Best 2001; Scott 2005), including media research.[1] To understand their relationship, I will focus primarily on the United States, with which I am most familiar and where communication research first gained institutional independence as a discipline.

Sociologists were some of the first researchers of twentieth-century media in the United States. They were interested in communication as fundamental to societies and particularly mass media in modern industrial democracies. Sociologists and sociology-based research continued to play a role in the development of communication research until the postwar era, when it became an independent field with its own departments, PhD programs, and journals. Sociology again became an important influence in the 1970s, but less directly, through its influence upon active audience approaches.

Throughout the twentieth century, there were two main sociological threads of influence on media studies. Together, these represent the core concerns of sociology more generally, i.e. the understanding of structure, culture and agency and their interdependence. One thread of influence focused on structure and included the political economy of media industry macrostructure and culture production in those industries' microstructure. Other chapters address this topic. The second thread focused on the agency of audiences, or what has become known as active audiences, which is the focus of this chapter.[2] Agency is an underlying assumption in sociological understanding of social interaction. Sociology's unique contribution to studies of audiences has been to approach them in terms of agency and social interaction, introducing questions and research methods that presumed and captured these in data.

By "agency," I mean the capacity to choose one's actions. Consciousness, reflection, thinking, acting – experiences we regard as essentially human – entail agency. It may seem at first a peculiar concept for sociology, concerned as it is with social structure and culture. Peculiar, too, in the minds of lay people, who more likely imagine psychology as the agency-friendly study of intimate relationships, and sociology as the study of structure that pushes people around and thus would seem more deterministic. But agency is how sociology explains the origins, changes in, and ongoing existence of structure and culture, through collective, collaborative, and conflictual actions and interactions among people, even though actors' agency at the same time is constrained by society.[3] As Marx famously stated in the second paragraph of his *Eighteenth Brumaire*, "Men make their own histories but not just as they please . . ." (Marx 1994 [1852]). They make their own history, not singly, but collectively, and that means through social interaction. Audiences are an example of people interacting and acting collectively. Sociologists studying audiences have tended to be those whose interests included people's interactions, micro-sociology, and who were therefore accustomed to thinking in terms of agency. It is no accident then that the Chicago School of sociology, as the center of American micro-sociology, was central to the early studies of audiences, and that its descendants influenced the rebirth of an active-audience approach.

Not all sociologists address agency and social interaction; many focus on large structures without much consideration of these phenomena. A few may even be characterized as deterministic. But since sociology's beginnings, major theorists have incorporated agency as central to their understanding of society, among them Marx (quoted above) and Weber in his concept of *verstehen*. Most structuralists do not deny agency but demonstrate that, as Marx notes, available choices and their consequences are enabled and constrained by social structure and culture. There was a renaissance of agency in sociology in the 1970s, at the same time as a renewed influence of sociological ideas upon communication and media studies. Even as some advocated Althusser's severe structuralism, others attempted to integrate Marx and George Herbert Mead, the "father" of symbolic interactionism, and hailed the social constructivism of Peter Berger and Thomas Luckmann's *Social Construction of Reality*.

Sociology, in its assumption of agency, has been an important long-term, although intermittent, influence on audience studies' evolution. The fluctuating influence has been partly due to contrasting conceptions of audiences: as active or passive – agent or acted upon – and as individuals alone or interacting in groups. These two approaches are commonly labeled on the one hand as "effects" and on the other as "uses and gratifications" and "cultural resistance." The two approaches pose different questions: what do media *do to* audiences versus what do people *do with* media (Katz, Blumler, and Gurevitch 1973/4), opposite presumptions of whom or what is doing the doing.[4] These two questions and their associated research methods belie fundamentally different conceptions of human behavior, media, and society. The former question gives weight to approaches that emphasize determination over agency; the latter to approaches that presume agency. They largely emanated from different disciplines, psychology and sociology, particularly as they evolved in the United States. Through a century, media-audience research has shifted focus repeatedly between what audiences do and how media affect them. This shift was aligned with the ebb and flow of sociological versus psychological influence in audience studies. This chapter traces the history of twentieth-century audience research in terms of the shift from agency to determinism and back. It ends by considering audience research's consequent compatibility with and potential contribution to sociology today.

Another way to assess agency's presence in sociology is to start with the negative: what does sociology not do? It generally does not take a deterministic approach in its explanations of human actions. As a field, sociology has mostly not been deterministic; micro-sociology almost uniformly starts from the assumption that people are agents who choose their actions, albeit within constraints of social structure and culture.[5] This distinguishes it from experimental social psychology, the other significant disciplinary contributor to audience research. Experimental method has steadily influenced psychology since William Wundt.[6] But after World War II, when there was a major push to emphasize "scientific" approaches, American social psychology shifted noticeably more to laboratory experiments. In American sociology, too, the balance of "power" shifted to quantitative quests, and influential centers of research moved away from agency and, for a variety of other reasons, from communication research generally.

Audience studies before World War II

Wilbur Schramm (1983), prime mover in establishing communication research as a discipline in the mid-twentieth century, cited early sociologists as pioneers. Making a similar observation about its more recent influence, Elihu Katz attributed a new "ferment" in communications research in the early 1980s to a "return of the humanities and sociology" and to a "requiem" for sociopsychological study of the persuasive powers of mass media. He wrote "the best thing that has happened to communications research is that it has stopped frantically searching for evidence of the ability of the media to change opinion, attitudes and actions in the short run" (1983: 51–2). Between the pioneers and the ferment, sociology's participation had waned and communication research was dominated by experimental social psychology.

Sociology arose in the late nineteenth century as an intellectual effort to understand industrialization, its disruptive effects on society and its impact on people transplanted from rural agriculture to urban industrial lives. In the United States, social change related to industrialization was compounded by a huge wave of immigration, with the foreign-born in 1910 constituting 15 percent of the nation's population and over a third of the population in the five largest cities (Gibson and Lennon 1999), the vast majority of them working-class, and many of them from agrarian backgrounds and newly proletarianized. This triggered fear and reaction among elites and upper-middle classes, leading some to depict these immigrants as racially inferior and generally un-American. In contrast, Progressives strove to help and to Americanize new arrivals, with settlement houses on the local level and labor and child protection legislation on the state and national level. American sociologists were similarly preoccupied with issues of the social control of these working-class immigrants and with understanding the cities and neighborhoods they inhabited (Corman 1996).

Some of the earliest sociological work on media concerned newspapers and nickelodeons in these neighborhoods. In the early twentieth century, faculty at the first sociology department in the United States, at the University of Chicago, pioneered participant observation research to study the city and its working-class immigrant neighborhoods. As part of this, they studied their use of newspapers. The Department's first chairman, Albion Small (Small and Vincent 1894), included a chapter on communication, newspapers as one example, in one of the first sociology textbooks, as did Robert Park and Ernest Burgess (1921) in their influential early textbook. Park, a former journalist and later departmental chair at Chicago, focused on the importance of newspapers for public opinion and for immigrants (Park 1922, 1923; Jacobs 2009), building on his dissertation about crowds and publics (1904), categories which included audiences. W. I. Thomas (1914: 635–7) described the role of newspapers in the collective actions of Polish peasants resisting their Prussian rulers. In each case, these researchers considered newspaper use as an activity embedded in everyday life, rather than as a singular stimulus causing individuals to think and act singly. Their focus was on social interaction through the medium of newspapers. The Chicago School showed more generally a substantial interest in communications as an important part of sociology (Buxton 2008).

Their ties to reformers and research on immigrant neighborhoods led some to become involved in studies of nickelodeons and their audiences (Lengermann and Niebrugge-Brantley 2002). The first research on twentieth-century media was conducted by social workers and reformers, often with the advice and collaboration of sociologists like those at Chicago, as part of a larger agenda confronting what they saw as the immigrant problem. The sudden explosion of cheap nickelodeons around 1905 precipitated a quick reaction from reformers and religious leaders to nickelodeons encouraging delinquency. These moral entrepreneurs (Becker 1962) were first concerned that children and teens were very attracted to "moving picture shows," and that they 'misbehaved' there in the dark. To provide evidence that something needed to be done, reform groups in major US cities, including New York, Boston, Chicago, Philadelphia, Cleveland, and Cincinnati, and even smaller cities such as Worcester, Massachusetts and Lexington, Kentucky,[7] went to nickelodeons to count unescorted children and observe their behavior (Butsch 2000: 150–7).

Quickly, however, concern turned to the impact of films themselves on children. Evaluating film content and theories about their effects on viewers replaced earlier observations of nickelodeon audiences. Critics from various quarters soon began reporting incidents of "youths" (teens) imitating behavior they had seen in movies, girls reporting that they learned how to kiss, boys how to steal. They expressed fear that movies were corrupting these youths and called for censorship. This soon led to censorship at city- and state-levels and even to the threat of a national censorship board (Grieveson 2004). This moral panic was based on mostly unverified anecdotes presented by moral guardians of various sorts and reported in newspapers, rather than on surveys or other systematic observation. However, this fear was soon increased by well-known theories purporting to explain the psychology of individuals in crowds. Prominent Harvard psychologist Hugo Munsterberg (Munsterberg and Lansdale 2001) published one theory of the effects of film. Munsterberg's approach presumed each individual viewer was independent and isolated from each others in dark theaters, a purely psychological perception process and emotional reaction, stripped of social interaction. Consistent with racialist crowd psychology theories, he presumed certain types of people (women, "lesser" races and nationalities, lower classes, poor immigrants) were more susceptible to suggestion and more controlled by the film than others, and were less able to decide for themselves independent of suggestion or, put differently, their behavior was more determined by their hereditary traits, making them more vulnerable to their environment (the film), than by their own agency (Butsch 2008).

The emphasis on media controlling users' thoughts and behavior continued in the 1920s (e.g. Mitchell 1929) and culminated with the Payne Fund studies of the late 1920s and early 1930s. A minister and classic moral entrepreneur, William Short, who promoted this project, wished to prove the effects of film on children by recruiting well-known academic researchers and their graduate students to support a crusade for film censorship. Among those he convinced to participate were prominent psychologists L. L. Thurstone, Vernon Miller, and George Stoddard (later president of the University of Illinois, who had invited Wilbur Schramm to create its School of Communications), education researcher and director of the project W. W. Charters, and sociologists Robert Park, Herbert Blumer, Philip Hauser, Paul Cressey, and Frederick Thrasher (Jowett, Jarvie, and Fuller 1996: xv–xxiii), faculty and former students at the University of Chicago Department of Sociology. Despite the sociologists' background in participant observation and community studies, most research emphasized children's psychological and physiological reactions to movie content. Cressey (1938) later criticized the research for its lack of sociological context and narrow-effects approach. He came close to arguing instead for an approach focused on what people do with media.

W. W. Charters turned his attention in the 1930s to his Bureau of Education Research at Ohio State University. With further Payne funding, he researched radio audiences (Butsch 2000). Influenced by that work, Princeton psychologist Hadley Cantril began experimental research on the effects of radio broadcasts, which he published with his Harvard mentor Gordon Allport (1935: x). Cantril was one of a group of academics and public intellectuals in the 1920s impressed or alarmed by the apparent effectiveness of World War I print propaganda upon opinions and beliefs of civilian populations in the United States (Gary 1999). Combined concerns about the dangers of propaganda in a democracy and the influence of films on children ushered in an effects approach to studying audiences, and lurking within it, presumption that media messages *caused* people to think and act accordingly. Yet, too, Cantril exemplified the predominant approach in pre-1950s' American social psychology, which was more concerned with groups and social interaction and more compatible and collaborative with sociology. Although he sometimes used experimental methods, he also conducted research in natural settings (Cantril 1940; Hastorf and Cantril 1954), including field experiments, and emphasized social processes and social interaction rather than simply the one-way effect of messages upon isolated individuals in a laboratory setting. He was also a pioneer in opinion polling and founder of *Public Opinion Quarterly*.

It was not so much that these researchers denied human agency as that their approach neglected agency. Since crowd psychology of the late nineteenth century, terms such as implanting, suggestion, emotional contagion, emotional possession, and impulse, combined with claims about lower status groups' genetic susceptibilities to these phenomena, were used to explain hypnosis, crowd behavior, and imagined direct effects of radio, film, and live speakers. All of these theories – some even adopted by racially inclined early sociologists – presumed that these processes supplanted agency. Explanations in terms of biological inequalities enabled theorists to exempt themselves and other elites from these influences and retain their own agency, while denying it among women and the masses.

In the late 1930s, the Rockefeller Foundation recruited Cantril to establish a Radio Research Project at Princeton. However Cantril soon withdrew from the directorship to pursue other research, replaced by recent European émigré Paul Lazarsfeld, on the recommendation of Columbia University sociologist Robert Lynd. Lazarsfeld would change the course of the embryonic field of communication research, from experimental research to surveys revealing social processes of opinion formation. He moved the project to Columbia University, where he and his center were affiliated with the Department of Sociology, and where his center quickly became the foremost source of audience research (Morrison 1998; Glander 2000). In 1944, in a study of radio's impact on voters' choices, he and his colleagues documented a two-stage opinion formation process. In a study of women, he found that after listening to radio they conversed with friends whose opinion they respected and trusted to evaluate the broadcast and form their own opinion. Lazarsfeld and his co-authors labeled these friends, "opinion leaders" (Lazarsfeld,

Berelson, and Gaudet 1944; Katz and Lazarsfeld 1955).[8] This was an important turning point, as it debunked the belief that radio affected listeners directly and caused them to think and act accordingly. It indicated instead that radio listeners did not simply swallow whole what they had heard, but engaged in a social process, discussing with peers before deciding their views, a clear case of agency and social interaction and a real-world example of publics as theorized by Tarde, Park, Dewey and others (Butsch 2008). This opened the door for the reintroduction into audience study of agency and the question "what do people *do* with media?"

This is not to say that media had no effect. Lazarsfeld's research enterprise was devoted to the study of effects and quantitative measurement. Even after demonstrating that direct, short-term effects were limited, he hoped eventually to demonstrate broader, "long-term" effects. Recognizing audience agency does not require denying media effect; it redefines "effect" from determinate to influential and shifts attention to what audiences do with that influence. Almost every public or scholarly interest in media has been motivated by the expectation that media do have some influence on audiences and on society, but not necessarily a determinate influence.

Community study methods used in *The People's Choice* went beyond effects, allowing room for respondents' own voices and designing interview questions to reveal interactions among voters. Focus on interaction facilitated the inclusion of agency, since interaction lends itself to a model based on deciding to act. *Personal Influence* would continue this focus on group interaction rather than media effect (Park 2008: 254–5; see also Rossi 1959). This different emphasis is characteristic of the sociological tradition in community studies and micro-sociology rather than that of postwar American experimental social psychology. Lazarsfeld and his co-authors introduced it almost serendipitously as they researched the effects of radio, which shifted attention to agency, social interaction, and active audiences. (Ironically, Lazarsfeld had an applied mathematics degree and had been a psychology professor in Austria and some of his co-authors had been trained in psychology. See Robinson 2011). Events during World War II would soon shift research toward experimental methods, but this opening to agency would be pursued by his co-author, sociologist Elihu Katz, and would gain new influence in the 1970s.

World War II to the 1970s: experimental social psychology

During World War II, US government funding redirected communication research again to media effects and to experimental psychological research. The military invested heavily in experimental research on "persuasion" – a word free from the tarnish of the term "propaganda." Sociologist Samuel Stouffer was appointed head of the Research Branch of the Information and Education Division of the War Department to direct a grand research enterprise on soldiers' morale. In his preface to *The American Soldier* (Stouffer et al. 1949), he stated that his colleagues preferred experimental research methods establishing causes, in contrast to Lazarsfeld and associates' focus on social processes. At a public relations conference, Stouffer (1953: 9) asserted his own preference for the laboratory experiment approach.

The list of psychologists employed in this and other similar government offices during the war reads like a "who's who" in American social psychology of the 1950s and 1960s.[9] When they returned to their universities after the war, a core group formed at Yale, in its new psychology building and department, generously funded by the Rockefeller Foundation (Butsch 2008). The US government, and especially the Department of Defense, continued to heavily fund experimental social psychological research. Many articles published in the *Journal of Personality and Social Psychology* and the *Journal of Experimental Social Psychology*, the leading US journals in the field at the time, acknowledged government and military funding. This enabled the institutionalization of experimental method as the dominant paradigm and attitude change (the new term for persuasion) as the major research topic in social psychology for three decades.

The shift toward experimental method is more significant for its assumptions than its conclusions. It was not that social psychologists themselves assumed that people lacked agency, or that actions were determined only by forces acting on people, but that there was a powerful professional preference for experimental method that was based on these assumptions. Experimental method is quite valuable in addressing causal questions. But to do this, it excludes consideration and precludes observation of the *inter*action and agency implicit in communication. Experimental method considers only the one-way action of independent upon dependent variable. It thus led to constructing audiences as isolated individuals stimulated by a media message which caused their thinking and behavior, not as people in groups interacting with each other. By virtue of the question asked (about media causing effects) and the experimental method used, action, and especially interaction, *by* audience members was seldom part of the research question.[10] The method effectively assumes that there is no agency, only unaccounted for independent variables, and that, by accounting for enough independent variables, one could apportion cause to account for all variation in response, leaving no place for agency in methodological and statistical logic. The only place for agency in equations for analysis of variance, the statistic for experimental design, would be as part of the error term, which is assumed to be composed of effects not yet determined. The goal of the method is to reduce this error term by progressively adding more terms for the effects of additional independent variables in the equation.[11]

After the war, communications research began to gain institutional status independent of its parent disciplines. Wilbur Schramm founded doctoral graduate programs in communication research at Iowa, Illinois and Stanford with a regular stream of large research grants from government agencies (Rogers 1994). The new discipline adopted the methods of experimental social psychology that were so well funded by the US government. Hundreds of studies from the 1950s through the 1970s tried to determine the effects of media on individuals (Gordon and Verna 1978).

The disappearance of agency and social interaction from audience research occurred as part of broader cultural changes that implicitly accepted the idea that people's agency could be overridden by the power of media. Widespread concerns about propaganda and other dangers of media took a darker turn with the Cold War. Public intellectuals as well as academics decried mass society, mass culture, and mass man (Jacobs 1959; Kornhauser 1959; Rosenberg and White 1957). Politicians and popular media proclaimed that communist brainwashing and corporate subliminal advertising could manipulate peoples' thoughts and desires without their conscious awareness (Butsch 2008). Churches, medical associations, and others advocated censorship and government regulation of media, particularly television. Congress repeatedly held investigative hearings on the dangers of media (Gilbert 1986). Within this climate of fear and moral panic, it is unsurprising that research presuming passive audiences seemed reasonable, even when the research itself contradicted those fears, indicating that media had only "limited effects" in the short term. One consequence was that audiences became the principal focus of communication research and the idea of active audiences choosing how to use television and other media for their own purposes was discarded.

Rediscovering active audiences since the 1970s

In the late 1950s, the civil rights movement shifted from its legal strategy to sit-ins, which began to appear on television for all America to see (Torres 2003). By the mid-1960s, others, not only in the United States, were agitating against institutions and their policies: youth opposed the Vietnam War, students opposed university administrations, women protested their subordination, and the elderly demanded poverty relief. These movements also created new styles and music to express their new values. With so many actively challenging authority, the image of the conformist, passive, media-manipulated mass man lost relevance. Furthermore, in the late 1970s, television itself began to change, as cable, VCR and remote controls gave audiences greater control over viewing (Butsch 2000), making active audiencing undeniable.

Academic attention shifted from what media did to audiences to what audiences did with media. American and British researchers independently initiated new developments in this direction. In the United States, Lazarsfeld and associates' social process approach reappeared as a "uses and gratifications" approach that initiated a shift of the center of gravity from effects to audience actions (Katz, Blumler, and Gurevitch 1973/4). Katz and Lazarsfeld's *Personal Influence* could not carry the day in the 1950s, when the experimental effects approach was rising in an era of unquestioned faith in science and lavish government research funding.[12] But the idea of audiences with agency began to regain traction in the 1970s. While *Personal Influence* (1955) might be considered a closing statement of the Lazarsfeld era, Katz, Blumler and Gurevitch's "Uses and Gratifications" (1973/4) might similarly be considered the symbolic beginning of a new era. By that time, research had established that short-term effects of media were limited, government funding of it began to shrink (Gans 1972), and experimental social psychologists began to question their own methods (Faye 2012; Greenwood 2004; McGuire 1976; Sherif 1977).

While the Lazarsfeld tradition was based on surveys, the revival was founded on another traditional sociological research method, observation in natural settings, a striking contrast to the laboratory conditions of experimental effects research and a revival of Chicago School methods. Buried in the five volumes of research reports from the US Surgeon General's Commission on Television and Social Behavior (Comstock et al. 1972) was a study that attached a camera to televisions in the homes of volunteer families and recorded what people were doing while the television was turned on (Bechtel, Achelpohl, and Akers 1972).[13] This study documented what Roger Silverstone (1994) later described as the embeddedness of television in everyday life and relationships. Although this study itself had little traceable influence, it seemed to presage the coming shift in research approaches to television. By the 1980s, American communication researchers increasingly observed what people said and did with television in their homes and elsewhere (Lindlof 1987; Lull 1990; McCain 1982), following the directive to focus on how people *use* television and other media. This new initiative also went beyond the uses and gratifications approach, which at its core still examined the individual user. In contrast, the new approach attended to people's interactions in using media – thus the observation of television embedded in family interaction, and the interpretation of audience practices as culture.

In Britain, the new Centre for Contemporary Cultural Studies (CCCS) at the University of Birmingham also adopted participant observation methods to study how the British working class used mass cultural goods and media to create their own culture. The work was partly inspired by British postwar youth subcultures of the 1950s and 1960s. It first drew upon American sociological studies of deviance (Critcher 1979; Gray et al. 2007: 3). Literature professor Richard Hoggart founded the Centre in 1964 for the purpose of exploring working-class culture in the way that academics had explored upper-class cultures of literature and art. Stuart Hall directed the Centre from 1968 to 1979, during which time what became known as British cultural studies emerged. In the early 1970s, Hall (1980) rejected the premises of effects research that meanings were fixed in messages and consumed whole by receivers. Instead, he argued that messages are always open to multiple interpretations, even though there are intended "preferred readings," thus positioning audiences as active interpreters rather than as passively programmed. This led to research on audiences constructing their own meanings from media texts and all sorts of other mass-produced culture, sometimes resisting preferred readings and substituting alternative or oppositional ones (Hall and Jefferson 1976; Hebdige 1979), the cultural studies version of how people use media.

Much has been made of CCCS foundations in the work of Raymond Williams, Edward P. Thompson, and Antonio Gramsci, so much so that its sociological roots are often scarcely mentioned (but see Denzin 1992; Wolff 1999). Yet in its focus on class and culture, its research methods and its presumption of agency, cultural studies was thoroughly sociological. This is not to deny that CCCS drew on many sources, including radical structuralism, for theory and inspiration, and was insistently eclectic, absorbing ideas from any field, indiscriminate about disciplinary boundaries, so long as they served a purpose. The purpose, the research question, however, was almost always sociological. The 1970s' working papers and books, the "classics" that established this new field, are filled with citations of and engagement with sociology and particularly American sociology's participant observation research tradition rooted in the Chicago School (Gray et al. 2007). Its student "working groups" that produced the "classics" began by studying and evaluating sociological research on deviance and working-class culture, using it as a source of research methods and the starting point for its own studies of working-class youth subcultures (Critcher 1979). For example, the path-breaking *Resistance Through Ritual* (Hall and Jefferson 1976) that introduced the concept of cultural resistance opens with John Clarke's sociological critique of the construction of working-class youth as deviant. Throughout, it draws on sociological concepts and literature on subcultures and deviance. The book ends with two essays on participant observation research methods (Butters 1976; Roberts 1976).

CCCS contributions to audience studies were similarly rooted in sociology and its research methods. Studies of television audiences (Brunsdon and Morley 1978; Hobson 1982; Morley 1986) used participation observation and in-depth, open-ended interviews with television viewers expressing what the shows meant to them. Both British and American studies became labeled as audience "ethnographies," although the label misrepresented their methods and was criticized for not being anthropological (McGuigan 1992; Nightingale 1993). Ethnography and participant observation both share the same goal – "to grasp the native's point of view," as anthropologist Bronislaw Malinowski (1922: 25) put it. The problem was the label: the studies themselves clearly and explicitly draw upon methods rooted in sociology.

Work at the CCCS soon attracted wide attention, probably because much of it focused on and tried to explain a controversial contemporary topic, 1960s' youth culture, and because it resonated with young scholars who had participated in the movements and youth subcultures of the 1960s in the United States and Britain, and who were beginning academic careers in the 1970s (Maynes 1982: 4). It was also reinforced by new initiatives in British and American sociology and history that similarly focused on working-class cultures (e.g. Samuel 1981). In sociology, changes were also brewing in approaches to the study of youth and deviance in the United States (Becker 1962; Chambliss 1973) and Britain (Cohen 2002), notably more sympathetic studies of working-class cultures.

The considerable research literature that we now have on media audiences and the active role they play as they use media, including a rich body of newer work on people *using* the internet, has continued to draw upon these sociological questions and methods. Even the history of audiences that has grown as part of this work has been based on applying sociological thinking to the past, using documents to hear audiences speak for themselves and others speak about audiences (Butsch 2000; Fuller 1996; McCarthy 2001). The focus on what people *do* with media has grown more necessary with greater convergence and mobility of media technologies, reaffirming the continuing importance to audience studies of sociology's research methods and presumption of social constructivism.

Media studies contributions to sociology: media sociologists seek a home

Audience studies has grown dramatically, venturing far beyond the television and the individual, attracting scholars from many disciplines, and drawing upon the legacy left by past sociologists. Today, media studies offers back to its parent discipline a sociologically grounded body of research compatible with other areas of sociology and with sociology's mission.

However, despite this growth, in the United States at least, sociologists interested in media must look outside sociology for publishing and recognition (Katz 2009; Pooley and Katz 2008). Introductory sociology textbooks provide no chapters and little discussion of media and its social significance. There are no sociology-sponsored journals devoted to media, at least in the United States. There is no section on media in the American Sociological Association. Closest to it is a section on culture (Wolff 1999). It was originally inspired by an organizational approach that focused on the production end of media and culture. As it grew, it defined culture quite broadly, encompassing topics from hobos to the death penalty, civility to childhood and the politics of water. Through three decades, less than 10 percent of the section's awards for books and articles were on topics concerning media.

In 1972, Herbert Gans decried sociology's neglect of media:

"Once upon a time, especially in the 1930s and 1940s, mass communications was a vital and productive field in academic sociological research, but ever since it has suffered from a drastic famine that shows no signs of abating." That neglect could be explained by the dominance then of experimental effects research that was of slim sociological interest. The recent neglect, however, comes during a renaissance in active audience research that is thoroughly imbued with sociological ideas and interests and to which sociologists continue to contribute.

What could sociology gain from audience studies? First, as the field that encompasses *all* aspects of modern society, it needs to include media in order to understand today's societies which are infused with media at both the macro and micro levels. Second, audience studies, built with sociological imagination and based on sociological questions, could readily be incorporated into sociology proper to fill the gap left by the sociology discipline proper. Third, sociology could weave this knowledge into its broader understanding of society and social institutions as well as of social interaction, community, and collective action. For example, audience studies in particular are relevant to sociologies of collective behavior and politics through their association with moral panics, crowds, and publics (Butsch 2008; Critcher 2003; Livingstone 2005). Audience "ethnography" studies provide new understandings of families at home (Lull 1990; Morley 1986) and more recently of small groups via social media and the internet. Fourth, sociology could become more relevant and useful addressing public issues concerning media use and policy. Last, sociology could build a partnership with audience studies to further sociology's influence. Just as sociology needs audience studies, so, too, audience studies continues to need sociology. It is important that a sociological imagination informs understandings of media, as it has in the past, lest the subtlety and complexity of their social and political significance be lost.

Notes

1 Thanks to Elihu Katz and Jefferson Pooley for reading earlier drafts of this chapter and providing helpful comments.
2 For other discussions of the history, see Park and Pooley (2008), Pooley (2006), Pooley and Katz (2008), and Katz (2009). In this short chapter, I cannot address the history of sociology and audience studies in other nations, except to discuss the development of cultural studies in Britain. Some discussion can be found in Blumler (1981).
3 On sociological conceptions of agency, see Sewell (1992), Hays (1994),

Emirbayer and Mische (1998), Fuchs (2001), and Wang (2008). Culture and agency are often theoretically subsumed together and juxtaposed to structure (Hays 1994), as sociological studies of culture have often been microcosmic participant observation studies of actors, from early studies at the University of Chicago to Howard Becker to 1970s' cultural studies and "history from below."

4 I recognize that the uses and gratifications approach still focused on the individual and not on social interaction, but its formulation could easily accommodate this addition, which seems to have happened in the United States through connecting studies of family communication with mass communication (Bryant 1990; Lindlof 1987; Lull 1990).

5 Methodologically, a deterministic approach is exemplified by experimental research, the purpose of which is to demonstrate that changes in independent variables *cause* changes in the dependent variable. Quantitative sociological research on the other hand tends to use correlational analysis designed to indicate *association* rather than deterministic cause, leaving a causal gap through which agency can enter.

6 Robert Park wrote about laboratory experiments, "I was more impressed by [Hugo] Munsterberg's discussions of the distinctions between history and natural science than I was in his laboratory psychology. James's description of laboratory psychology as little more than an elaboration of the obvious struck me at that time as it does now, as a particularly happy and accurate description" (Baker 1973: 256). Munsterberg had created at Harvard the first psychology research laboratory in the United States and published an influential theory base on crowd psychology, *The Photoplay* (Munsterberg and Lansdale 2001 [1916]), about the psychology of watching a film (Butsch 2008).

7 In Boston, the Twentieth Century Club issued a report in 1910. The Cleveland City Council funded a study of the theaters there in 1913. In Chicago, it was the Juvenile Protective Association, led by wealthy do-gooder Louise de Koven Bowen, issuing reports in 1909 and 1911. In New York and Chicago, settlement house workers also took up this issue.

8 About the significance of Katz and Lazarsfeld, *Personal Influence*, see Simonson (2006).

9 Employed in this research were: Leonard Cottrell, Carl Hovland, Arthur Lumsdaine, Nathan Maccoby, M. Brewster Smith, Hadley Cantril, Louis Guttman, Rensis Likert, Quinn McNemar, Fred Mosteller; Irving Janis, Harold Kelley, Leonard Doob, Fred Sheffield, Muzafer Sherif, Daniel Berlyne, Seymour Feshbach, Herbert Kelman, Robert Abelson, Solomon Asch, Irving Child, Neal Miller, and Theodore Newcomb. See Stouffer et al., *The American Soldier* (vol. 1: xi–xii, 22–7).

10 Some experiments included in the 1972 Surgeon General's research reports (Comstock et al. 1972) did include effects of a parent or older sibling upon a child watching television, but conceived this as an

additional independent variable, and did not consider any *inter*action between them.

11 Further, establishing cause was funded for the purpose of and led to certain practical goals. In experimental method, social and cultural pressures on individuals are defined as independent variables, and the behavior they affect as the dependent variable. To observe the effect, a single independent variable is "manipulated," i.e. varied from group to group of "subjects," while all other variables are "controlled," i.e. held constant across all groups. This language, used in experimental method, expresses not only a deterministic assumption, but also a practical goal, to manipulate people's attitudes and behaviors. This was the explicit goal of experimental research on persuasion and attitude change from World War II through the 1970s in American social psychology, to discover how to manipulate and control people's opinions, beliefs, and behaviors. In wartime, the purpose was to get soldiers and civilians to obediently and enthusiastically support the war effort. Postwar, many researchers hoped their research would reduce racial prejudice and discrimination (Allport 1954).

12 Nevertheless, Katz (1957, 1963) continued to use and promote the thesis of two-step communication process and focus on audience "use" rather than effects. He applied the idea to communication social processes, for example, to explain the diffusion of innovations.

13 Peter Collett (1987) repeated the method in British homes, amidst the rise of cultural studies.

5

Media Industry Sociology: Mainstream, Critical, and Cultural Perspectives

Timothy Havens

Sociological inquiry into the media industries traces its roots to Max Horkheimer and Theodor Adorno's (1996) "Culture Industry" essay in the *Dialectic of Enlightenment*. We can distinguish between both critical and noncritical versions of the sociology of media industries, despite their shared roots in critical social theory. Political economy, in particular the cultural industries strain of European political economy, generally adopts a critical sociological approach, as do cultural studies inquiry into media industries. Meanwhile, production of culture studies, rooted in organizational sociology, tends to produce noncritical scholarship.

Perhaps the two most enduring theoretical issues in critical studies of the media industries are the impact of corporate capitalism on creative workers' autonomy and the diversity of content that media industries produce. These are related, yet separable questions: theoretically at least, an industry could have quite low levels of creative autonomy, yet still produce a diverse range of texts. On the other hand, workers in the commercial media industries might have a high degree of creative autonomy, yet produce a limited diversity of content. Cultural industries scholarship and some strains of organizational sociology focus on creative autonomy, while the majority of organizational sociology and cultural studies scholarship explores content diversity. However, as media industry studies has come into its own, new theoretical questions are being asked, in particular from the perspective of cultural studies and economic anthropology.

Defining media industries

Different definitions of the media industries have been proposed in different fields, including "the entertainment industries," "the cultural industries," and "the creative industries." More than mere differences of diction, these distinctions have a fundamental influence on what kinds of organizations and processes get studied, as well as the theoretical tools that are used and conclusions that are drawn. The term "entertainment industry" obviously excludes such informational media as newspapers and even television journalism, while its focus on *entertainment* (rather than, say, culture or ideology) works to minimize serious consideration of the industry's products, and so is rarely used in academic settings. "Cultural industries," by contrast, both identifies the shared product of these industries – what David Hesmondhalgh (2012) calls "symbol production" – and conceives of the related industries broadly, including fine art as well as popular media and journalism. Again, the assumption behind this definition is that all capitalist institutions engaged in the production of symbolic commodities share some specifiable traits, operate under similar kinds of pressures, or respond to environmental changes in similar ways.

As Hesmondhalgh (2008) notes, the term "creative industries" has become particularly popular in recent years in academic and policy circles, usually as part of an effort to attract light industry and creative work to particular locales. By affixing the term "creative," rather than "cultural," proponents of creative industries avoid critical resonances with the phrase "culture industry." At the same time, the term marks particular kinds of occupations and workers as especially desirable, namely jobs oriented toward the global information economy and workers in those industries, who are often seen as ideal citizens and consumers. The tech industry, fashion, design, and software development – along with traditional media industries like film and television – appeal to politicians and policy makers because they are cutting-edge and seemingly integrated into the growing global economy, because they attract young workers with high salaries and large disposable incomes, and because the workforce is supposedly cosmopolitan and diverse, a fact often seen as supporting broader policy goals of establishing "global cities."

Much like media industries work in general, creative industries scholarship can be both descriptive and critical. However, as Hesmondhalgh (2008) rightly emphasizes, in its acceptance of the definitions of creativity provided by the industry, its close ties to policy makers, its government funding, and its proscriptive, goal-oriented conclusions, even critical forms of creative industries scholarship risk accepting as inevitable the historical process of neoliberalism. For this reason, he prefers the term "cultural industries" because it maintains the traces of critical social theory associated with the original "Culture Industry" essay. Additionally, Hesmondhalgh urges us to focus on the cultural industries writ large, rather than any specific industry, as a way of capturing and theorizing broad historical trends that cut across specific industries.

Ironically, a form of noncritical organizational sociology likewise lays claim to the term "cultural industries." Inspired by Paul Hirsch's 1972 article, "Processing Fads and Fashions: An Organization-Set Analysis of Cultural Industry Systems," this variant of cultural industries research seeks a functional analysis of how the cultural industries are organized to cope with the unique risk environments they face, in particular high costs and highly unpredictable profits. The goal is to describe the entire process of cultural production, from discovering new talent through marketing, promotion, exhibition, and assessment. Taken together, then, critical variants of the cultural industries approach insists on studying across multiple cultural industries, while noncritical variants insist upon studying the broadest possible range of stakeholders, decision makers, processes, and practices that these industries encompass in bringing cultural products to market.

Sociological work on the media – or cultural – industries, then, seeks to describe how the industrial production of culture occurs across multiple organizations, as well as all facets of work in the organization. Furthermore, it seeks to connect these descriptions to broader historical and social trends and theoretical concerns, particularly those having to do with the autonomy of creative workers and the diversity of textual commodities.

Media industries – newspaper, magazine, television, film, gaming, and popular music –are a distinct subset of the cultural industries, concerned fundamentally with telling stories. For many media and cultural studies scholars, the telling of stories sets these industries apart and gives them unique social influence since it is through narrative processes that we come to know ourselves and the world around us. Therefore, though I draw on a range of sociological inquiry into the cultural industries in this essay, I primarily focus on the institutions that I have defined here as members of the media industries.

Culture industry or the cultural industries?

Although Adorno and Horkheimer's (1996) influential essay was not in any sense sociological, it did spur a good deal of sociological research designed to critique their premise that the industrialization of cultural production inevitably produced standardized, bourgeois cultural forms, scrubbed of both the nobility of high art and the raucousness of popular art. Responses to the culture-industry model developed in both the critical and noncritical human sciences. The French media sociologist Bernard Miège, for instance, took Horkheimer and Adorno to task for conflating a range of quite different cultural production activities under a single heading – *the* culture industry – and for ignoring the actual operations of cultural production in favor of analyses of a limited range of industrialized cultural products. In his collection of translated essays, *The Capitalization of Cultural Production*, Miège distinguished between three distinct organizational models, depending on the kinds of cultural commodity being produced: publishing, flow, and press. In the publishing model, organizations such as film and book publishers seek to amass large libraries of content so that they can offset the losses from unsuccessful properties with the profits from successful ones. In the flow model, organizations such as television broadcasters provide a constant stream of content and seek to amass the largest possible audiences. And in the press model, organizations including newspapers and magazine publishers attempt to provide a regularly scheduled, quickly obsolescing product that encourages frequent purchase. Because of the distinct logics at work in each type of cultural industry, creative workers have varying degrees of freedom that may or may not entail stamping out largely indistinguishable cultural products, as Adorno and Horkheimer (1996) suggest.

Miège (1989) likewise identified the role that technology and technological change play in altering the operations and power relations in the media industries. Derek Kompare (2006), for instance, has shown how the introduction of the DVD player and the DVD box set, which packages one or several seasons of a television series together, has changed television from an industry built around the logic of flow to one built around the logic of publishing. Today, channels such as Home Box Office (HBO) operate via a hybrid publishing-flow logic, in which they generate perhaps a quarter of their profits from DVD box set sales (Flint 2005). This hybrid model helps explain in part both the autonomy of HBO's producers and the diversity of the content that HBO produces in terms of genres, topics, episode run times, and ideological perspectives.

Miège's more sociological "cultural industries" approach was picked up in the United Kingdom as well, most notably by Nicholas Garnham and, more recently, David Hesmondhalgh. Meanwhile, in North America, a more polemical and less sociological version of critical political economy has tended to dominate the academy (Hesmondhalgh 2012). This North American variant, including the work of Ben Bagdikian, Noam Chomsky, Edward Herman and Robert M. McChesney, and Herbert Schiller, is quite good at documenting the worldwide consolidation of ownership among media and telecommunications corporations, as well as the role that powerful states play in facilitating consolidation. However, it is much less thorough and empirically rich when it comes to exploring the two theoretical questions I identified above that lie at the heart of critical media industries scholarship: workers' autonomy and the diversity of textual output.

In recent work, Hesmondhalgh and Sarah Baker (2011) theorize and research in detail how commercial industrialization has influenced creative autonomy. Beginning with a careful review of the literature on good and bad work, Hesmondhalgh and Baker argue that creative work, or work which results in primarily symbolic commodities that circulate broadly, has the potential to have many attributes of good work: it can be independent, self-directed and capable of producing feelings of self-worth and accomplishment. Taking this model, then, the authors analyze findings from sixty-three interviews conducted with creative workers and managers in the television, magazine and music industries. They find that several factors degrade the quality of creative work today, especially privatization of the cultural industries and the rise of neoliberal economic regimes. They identify the sacrifices necessary, especially at the beginning of one's career; difficulties balancing work and life; increasing need to spend time on noncreative work, such as networking and fundraising; and how the present market for creative professionals makes it particularly difficult for women and middle-aged workers to participate.

Hesmondhalgh and Baker's (2011) work demonstrates the continuing vitality of cultural industries scholarship and the enduring importance of its central questions. Bringing on board both structuralist and post-structuralist theories of identity formation and work, and combining these insights with extensive field work and conventional industry analysis, they chart significant changes in the industry and how they affect one of the central features of media work.

Production of culture studies

A second strain of scholarship that developed in response to Horkheimer and Adorno's essay has come to be dubbed the "production of culture" perspective. Rooted in organizational sociology, the scholarship in this area is decidedly functionalist, designed, as one of its founding figures writes, as a "depoliticized exploration of what Adorno . . . had earlier characterized as the industrialization of high culture" (Hirsch 2000). Production of culture studies recognizes that the cultural industries share several formal features, including the need to employ and manage creative workers, the constant need for new talent and new content, and the highly unpredictable nature of popular success. Scholars in this tradition seek to understand how the organizational features and practices of the industry shape the products that the cultural industries produce.

In their synthetic review of production of culture studies, Richard A. Peterson and N. Anand (2004) identify six distinct forces that cumulatively shape the cultural output of the industries: technology, law and regulation, industry structure, organization structure, occupational career, and market. In recounting how rock music became the dominant popular music form between 1954 and 1956, Peterson (1990) argues that technological and regulatory changes increased the number of firms operating in the popular music industry, which led to a reconceptualization of the audience market as a set of differentiated niches, rather than a homogenous mass. These newcomers, moreover, were more aware of changing popular tastes than the large oligopolies. Finally, because most rockers were only contract employees of the labels, rather than lifetime employees, they had greater freedom (and greater risk) to innovate.

Generally speaking, production of culture scholarship eschews questions of social power and the role that cultural production plays in the maintenance or challenging of social relations. Instead, it is content to describe interrelations between the six "facets" of industrial practice identified above, and the content of cultural industries productions, while searching for testable hypotheses about how these facets of production interact, evolve, and function. Little discussion of the broader implications of the commercialization of culture or the relations between culture and the maintenance of social power occur. Nevertheless, the descriptive acuity of this perspective and its capacity to theorize in detail the facets of industrial production that have an impact on cultural products are significant. These studies point to the complex and multifaceted relationships that exist between seemingly mundane business, regulatory, and technological practices and the cultural experiences that fill our lives.

Current research in the production of culture perspective seeks to examine what forms of management are most effective for the cultural industries; how decisions about production and circulation get made (see Bielby and Harrington 2008 for a discussion of decision making in international television distribution); how increasingly complex, fragmented, and transnational business networks shape perceptions of markets and products; and the ways in which competition between large and small firms affects the diversity of cultural output (see Greve, Pozner, and Rao 2006 for an analysis of how social movements can destabilize organizational structures and produce cultural diversity).

Alongside the production of culture perspective, business management scholars developed their own "cultural industries" perspective, identified most strongly with Paul M. Hirsch. Hirsch (1972) initially theorized that the unique conditions of the cultural industries – highly unpredictable profits, the need for constant turnover of products – lead to distinct organizational structures and practices, in particular the proliferation of "contact people" at the "input" and "output" boundaries of the organization who search out new talent and products or ensure that finished products are effectively differentiated from potential competitors. Since the publication of Hirsch's article, a good deal of research has focused on understanding how the "throughput" portion of his model is dealt with organizationally, and why these particular organizational structures have developed. How, for instance, has the fragmentation of cultural industry markets altered power relations among organizations involved in cultural production, as well as the role of independent firms that operate between distinct organizations?

While the majority of production of culture scholarship focuses on the relationships between organization practices and cultural products, a handful of scholars rooted in organizational studies also examine worker autonomy. Curiously, these studies also tend to be the ones most invested in critical social theory. Joseph Turow (1997), for example, introduced power relations in organizational studies of the cultural industries through his power-roles framework, which theorizes how different organizations involved in the production of culture gain power and acquiescence over others. Defining power as the capacity to provide or deny resources to other organizations, Turow demonstrates how all types of organizations involved in cultural production – even the caterers – wield power over other organizations. He identifies seventeen distinct forms of organizational power, and provides a framework that is particularly effective for analyzing controversies among firms in the cultural industries. Ultimately, however, Turow's interests here lie less in understanding *worker* autonomy than *organizational* autonomy, though undoubtedly the two concepts are intimately linked.

Finally, Mark Deuze (2007) draws on continental sociological theory, in particular Zygmunt Bauman's theories of "liquid life," in which the distinctions between life and work, production and consumption, public and private, unity and fragmentation, and so on have blurred. Deuze surveys creative work and management in advertising, journalism, film and television production, and gaming to demonstrate how, across these industries, the introduction of digital technologies has "supercharged" the dissolution of work and leisure, of autonomy and exploitation, in the current era.

Cultural studies of media industries

In the early years of cultural studies scholarship, several researchers conducted studies of television production, especially at the British Broadcasting Corporation (BBC). Perhaps because of its noncommercial status, this scholarship generally eschewed many of the questions raised by the "Culture Industry" essay and its subsequent uptake among critical cultural industries scholars, focusing instead on how conceptualizations of the audience and the nation shaped representational choices.

In the 1980s, however, cultural studies scholarship tended toward textual and reception analysis, eschewing serious discussion of how the industry itself works and influences popular representations. Indeed, according to John Fiske (1992), one of the most prominent cultural studies figures in the 1980s and 1990s, popular culture circulated within two distinct economies: a cultural economy, where audience circulated meanings; and a money economy, where corporations earned profits.

Fiske's formulation freed discussions of the cultural consequences of popular culture from derivative theories of media conglomeration and proved useful for a wide range of cultural scholars. However, in its focus on the articulations between text and audience, this strain of cultural studies scholarship tended to set aside questions about the articulations between industry and text. This latter set of questions, though, had been on the cultural studies agenda, albeit frequently in the background, at least since Raymond Williams's (1980) essay, "Base and Superstructure in Marxist Cultural Theory" which sought to retheorize the relationships between the economic base of capitalist societies and their cultural superstructure. Williams advocated reconceptualizing superstructural activities, such as television programming, as sets of practices that occur within and are articulated to the practices of the economic base. "I am saying that we should not look for the components of a product (i.e. textual analysis) but for the conditions of a practice," he writes in regard to cultural texts. "We should find ourselves attending first to the reality of their practice and the conditions of the practice as it was then executed" (1980: 143). In other words, Williams calls for sociology of cultural production that attends to both how cultural works are created and their aesthetics and meanings.

Amanda Lotz, Serra Tinic, and I (Havens et al. 2009) dubbed this strain of cultural studies scholarship "critical media industry studies," though others have called it production studies (Mayer, Banks, and Caldwell 2009) or, merely, media industry studies (Holt and Perren 2009). Our particular phrasing was chosen to distinguish such scholarship from noncritical media industries scholarship in organizational sociology, though certainly such scholarship informs our own understanding of the unique properties and practices of these industries. At the same time, we wanted to transcend conventional understandings of production as the work of creative workers alone, to include a range of corporate executives, outside interest groups, regulators, and below-the-line workers who often put their distinctive stamp on cultural products circulating throughout contemporary societies. Regardless of what we call it, however, this strain of cultural studies scholarship shares an emphasis on understanding the particularities, complexities, and contradictions inherent in cultural production and cultural representation, as well as the ways in which these two fields are articulated to produce specific cultural practices. Of particular interest to critical media industries scholars are the lifeworlds that media industry professionals inhabit, the discourses through which they understand those lifeworlds, how those discourses arise and change, and how they produce particular representational regimes within commercial media texts.

The original scholarship in this area comes from the field of sociology, in particular Todd Gitlin's (1983) *Inside Prime Time*, which reports interviews conducted with television executives and producers about how programs get on television. Gitlin maps both the barriers to and incitements toward socially conscious, aesthetically innovative programming on American network television by exploring how and why television executives make programming decisions. He discovers that the "nobody knows" principle, which holds that popularity and success are impossible to predict, gives executives a good deal of leeway in making decisions, and prompts them to rely more on gut instinct than hard research. In one chapter, Gitlin examines how technological and industrial changes, particularly the growing threat from cable television and the introduction of home video, created conditions that allowed Steven Bochco considerable artistic and thematic freedom in his 1980s' hit series *Hill Street Blues*.

While Gitlin's study did not spawn a critical mass of related scholarship, industry studies did resurface in cultural studies throughout the 1980s and 1990s. Perhaps most notably, Julie D'Acci's (1994) analysis of the female buddy police drama *Cagney and Lacey* put such industrial considerations as niche marketing, promotional materials, conservative pressure groups, and the personal histories of the series co-creators at the forefront of her analysis of the ambivalent feminist politics of the series. While her scholarship can most accurately be defined as an attempt to integrate industrial, textual, and reception analysis into the study of a particular popular phenomenon, D'Acci does devote a good deal of her analysis to exploring the lifeworlds and industrial surrounding that the show's creators inhabited, and how they influenced representational decisions.

Jennifer Holt and Alissa Perren (2009) identify three distinct ways in which cultural studies scholars have imagined the relationship between industrial and representational practice, including issues of style (e.g. Caldwell 1995), authorship (e.g. Mayer 2011), and genre (e.g. Shattuc 1997), as well as industrial histories that address one or more of these textual concerns (e.g. Hilmes 2007). To these three issues, I would add a fourth: the relationship between industrial practices and representations of social differences such as gender (Lotz 2006), sexuality (Becker 2006), regional identity (Johnson 2008), and race (Smith-Shomade 2007). Again, the uniting theme of this scholarship is the articulation between the worldviews of a wide range of industry executives and creative workers, and the representational politics of the texts they produce.

While the focus on texts distinguishes cultural studies approaches to media industries from cultural industries approaches, Hesmondhalgh (2010) suggests that the best critical insights in the sociology of media industries have always come from the dialogue between these two camps. While he specifically identifies the question of autonomy of creative workers, the productive tension between a focus on worker autonomy and textual diversity also animates this interdisciplinary dialogue, and accounts for much of the cross-fertilization among approaches. An exemplary study here is Vicki Mayer's analysis of the autonomy of media workers who are frequently considered non-creative, or "below-the-line" workers. In *Below the Line: Producers and Production Studies in the New Television Economy* (2011), Mayer makes a strong argument for expanding our notion of what constitutes media "production" to include a range of trade workers, production assistants, manufacturing workers, and even regulators, all of whom contribute to the creation of media texts. Mayer here explores one of the main topics of cultural studies of the media industries, namely the attempt to map who exercises authorial control over media texts, but deploys this to make an argument more germane to cultural industries concerns about the autonomy of creative workers. In other words, she uses cultural studies themes to demonstrate that the work of these below-the-line workers is creative, then assesses their creative autonomy from a cultural industries perspective.

Economic anthropology and the construction of value

A relatively new approach to the sociology of the media industries, at least to those of us in media studies, comes from scholars interested in economic anthropology. Much of this scholarship addresses material culture produced in nonmarket economies, and is thus not directly relevant to media studies questions. However, among a small group of scholars who do study contemporary media industries, two particular theoretical insights – the distinctive features of "gift" economies and the social construction of "value" in organization – offer the opportunity to introduce new theoretical questions in the sociology of the media industries.

Arjun Appadurai (1986) broached the question of how "value" gets constructed in gift economies in his analysis of Melanesian kula rings, or exchanges of necklaces and armbands among men. Unlike commodity exchanges, these gift exchanges are temporary (though one can regift them), and the traded objects derive their value not from their physical properties but rather from the identity and status of the gift giver. Gift economies, then, are primarily involved in the reproduction and display of status through the exchange of nonutilitarian goods.

A good deal of scholarship in recent years has focused on the gift economies prevalent in social media and open source software, while bemoaning its disappearance due to the introduction of market forces, but economic anthropologists see the continuation of gift-economy practices even in commercial creative industries. Brian Moeran (2010), for instance, examines book publishing and argues that the intense personal relations among industry workers, the importance of corporate and author reputation in publishing and marketing decision, and the continued use of authors' names on books all trace back to the status of the book commodity as a gift. Put slightly differently, the reason that books can accrue monetary value is because they accrue status value through the operations of the gift economy.

Appadurai (1986) refers to kula rings as a "tournament of values," where participants strive for status with regard to the major values of the society, which are vividly on display in kula exchanges. They are competitions for status and power. Moeran (2010) applies the concept of a tournament of values to the book fairs he studies, arguing that such values as literary quality and price are constantly challenged, negotiated, reworked, and reaffirmed. Likewise, I (Havens 2011) applied the tournament-of-values framework to international television trade shows, demonstrating how the formal features of television markets like MIP-TV and NAPTE, combined with an array of differentially available perquisites given to attendees, create status values for television distributors. These status values, then, are translated into discursive power, as respected distributors define the terms of what constitutes "universal cultural themes" among industry insiders, helping erase the local particularities of their program offerings in the minds of buyers. Thus, while the prize of the kula ring is social power, the prize of television and bookfairs is sales. However, media executives and firms need to win the tournaments of values in order to gain sales.

The focus on values among economic anthropologists recognizes that the monetary value in cultural goods is inseparable from a host of other cultural values. In this way, the perspective can help reconcile our theoretical considerations of the money and cultural economies, which Fiske (1992) claimed were distinct. Trade fairs and other such high-visibility industry gatherings provide a sort of "high holiday" for media industry executives where these values are not only displayed and negotiated, but also where transaction from one form of value to another occurs. All media industries have such events for this reason. As Moeran and Strandgaard Pedersen explain,

> Fairs, festivals, and competitive events provide a venue for the (re) enactment of institutional arrangements in a particular industry's field

and for the negotiation and affirmation of the different values that underpin them. Thus, while the function of economic exchange may be to create value, all sorts of other, different kinds of – material, social, temporal, spatial, appreciative, and other – values are introduced and promoted as part of the negotiation of the economic worth of [a cultural commodity]. (2011: 10)

The focus on values and how they interact to construct profit in economic anthropology does not inevitably address questions important to critical media industries scholars, though certainly some of the more descriptive explanations of these processes can prove enlightening. But critical cultural studies scholars are well poised to bring questions of social power into these kinds of analysis.

Perhaps most interestingly, a focus on how cultural values get transcoded into economic value helps erase distinctions between text, industry, and audience that have animated much of the scholarship in media studies as a field. With such a focus, we can conceptualize industry executives as an audience that understands media texts within a particular interpretive community. Much like popular audiences, executive audiences only adopt those elements of popular texts that they find valuable within that community, rejecting elements or entire texts that they do not see as valuable. The only real difference, in this sense, between executive and popular audiences is that the former are looking primarily for economic values, rather than values of community, identity, resistance, recognition, or reassurance that popular audiences seek.

Conclusion

If we take seriously the insights of the various traditions in media industry sociology outlined here, we can see that the topic is remarkably broader and more complex than it might at first appear. A thorough sociology of these industries would need to include above-the-line and below-the-line producers and creative workers, and the vast array of executives involved in these and other ancillary industries, including ratings and measurements, toy merchandising and several other industries. We would need to understand power relations within organizations, as well as across organizations, and how different categories of industry workers interact with one another to form distinct fields of knowledge. For example, computer game creators may have a very different conceptualization of their audiences than do game retailers, but both kinds of workers influence the formal properties of games and experiences of creative autonomy in the industry.

These are just a few of the sites available for media industry sociology. They have expanded significantly over the past thirty years, from a time when both cultural studies and organization sociologists agreed that television producers were the primary objects of analysis (Newcomb and Hirsch 1983). In addition, the theoretical questions and models for conducting media industry sociology have also grown. As we have seen, media industry sociologists have developed frameworks for understanding interfirm power relations, what constitutes creativity, how technological and economic changes affect media industry work, the various types of authorship that exist in the industries and how they feed into representational strategies, and how distinct fields of knowledge within the industry form, change, and interact with other industrial fields.

With all of this diversity of topic, approach, and industrial conditions, it may be folly to suggest areas for future scholarly investigation. And, indeed, any such suggestions would need to remain illustrative of interesting questions, not proscriptive of what questions are and are not worth pursuing. However, I wish to end this overview with a couple of observations about promising areas of scholarship that, to me, seem worth pursuing. I am particularly interested in those questions that extend beyond conventional critical questions about creative autonomy and textual diversity.

While economic anthropology has provided compelling accounts of how fields of knowledge develop and change *within* one or two fields in specific industries, we know little about power relations *among* different fields. How do discourses about audiences, for instance, circulate between, say, programming executives in the television industry and production crew? Which discourses have more power, and how are those power differentials influenced by new technologies. Take, for example, the case of the 2010 Fox Broadcasting series *Lone Star*, produced and written by Kyle Killen. When Fox cancelled the series after only a few episodes due to low ratings, Killen took to Twitter to get his fans to lobby the executives on his behalf. Though ultimately unsuccessful, here was an example of a television producer having a very different perception of his audience than network executives, and an attempt to use social media to alter power dynamics between executives and producers. To put this question into different language, we might explore the interactions between different fields of discourse within the industry and how the struggle over meaning and decision-making power occurs. Of course, this set of questions might touch on such topics as creative autonomy but need not be limited to them.

Second, while economic anthropologists are correct that value gets exhibited and negotiated at industry fairs and festivals, it may not be the case that this is the primary site for those processes, and it would be worthwhile exporing how this process operates in more mundane business conditions. Much as Michael Billig (1995) has argued that the discourse of nationalism is sustained in daily life in subtle, barely recognized ways, so might discourses of media industries and their imaginations of value be constructed and reinforced primarily in day-to-day business activities. Studying and theorizing the internal discourses of the media industries presents challenges of access, and such scholarship is therefore not widespread. However, scholarship in "cultural economy" (Du Gay and Pryke 2002) may offer a good model for such questions in its insistence on understanding the cultural construction of monetary value in day-to-day business operations. For instance, in recent research, I (Havens 2012) identified a shifting discourse among certain segments of the global television industries where particular buyers and sellers no longer discussed the "universal themes" inherent in globally popular shows but instead discussed television viewing as a "cultural journey" in trade journals and email exchanges. This altered discourse, I observed, produced – and responded to – the global circulation of locally specific, minority-themed television programming.

Finally, sociology of media industries, integrated with and inflected by sociology of regulatory policy making, promises to provide fertile ground for new kinds of topics and questions. In some ways, this is what Brian Larkin (2008) accomplishes in his history of media technologies and industries in Nigeria, as he charts the relationships between government policy, colonialism, and postcolonialism, and the uses of media in West Africa, although it would be a mistake to claim that such an integrated sociology of regulators and industry workers is his primary goal. Likewise, Aswin Punathambekar (in press) executes a critical sociology of Indian filmmaking, examining how the industry has evolved from a semi-legal, local, and informal business to an organized, state-supported global force. The success of Bollywood is largely due to efforts to rebrand India as a legitimate destination for global capital, especially among nonresident Indians. Again, Punathambekar's sociological work is largely confined to industry workers and audiences, but it makes clear the potential benefits and contours of an integrated sociology of industry and state regulators.

My suggestion that critical scholars working in the sociology of the media industries move beyond questions of creative autonomy and textual diversity should not be read as a call to abandon those questions. Rather, I believe such questions remain vital as the transnational pressures of capital meet the politics of social conservatism in reshaping the media industries in many parts of the world. Furthermore, even these "other" questions involve issues of autonomy and diversity. But the field of critical media industry sociology has expanded significantly over the past fifteen years, encompassing an ever-wider range of scholars and approaches, and the time to expand the theoretical questions we ask has come as well.

6

The Political Economy of Media Work and Watching

Toby Miller

Numerous tendencies across the human sciences study the media.[1] Each one is tied to particular interests of state and capital:

- engineering, computing, public policy, and "film" schools enable media production via business, the military, the community, and public service;
- communication studies focuses on socioeconomic projects such as propaganda, marketing, social control, and citizenship;
- economics and law theorize and police doctrines of scarcity and manage overproduction through overseas expansion; and
- Marxism points to the impact of ownership and control and cultural imperialism on TV and consciousness.

Within and between these areas, the political economy of the media has given rise to several major topics that connect to sociology. Its central organizing precepts typically pose the following questions of the media in terms of infrastructures, institutions, and images: who controls, owns, regulates, and benefits from them; the latest query is, who suffers environmentally? This analysis draws on numerous sources, such as laws and legal cases, business magazines, corporate reports, regulatory discourse, union actions, social movements, and lived experience. At its best, political economy combines the structural analysis of ownership and control with sensitivity to everyday life through ethnography.

Political economy is as concerned with justice as science, in keeping with its origins as an Enlightenment project dedicated to bettering the lives of ordinary people in a democratic and secular way that rejected sectarian tendentiousness other than on behalf of the socioeconomically disenfranchised. It blends social struggle and knowledge with an abiding concern for class interests and other forms of inequality. It focuses on material power, the capacity to mobilize resources, the warp and woof of history, and the correlation of meanings with economic and political interests. Political economy sees culture as made through struggle, with an emphasis on social power as a determinant. It is linked to sociological studies of the relationship between political consciousness and industrial organization, state and citizen, and government, labor, and capital (Amariglio et al. 2009; Chakravartty and Zhao 2007; Maxwell 2001; McChesney 2013; McKercher and Mosco 2007; Meehan and Riordan 2001; Mosco 2004; Mosco and McKercher 2008; Mosco, McKercher, and Huws 2010; Ruccio and Amariglio 2003; D. Schiller 2007; H. Schiller 1989; Wayne 2003; Wasko, Murdock, and Sousa 2011). Such work seeks to erase "the tenacious division that for so long separated sciences of description and sciences of interpretation, morphological studies and hermeneutical analysis" and recognize that the "'world of text' . . . [is] a world of objects and performances" (Chartier 2005a: 38–9). This is in keeping with attempts to blend cultural and political-economic analyses as per the New International Division of Cultural Labor (Kavoori and Chadha 2009; McPhail 2009; Miller 2012; Miller et al. 2005).

Unlike *bourgeois* or neoclassical economics, which is dominant in economics and political science departments, political economy does not take as its lodestone the individual rationality of consumers and firms. Rather, it starts from an historical understanding of how power operates in everyday work and domestic life, stressing that value is generated by workers, who rarely benefit from it – unlike owners of capital. Political economy concentrates, in the words of the physicist-novelist C. P. Snow, on people "lost in the great anonymous sludge of history," where life (troping Thomas Hobbes) "has always been nasty, brutish and short" (1987: 26–7, 42). Where orthodox economics assumes that supply and demand determine price, political economy examines the role of the state and capital in controlling labor and ideologizing consumers and citizens. In other words, the orthodox approach looks to increase the role of markets, regarding them as jewels of human behavior. The heterodox approach challenges this focus on consumption and looks instead to production.

These differences have significant consequences. For instance, *bourgeois* economists claim that cell phones have streamlined markets in the global South, enriching people in zones where banking and economic information are scarce thanks to the provision of market data. Claims include "the complete elimination of waste" and massive reductions of poverty and corruption through the empowerment of individuals (Jensen 2007). This utopianism has seen a comprehensive turn in research away from unequal infrastructural and cultural exchange towards an extended dalliance with new technology and its supposedly innate capacity to endow users with transcendence (Ogan et al. 2009). New media technologies are said to obliterate geography, sovereignty, and hierarchy in an alchemy of truth and beauty in a deregulated, individuated, technologized world that makes consumers into producers, frees the disabled from confinement, encourages new subjectivities, rewards intellect and competitiveness, links people across cultures, and allows billions of flowers to bloom in a post-political cornucopia where people fish, film, fornicate, and finance from morning to midnight. Consumption is privileged, production is discounted, and labor is forgotten. The *Magna Carta for the Information Age*, for instance, proposes that the political-economic transformations toward democracy in the thirteenth century and since have been eclipsed by technological transformations:

> The central event of the twentieth century is the overthrow of matter. In technology, economics, and the politics of nations, wealth – in the form of physical resources – has been losing value and significance. The powers of mind are everywhere ascendant over the brute force of things. (Dyson et al. 1994)

> *Time* magazine exemplified this love of a seemingly immaterial world when it chose "You" as 2006's "Person of the Year," because "You control the Information Age. Welcome to your world." (Grossman 2006)

This discourse buys into individualistic fantasies of reader, audience, consumer, and player autonomy – the neoliberal intellectual's wet dream of music, movies, television, and everything else converging under the sign of empowered and creative fans. True believers invest with unparalleled gusto in Schumpeterian entrepreneurs, evolutionary economics, and creative industries. They've never seen an "app" they didn't like, or a socialist idea they did. Faith in devolved media-making amounts to a secular religion, offering transcendence in the here and now via a "literature of the eighth day, the day after Genesis" (Carey 2005). Machinery, not political-economic activity, is the guiding light.

But the story is more complex. Max Weber insisted that technology was principally a "mode of processing material goods" (2005: 27) and

Harvey Sacks emphasized "the failures of technocratic dreams[:] that if only we introduced some fantastic new communication machine the world will be transformed" (1995: 548).

Being mindful of these warnings, rather than seeing cell phones, for instance, as magical agents that can produce market equilibrium and hence individual and collective happiness, allows us to note their other impacts. The new freedoms associated with cell-phone usage have created nightmares for workers, public health professionals, and environmentalists.

In the Democratic Republic of Congo, which has a third of the world's columbite-tantalite (coltan), a crucial ingredient of cell phones, more than 90 percent of eastern mines are controlled by militias, which use threats, intimidation, murder, rape, and mutilation to enslave women and children for work in the mines, extracting profits to buy more weapons. More than five million people have perished in the civil war over the past decade (Maxwell and Miller 2012). Sex workers at risk of sexually transmitted disease increasingly communicate with clients by phone and are less easy to educate and assist than when they work at conventional sites (Mahapatra et al. 2012). And when old and obsolete cell phones, like other media technologies, are junked, they become electronic waste (e-waste). E-waste is the fastest-growing part of municipal cleanups around the global North. Its salvage yards have generated serious threats to worker health and safety wherever plastics and wires are burnt, monitors smashed and dismantled, and circuit boards grilled or leached with acid, while the toxic chemicals and heavy metals that flow from such practices have perilous implications for local and downstream residents, soil and water. Most electronic salvage and recycling is done in the global South by pre-teen girls, working with discarded television sets and computers to find precious metals, dumping the remains in landfills. E-waste ends up there after export and import by "recyclers" who eschew landfills and labor in the global North in order to avoid higher costs and regulatory oversight of recycling in countries that prohibit such destruction to environment and workers. And businesses that forbid dumping in local landfills as part of their corporate policies merrily mail it elsewhere (Maxwell and Miller 2012). Clearly, we need to transcend the beguiling simplicity of dominant economics. Political economy offers an exit.

Antonio Gramsci may be the foremost media theorist bringing together issues of ideology and economics. In his Communist Party activism against the fascists in 1920s' and 1930s' Italy, Gramsci sought to understand the far Right's appeal to disaffected working people, given that its policies clearly favored the interests of corporations over the proletariat and were fundamentally opposed to democracy and human rights. He explained the appeal of fascism in the media as hinges between physical and intellectual power, between force and culture.

Gramsci recognized that each social group creates "organically, one or more strata of intellectuals which give it homogeneity and an awareness of its own function not only in the economic but also in the social and political fields." He argued that "'organic' intellectuals[,] which every new class creates alongside itself and elaborates in the course of its development," assist in the emergence of that class, via military, entertainment, political, propagandistic, or educational expertise. These intellectuals operate in "civil society . . . the ensemble of organisms commonly called 'private,' that of 'political society' or 'the State.'" They enable the "'hegemony' which the dominant group exercises throughout society" as well as the "'direct domination' or command exercised through the State and 'juridical' government." Ordinary people give "spontaneous consent" to the "general direction imposed on social life by the dominant fundamental group" as a consequence of this exercise of hegemony in such fields as the press and schools (Gramsci 1978: 5–7, 12).

Gramsci argued that, although the media legitimize sociopolitical arrangements, they can be sites of struggle as well as domination because hegemony is contested between and among classes. While Gramsci acknowledged, and fought against, the dominance of fascism, he also saw that its mobilization of populism could be countered. The Welsh critic Raymond Williams (1977) adapted Gramsci's model, referring to residual, dominant, and emergent hegemonies to describe the process whereby different class formations compete for control of the narratives that legitimate social control. An example might be the hegemonies of the remains of an empty empire, a modern mixed economy, and a neoliberal transformation.

Conversely, some political-economic studies of the media suggest they "impress . . . the same stamp on everything" because their organizational form necessitates repetition rather than difference: factory-like films, songs, news bulletins, radio formats, and programs are made in the same way as cars. This perspective derives from the Frankfurt School, anti-Nazi scholars writing around the same time as Gramsci. The principals of this school, Theodor Adorno and Max Horkheimer (1977), saw consumers and citizens as manipulated from the economic apex of production. "Domination" masquerades as choice in a "society alienated from itself" and culture becomes just one more industrial process, subordinated to dominant economic forces within society that insist on standardization in order to reduce ideological or generic innovation.

Since the time of Gramsci and the Frankfurt School, the media have become even more central to economic and social life. The inaugural president of the European Bank for Reconstruction and Development, Jacques Attali, explains that a new "mercantile order forms wherever a creative class masters a key innovation from navigation to accounting or, in our own time, where services are most efficiently mass produced, thus generating enormous wealth" (Attali 2008: 31). His remark indexes recognition that a prosperous economic future lies in finance capital and ideology rather than agriculture and manufacturing – seeking revenue from innovation and intellectual property, not minerals or masses. It is no surprise that global trade in the culture industries increased from US$559.5 billion in 2010 to US$624 billion in 2011 (United Nations 2013).

As a consequence, the canons of aesthetic judgment and social distinction that once separated humanities and social science approaches to the media, distinguishing aesthetic tropes, economic needs, and social norms, have collapsed. The media are more than textual signs or everyday practices. Art and custom are now resources for markets and nations, reactions to the crisis of belonging and economic necessity occasioned by capitalist globalization. They are crucial to advanced and developing economies and provide the legitimizing ground on which particular groups (e.g. African Americans, lesbians, the hearing-impaired, or evangelical Protestants) claim resources and seek inclusion in national and international narratives (Martín-Barbero 2003; Yúdice 2002).

These transformations in turn create their own textual, cultural, and economic effects. Beginning as reflections of reality, commodity signs such as factual media texts are transformed into perversions of reality as representations of truth are displaced by false information. Then these two delineable phases of truth and lies become indistinct. Once underlying reality is lost, signs refer to themselves, with no residual correspondence to the real: they have adopted the form of their own simulation (Baudrillard 1988). People buy things to give meaning to their world because societies no longer provide them with belonging. The desire that audiences exhibit for media entertainment represents a never-ending treadmill in search of purpose (Bauman 2001): "human needs, relationships and fears, the deepest recesses of the human psyche, become mere means for the expansion of the commodity universe" (McChesney and Bellamy Foster 2003: 1).

This concatenating simulation has implications for the aesthetic and social hierarchies that "regulate and structure . . . individual and collective lives" (Parekh 2000: 143) in competitive ways that harness art and collective meaning for social and commercial purposes. For this reason, political economists discern close ties between the ideological content of the media and their industrial impact. The Frankfurt School may be contested via Gramscian theories of hegemony, but its insistence on a multisited analysis of power remains influential.

I concentrate here on two themes from political-economic analysis of the media that bring questions of consciousness and industry together: Hollywood workers, notably stars, and media audiences. These topics are familiar to us all. They address the human figures that dominate our screens and the experience of hearing and watching them. We are accustomed to moral panics about stars and audiences. Consider two classic questions that seem to recur every week: are stars good or bad role models for the young; and are audiences driven to violent or civilized conduct by the cinema? This chapter uses political-economic approaches to query these seemingly perennial shibboleths and exemplify two core themes of sociology: the conduct of institutions and populations.

Not all the research summarized below was undertaken by people calling themselves sociologists, but it draws on social science methods and preoccupations that derive from and inform the discipline. These include participant observation, critical analysis of monopoly capitalism, regression, content and textual analysis, archival research, questionnaires, and interviews. Binding these methods together with an eye to social justice concerns permits political economy to assess the issues with which we began, of control, impact, and benefit.

The car-assembly-like Hollywood studio-system of production applied between about 1920 and 1970 but began to erode in the late 1940s due to vertical disintegration, suburbanization, and televisualization (Miller et al. 2005). Since then, the US film industry has been a pioneer in the model of employment beloved of contemporary management. As such, it may be more complex than the Frankfurt School's Fordist analysis allows, and closer to Gramsci's conflict-based account. With jobs constantly ending, starting, and moving, Hollywood exemplifies "flexible specialization" – a shift from lifelong employment to casual labor. It has an economic commitment to "permanent innovation," and a political commitment to control its environment (Piore and Sabel 1984: 17).

For decades, Hollywood has sustained horizontal unionization, rather than an enterprise-based system. Within this context, workers and bosses strike complex, transitory arrangements on a project basis via temporary organizations, with small numbers of diverse hands involved at each stage other than production, when sizeable crews function both together and semiautonomously. Places and networks matter in terms of textual cues, policy incentives, educational support, financing, and skills. Time matters because of cost and marketing. Work may be subject to local, national, regional, and international fetishization of each component, matching the way that the labor undertaken is largely fetishized away from the final text. Conventional organizational charts are inadequate to the task, especially if one seeks to elude the conventions of hierarchy through capital while recognizing the eternal presence of managerial surveillance. Businessmen want flexibility in the numbers they employ, the technology they use, the place where they produce, and the amount that they pay – and inflexibility of ownership and control. The power and logic of domination by a small number of vast entities is achieved via a huge globalizing network of subcontracted firms and individuals, in turn mediated through unions, employer associations, education, and the state.

Many of the people working in the industry have highly-educated, middle-class backgrounds. Alvin Toffler invented the concept of a "cognitariat" a quarter of a century ago (1983) to describe them. The idea has since been taken up and redisposed for political economy by Antonio Negri (2007). He applies the term to people mired in contingent media work who have educational qualifications and facility with cultural technologies and genres. This cognitariat plays a key role in the production and circulation of goods and services, through both creation and coordination. As per Gramsci, the *culturalization of production* increases the importance of intellectuals because it places them at the center of world economies. But it simultaneously disables them, thanks to flexible production underwritten by the ideology of "freedom." What used to be the fate of artists and musicians – where "making cool stuff" and working with relative autonomy was meant to outweigh ongoing employment – has become a norm. The outcome is contingent labor as a way of life that is no longer defined in terms of location (factories), tasks (manufacturing), or politics (moderation of ruling-class power and ideology) and comprises people whose immediate forebears, with similar or less cultural capital, were confident of secure health care and retirement income. It lacks both the organization of the traditional working class and the political *entrée* of the old middle class.

Most of this work is invisible to viewers of Hollywood. The people

we see and remember are stars, i.e. celebrities. Their history pre-
dates film: celebrities have been around since the first portraits of
writers and painters in twelfth-century Europe, which marketed their
subjects to potential sponsors. In the seventeenth century, portraits
transformed into methods of instruction, as depictions of the daily
life of the court became model rituals for courtiers. Then democracy
and capitalism invented the idea of publicity, transferring esteem and
legitimacy from royalty and religion to upwardly mobile businessmen. Hence today's debates over stars' transhistorical as opposed to
ephemeral value, their authentic versus manufactured images, and
their public and private lives – in other words, the full catastrophe
(and pleasure) of forming a *nouveau riche* and providing popular
methods for measuring bodies, families, and lifestyles (Briggs and
Burke 2003: 11, 41).

Stardom is business. In 2005, the cost of celebrity endorsements
exceeded a billion dollars. This expenditure is predicated on a tie-in
between commodities and stars, such that the lifestyle of celebrities
can be purchased along with the products they favor. It is unclear how
well this works; research suggests minimal media attention to these
efforts, audience skepticism, and credibility that diminishes with the
contentiousness of the issues discussed (Becker 2013; Spears, Royne,
and Van Steenburg 2013).

As audiences, we may know less about stars than we imagine – for
instance, the public probably agrees with Hollywood that the key to
the industry's financial success is stardom, despite the evidence of
regression analysis, which highlight other factors such as genre, corporation, and directing (De Vany 2003). It is also common to negate
the centrality of institutions to stars. In many popular and academic
analyses, the dominant thesis is that actors become popular because
of individual abilities and characteristics. Four qualities associated
with stars encourage this view: beauty, age, skill, and screen image.
But stars have at least three faces: their characters in films, their
private selves, and their public *personae* (Clark 1995; Dyer 1986).

Rather than the culmination of emotional interiority or thespian
skill, stars are complex mixtures of marketing methods, social signs,
nationalism, capitalism, individualism, and consumption. Each
element imbricates the public with the private. Actors transmogrify
into stars when their social and private lives become more important
than their professional qualities, when the public wants to emulate
them, and artists do, too. They feed into and generate stereotypes of
success, power, and beauty, incarnating dramatic roles or fashions,
and indexing the limitations and the promises of the age. Each star

"es una imagen; pero no una imagen natural" [is an image; but not a natural image]. Their crucial transformation is from an "icono ideográfico en icono normative" [ideographic icon into a normative one] (Bueno 2002).

This is neither magical nor a reflection of some naturally occurring Zeitgeist determined by audiences. It is a result of corporate agility. For example, the major talent agencies in Los Angeles identify causes for their celebrity clients to endorse, based on visibility, publicity, subjectivity, interest, availability, and other pragmatic factors. Consider cause marketing, whereby stars associate themselves with political movements, perhaps most notably environmental activism. Now the major scholarly study on the topic names the motion-picture industry as the biggest producer of conventional pollutants in Los Angeles because it uses so much electricity and petroleum and releases hundreds of thousands of tons of deadly emissions each year. In the state of California overall, screen drama's energy consumption and greenhouse-gas emissions are akin to those of the aerospace and semiconductor industries (Corbett and Turco 2006).

We need to connect celebrity eco-activism and Hollywood ecological damage via political economy. Take the example of Leonardo DiCaprio, who announced a 2013 sabbatical from filmmaking to "fly around the world doing good for the environment." As part of this paradox, DiCaprio helped launch World Wildlife Fund's "Hands Off My Pants" campaign. With compelling solipsism, his accompanying press release focused on a country that had incurred the great man's particular displeasure, "calling on Thailand's government to show leadership on elephant conservation by shutting down its ivory market" (The Nation 2013).

Of course, some of the money DiCaprio uses to "fly around the world doing good for the environment" comes from his films, and political economy directs us to consider how those activities sit with his activism. Consider *The Beach* (2000), set in Thailand and directed by Danny Boyle, whose nationalism suffused the opening ceremony of the 2012 Olympic Games, encouraging *The Guardian* newspaper to ennoble him as a "champion of the people" and "the ultimate idealist" (Freedland 2013).

Like his fellow environmentalist DiCaprio, Boyle felt strongly about the need to elevate Thai environmental consciousness while filming. Boyle claimed *The Beach* was "raising environmental consciousness" among a local population whose appreciation of these things lagged "behind" US "awareness." He elected to "give something back to Thailand" by hiring Thai apprentices even though this meant "We were hauling 300 fucking people around wherever we went. And you know how hard it is to learn Thai names. Every lunchtime was like a prime minister's reception." Before the film was released – but no doubt having had their consciousness raised – environmental groups sued the studio and local officialdom for contravening the National Parks Act and the Environmental Protection Act. It took seven years, but the Thai Supreme Court found in their favor in 2006 (Maxwell and Miller 2012).

Despite these instances, the story of environmental celebrity does not have to be self-regarding. The key is unpacking the political-economic realities of such activism, especially the extent to which stars endeavor to be consistent across private and public spheres. For example, Darryl Hannah travels by train, even across the United States, and was arrested after chaining herself to the gates of the White House in protest at a proposed oil pipeline. This forms part of a serious engagement with issues that often sees her face media opprobrium and state violence (Goldberg 2013; Rowlatt 2009; Wood 2009). Such actions produce press coverage, photos, and popular discourse in a reflexive way that takes account of one's own complicity, as opposed to a hypocritical Messianic wish fulfillment fueled by the very actions it purports to change. When we examine Hollywood from this perspective, the tools of political economy unveil both its industry-wide exploitation of labor and natural resources and the gaps that its struggle for hegemony create.

Audiences

In addition to unpacking the labor of work in search of hegemonic probabilities and counter-hegemonic possibilities, political economy has contributed a great deal to understanding media audiences by historicizing the way that other forms of knowledge have researched them. Cinema's earliest critics were frightened of socialism, democracy, and populism. With civil society growing restive, the wealth of radical civic associations was explained away in social-psychological terms rather than political-economic ones, thanks to psychology, sociology, and education. Scholars at Harvard took charge of the theory, faculty at Chicago the task of meeting and greeting the great unwashed, and those at Columbia the statistical manipulation (Staiger 2005: 21–2). Such tendencies moved into high gear with the Payne Fund studies of the 1930s, which juxtaposed the impact of films on "'superior' adults – young college professors, graduate students and their wives" – with children in juvenile correction centers. This research inaugurated mass social science panic about young people at the cinema by collecting "authoritative and impersonal data which would make possible a more complete evaluation of motion pictures and their social potentialities" to answer "what effect do motion pictures have upon children of different ages?" Pioneering scholars set out to see whether "the onset of puberty is or is not affected by motion pictures." The researchers asked their subjects whether "all, most, many, some, few, or no Chinese are cunning and underhand" and investigated cinematic "demonstrations of satisfying love techniques" to establish whether "[s]exual passions are aroused and amateur prostitution . . . aggravated." Laboratory techniques used psychogalvanometers and wired beds with hypnographs and polygraphs (Charters 1933: iv–v, 8, 12–13, 314, 10, 15, 25, 32, 49, 54, 60; Wartella 1996: 173).

Effects research continues to have considerable traction across the human sciences, thanks to true believers and research-grant incentives. Sociology is not immune to such desires, but political economy is skeptical, despite the Frankfurt School tradition. Materialist and embedded, rather than psychological and experimental, methods have shown that communities frequently create syncretic cultures of reception. For although Adorno thought popular cinema's "infantile character, regression manufactured on an industrial scale" diminished audiences' capacities for social critique, he acknowledged that Hollywood's factory-like norms could never entirely control the camera's tendency to reference what actually lay before it: the art of filmmaking was unable to control the power of objects to express themselves and their histories (Adorno 1981–2).

In accounting for cult cinema, Umberto Eco suggests fans can "own" a text, psychologically if not legally, by quoting and imitating characters' escapades and proclivities. References to segments of an episode or the typical behavior of an actant catalyze collective memory, regardless of their significance for individual plotlines (Eco 1987: 198). Marie Gillespie (1995) illustrates how elderly Punjabi expatriates in London take the viewing of Hindi films with their children and grandchildren as opportunities to reminisce and educate family members about India. There was controversy and even violence among exiled audiences in Los Angeles in 1990 when their image of "home" was challenged during a film festival devoted to post-revolutionary cinema (Naficy 1993). Right-wing nationalist diasporic Vietnamese picketed a Los Angeles video store for 53 days in 1999 because its owner had displayed a picture of Ho Chi Minh in his Little Saigon shop (Shore 2004). Gay Asian-Caribbean-Canadian video-maker Richard Fung (1991) talks about "searching" for Asian genitals in the much-demonized genre of pornograph, an account not available in conventional denunciations of porn and its impact on minorities. When JoEllen Shively (2009) returned to the reservation where she grew up, her fellow Native Americans were reading western films as they had done during her childhood, in an actantial rather than a political way that found them cheering for cowboys over Indians, because heroic narrativization had overdetermined racial identification. Jacqueline Bobo's analysis of black US women viewers of *The Color Purple* (Stephen Spielberg, 1985) shows that watching the movie and discussing it drew them back to Alice Walker's novel, with all three processes invoking personal experience (Bobo 1995: 3). Such aberrant decoding seizes control of cinema, regardless of its factory norms or hegemonic meanings. It is observable through the sinews of audience reactions, the materiality of their intersections with texts.

Political economy tracks both what happens *in* movies and what happens *to* them as they travel, attenuating and developing links and discourses across their careers. In other words, we trace the "different and successive materialities" of texts – their open, malleable, polyphonic qualities (Chartier 2005a: 40, 2005b).

Such political-economic methods are also available to capital, which understands that audiences are not already-extant entities participating in the neoliberal wet dream of supply and demand. Most of the time, the media are not directly selling to their audience, and their audience is not buying from them. Fifty years ago, Dallas Smythe (2004: 319f) explained that audience attention was the key commodity that the commercial media sold to advertisers, even though it was not material and was difficult to define and measure: media texts are not so much commodities as "symbols for time" (Hartley 1987: 133). In fact, the media positions themselves "at the intersection of time and real estate."

Surveillance has long been a central strut of modernity, supposedly to make populations secure, content, and productive. With the expansion of state authority into the everyday, into all corners of life, the quid pro quo for the security afforded by governments became knowing everyone's identities and practices. The equivalent expansion of corporations into the everyday, into the same corners of life, had as its quid pro quo for the provision of goods and services that they, too, know more and more about us. The proliferation of methods for studying how people interact with the media may even infringe privacy and free speech, given the proprietorial methods used by corporations to undermine autonomous reading (Andrejevic 2006; Baruh 2004; Gandy 1989; Turow 2005).

For whether we see audiences as knowledgeable, ignorant, passive, active, powerful, weak, intelligent, idiotic – or none, all, or some of the above – their principal role for the media industries is to be known, to be investigated. As such, their active participation in watching texts or creating paratexts can be valuable to the industry because it offers corporations greater surveillance of them. For it is audiences' attention, their mental and emotional labour, that gives them value. The more visible that labor becomes – the more that is known about the audience's composition and conduct – the better off corporate capitalism is (Wasko, Phillips, and Meehan 2001).

Three basic fantasies about media audiences dominate marketing: the individual, the regional, and the global. The first is animated by classifications of race, class, gender, age, and psyche; the second by geopolitical clusters; and the third by a growing cosmopolitanism. So a visit to a Santa Monica British-style pub may offer football and rugby union on different walls at the same time, while a Clerkenwell gastro pub provides one television set dedicated to La Liga and another to the Barclays Premier League. Such viewing practices can be understood through three lenses: globalization also deglobalizes, in that it is not only about mobility and exchange, but disconnectedness and exclusion; cultural groups frequently emerge transnationally, due to migration by people who continue to communicate, work, and consume through their languages of origin; and demographic minorities within sovereign states may not form textually specific rather than profound minorities on their adopted terrain (García Canclini 2004). This is as per the concept of multi-sited ethnography (Marcus 1995), which insists on the need to examine groups based on all the spaces and forces affecting them.

Audience surveillance is alert to these sociological niceties and deploys them, for example before television programs have even been made, via the sociological staple of the focus group, which scrutinizes small numbers of people whose identities represent the social formations desired by advertisers. They are shown pilots of programs to judge the likelihood that people like them will watch shows that are picked up by networks. These groups are crucial to the arrival and departure of US TV texts (Miller 2010).

Some telling examples of intense audience targeting and surveillance come from sporting TV. For marketers in the global North, young, affluent men are the most desirable media spectators. By contrast with other segments of the population, they watch little television, have protean preferences for brands, and earn sizeable incomes. They often love TV sport, which makes their interest in it disproportionately influential on programming (Commission on the Future of Women's Sport 2010: 7).

At the height of the contemporary Great Recession, the premium-cable network HBO had 41 million US subscribers, paying US$3.84 billion a year. Their social identities and viewing interests are very precisely calibrated. For example, visitors to HBO's website on boxing encounter a section titled "TALK," which invites them to participate in polls, sign up for a newsletter and write on bulletin boards.[2] "TALK" is also and equally a system of surveillance that allows the network to monitor viewers' tastes and ideas without paying them for their intellectual property. The basic-cable sports network ESPN uses interactive TV fora such as "My Vote" and "My Bottom Line" to uncover audience drives in the name of enabling participation and pleasure in watching. ESPN has also purchased broadband portals that ensure global dominance. It now owns Cricinfo, Scrum. com and Racing-Live, which provide two-way exchanges with their audiences to build loyalty and deliver intelligence to advertisers. The US cable and satellite network Fox Soccer targets men aged 18–34 with annual household incomes of US$75,000 and above; it also undertakes surveillance of viewers on the Web. The station boasts that three quarters of its audience is male and half own their own homes. Commercials provide textual hints about the network's plan for matching viewers to advertisers: its advertisements concentrate remorselessly on regaining and sustaining hair growth and hard-ons, losing and hiding pimples and pounds, and becoming and adoring soldiers and sailors (pers. exp.; Miller 2010).

Online sites, such as Hulu, replaying network television and movies use "geo-filtered access logs" to identify audiences. These are measured each day, alongside confessional testimonies by potential viewers – if you tell us about your life and practices of consumption, we'll tell you about programs that may interest you. YouTube's Video Identification software, which was developed with Disney and Time Warner, is a surveillance device for tracking copyrighted materials on the site that follows the history of each uploaded frame, spying on users to disclose their internet protocols, aliases and practices to corporations. The software permits these companies to block or enable reuse of texts, depending on their marketing and surveillance needs of the moment. YouTube has thus become middle-aged media's valued ally, tracking intellectual property and realizing the

culture industries' paradoxical dream of engaging in product place-
ment each time copyright is infringed on line, while learning more
and more about their audiences (Miller 2009, 2010).

Conclusion

Focusing on corporate power, as I have done here, leaves one open to
the venerable, predictable charge of denying the pleasures of stardom
and the autonomy of audiences, of falling into the trap of a leftist
functionalism that focuses so tightly on political-economic structures
that it neglects cultural struggle.

But lest it be assumed that political-economic accounts of workers
and audiences are full of *données* and *nostra* rather than empirical
surprise and conflict, we should recognize that labor exploitation
and ideological mystification are routinely hidden from viewers,
while marketers like nothing better than active audiences who are
overflowing with knowledge about programs; nothing better than
diverse, articulate groups with easily identified cultural politics
and practices; nothing better than fine-grained ethnographic and
focus-group work in addition to large-scale surveys that provide
broad-based demographic data. The supposedly resistive social
identity is one more category for their delectation (Maxwell 1996;
Pendakur 1990; Rhines 1996; Wasko 2005). Marketers avow their
powerlessness over audiences when challenged in the public sphere,
but boast omnipotence over them in the private world: the essay that
won the oleaginous "Best New Thinking Award" at the 2003 Market
Research Society Conference acknowledged that successful marketing does not "view . . . the consumer as an individual" but "part of
the herd" (Earls 2003).

The task for sociologists who want the media to be more entertaining, informative, inclusive, and democratic is to alert our fellow
audience members how the "cognitariat" is exploited, the environment is polluted, and viewing and social identities are governed and
commodified by Hollywood and other media.

Notes

1 Some of this chapter draws on Maxwell and Miller (2012).
2 www.hbo.com/boxing/index.html#/boxing/talk/index.html, accessed
  September 2, 2013.

PART III
Media Representations

7

When Media Representation Met Sociology

Shani Orgad

We tend to take for granted images and narratives we encounter daily in the media; they function as a kind of background to our social lives, a constant flow of signs and symbolic content "that shape and inform a complex, unstructured, and not fully articulated understanding of life and the world we live in" (Orgad 2012: 9). However, as analysts, we pause to ponder their meanings. Semiotic analysis, which has been highly influential in the study of media representations, explores media images and texts as signs, seeking to discern the meanings generated by their discursive and visual properties. Similarly, popular (nonacademic) discussions of media representations, e.g. film reviews, analyze their textual, visual and auditory features, genres, and styles to contest their significance. But what does it mean to think *sociologically* about images and stories we encounter daily in the media? Sociological analysis of media representations – although it certainly may benefit from tools and concepts in other theoretical and methodological traditions, such as semiotics – foregrounds a different concern. Its interest is in the *social* role and *social* "work" (Hall 1997) performed by representations in particular contexts.

This chapter examines what a sociological focus entails, what sociology offers to media representation research and to understanding media representations' social "work" in the twenty-first century. As the chapter title implies, discussion is framed metaphorically as a meeting between sociology and media representation. I am interested in exploring what is productive in this meeting and, specifically, what it contributes to the study of media representations. The discussion starts by establishing briefly several "basic understandings" deriving from an analysis of media representations using a sociological lens. These understandings may depart from or be in tension with other approaches to studying media representations, e.g. semiotics, psychoanalysis, or post-structuralism. In other respects, they may complement non-sociological approaches and analyses. The chapter then examines "the meeting" between sociology and media representation analysis, and how media representation has been studied and theorized within sociology. The focus is on two central areas that have preoccupied the sociology of media representation and how they have been investigated empirically. The final part of the chapter reflects on future developments of this relationship. I discuss questions that sociological research of media representations ought to address and the directions in which it should develop to continue to be adequate for and relevant to understanding the contemporary, globalized media environment.

The interest in this chapter is biased toward contributions from a sociological perspective to the study of media representations. Equally important and interesting is how the meeting between sociology and media representations informs and enriches sociology. Although I do not address this question directly (and it would benefit from separate discussion), I hope the chapter offers some insights into how granting attention to media representations benefits sociology and why sociological studies should take media representation seriously and make it central to their analyses.

Establishing basic understandings

Media representations are images, narratives, accounts, and frames that circulate in the media and carry symbolic content: news photographs and reports, advertisements, radio programs, online videos, films, blogs, Facebook pages, and so on. These representations construct meanings, offering understandings of what the world is, and why and how it works in particular ways (based on Hall 1997).

The notion that representations construct rather than reflect reality is rooted in semiotics and other strands of the constructionist approach (see Hall 1997; Orgad 2012). The constructionist approach argues that any representation is inherently and inevitably a construction, a selective and particular depiction of some elements of reality, which generates certain meanings and excludes others. This view is premised on the recognition that: "we give things meaning by how we represent them – the words we use about them, the stories we tell about them, the images of them we produce, the emotions we associate with them, the ways we classify and conceptualize them, the value we place on them" (Hall 1997: 3).

Nevertheless, the mimetic (or reflectionist) approach, which assumes that representation's task is adequately to reflect pre-existing meanings of the "real," continues to underpin considerable debate and critique of media representations. For example, various research projects, often based on quantitative content analysis, and public discussions of media representations have been premised on the idea that media should mirror the society they represent (for specific examples, see Orgad 2012: 19). The view of media representations as mimetic devices can be found in McQuail's (1969) influential intervention, in what was the first concerted effort to develop a sociology of mass communications: "Perhaps the single most important issue in the sociology of mass communications which calls for the deployment of content analysis is . . . does the mass media content *mirror* social values and the prevailing social structure or does it independently originate change?" (McQuail 1969: 68, emphasis added).

In contrast to McQuail's sociological account, which relied heavily on then current Anglo-Saxon and particularly American quantitative research, twenty-first-century media sociology demands that representations are *reframed*: rather than "content" that "mirrors" society and its values, representations are seen as cultural resources produced by and for society, and as symbolic sites where issues, problems, tensions, and dilemmas are negotiated and contested. Methodologically, this view demands inclusion of other, including more qualitative and interpretive, methods of analysis. While content analysis remains important and useful in media representation analysis, it is underpinned by the assumption that reality can be reflected in more "accurate" and "truthful" ways. Thus, it records trends in representations of specific issues, and highlights problems, such as "bias," "disproportion," and "misrepresentation," and how they change (or not) over time. Methods such as Critical Discourse Analysis are unconcerned with whether and how truth is reflected, focusing instead on how meanings are produced and legitimized, and how power relations, hierarchies, and authorities are produced, reproduced, and transformed symbolically.

Sociological analysis should be able to advance our understanding of why media representations matter, why they are *not*, as some may contend, "just texts," insubstantial alongside the materiality of real occurrences. It demands that our semantic interpretations of images and texts are always grounded in social contexts giving rise to these representations: their production, circulation, and consumption. A sociological perspective steers researchers away from treating representations in isolation, a tendency of some semiotic and linguistic traditions and psychoanalytic approaches to text. Some film analysts, for example, write as if the concern is only with the mechanics of films (Barker with Austin 2000: 3). A sociological approach moves toward critical consideration of the social work that representations do in making sense of social life, binding everyday life to values and morality, and sustaining, reproducing, and contesting power relations – all of which aspects are discussed in more detail in the next section. While sociological analysis still may center on analyzing representations as texts, scrutiny of textual, auditory, visual, and discursive properties seeks to establish better understanding of representation as a process of producing meanings in particular social contexts, with particular social implications.

Thinking sociologically about media representations highlights their influence and centrality in the societies and cultures in which, by which, and for which they are produced, circulated, and consumed. It also offers an important reminder that representation is *one* component in a complex social reality and its meanings and consequences are contingent upon and interact with a range of other factors. In contrast to the omnipotence attributed to media representations in some earlier ("strong effects") research, and in moral panic and/or deterministic accounts of their impact, a sociological approach emphasizes the *conditionality* and *contingency* of the meanings and impact of representations. The sociologist's task is *not* to discover and determine the ultimate meaning or meanings of a text, but rather to identify the *proposals* that representations issue (based on Boltanski 1999), invitations they deliver to their audiences to think, feel, and act in certain ways, and possible meanings they block or suppress. Sociological analysis carries the inherent caveat that the *proposals* it identifies must be activated, negotiated, enacted, and/or rejected by particular people, in particular places and at particular times. In other words, exploration of texts, images and the "invitations" they issue are *one* element in the "circuit of culture" (Johnson 1986/7) since this includes consumption and production, moments that are crucial but whose investigation goes beyond the remit of textual analysis of representations.

Media representation meets sociology

Sociology has inspired two important areas of research in relation to media representations: the first focuses on the role of representations in sustaining community, social order, and orienting everyday life, and the second centers on their exercise of symbolic power.

Media representation, community, social order, and everyday life

This body of work underscores the central role of media representations in creating and sustaining social integration, order, and cohesion, and enabling management of social tension and continuity of society, culture, and values. Its main endeavor is to identify the collective narratives circulating in society at a certain time, and to explain their role in orienting and binding community. In this research, representations are not used (as McQuail (1969: 67) describes in relation to some "content studies") as "evidence about the culture in which [they are] produced and used" or as "evidence of intentions, attitudes and values of its producers." They are not illustrations of pre-existing cultures and values, but rather cultural constructions produced in and by societies in particular times and places, which in turn shape, orient, and inform frames of understanding and social action.

Durkheim's functionalist analysis is a major source of influence on this work. Media representations are understood to act as collective representations through which society tells itself what it is. The community projects its ideal, embodied in news stories and other media representations, which create a symbolic order operating to provide confirmation (Carey 1992). They construct society in an almost mystical way, as a sort of "super-being" enthralling its individual members (Giddens 1990: 13). The analysis focuses on media representations' role in symbolic construction and sustenance of community.

The study of *media events*, which is rooted in anthropological theory, has been constitutive in developing this area of inquiry. It developed an account of how, through ritual, media representations serve to integrate societies, sustaining symbolic order and control. Since Dayan and Katz's (1992) original study, numerous analyses have demonstrated the integrative function of media events. They show how ritualized representations, constructed and presented reverently within generic "scripts,"[1] articulate, reproduce, and deepen certain understandings and beliefs about society. Coronations (e.g. Wardle and West 2004), sporting events (e.g. Tomlinson 1996), political events (Lee et al. 2000), "traumatic events" (Katz and Liebes 2007) and national celebrations (Bin 1998; Lu 2009; Pan 2010), through their performative, ritualized, and spectacular character, have been shown to reaffirm the symbolic contours of communities, renewing the contract between members of the community and its imagined center, confirming traditional authorities (Couldry, Hepp, and Crotz 2010).

Empirically, research on media events (and media representations and community more generally) has focused on national community. Even global media events, e.g. the Olympic Games, analysts have argued, tend to be nationalistic displays and assertions of cultural distinctiveness foregrounding national over global considerations (e.g. Tomlinson 1996). More recently, media events analysis increasingly concentrates on other types, levels, and formations of community. This not only expands the empirical, analytical focus from national to global and other levels, it also complicates and unravels the neatness of the functional explanation, exposing contestation, contradiction, and competition as important features of contemporary media events. This line of research suggests the role and significance of media events may reside not so much in their cohesive function but in their capacity to provide a stage allowing many voices to compete and be heard. I argue later in the chapter that this is one area where sociological analysis of media representation should be developed further if it is to respond to and correspond with the changing, twenty-first-century media environment.

In contrast to media events, the "high holidays of mass communication" (Dayan and Katz 1992: 1) whose exceptional, extraordinary, outstanding, spectacular, and unusual character is constitutive of symbolic building of community, the other empirical focus in study of representations and community is *news*. Partly responding to the declining centrality of ceremonial media events (Katz and Liebes 2007), this research highlights the centrality of news representations – ongoing, repetitive, formulaic, and ritualized – in creating and sustaining the ordinariness and normality of everyday life, providing resources for social confirmation and reassurance (Silverstone 2005).

Carey's (1992) ritual model of communication, drawing on Durkheim and deriving from anthropological theory of religious ritual, inspired much research into news representations. News is conceptualized as "presentation of reality that gives life an overall form, order, and tone" (Carey 1992: 21); news creates an artificial, though nonetheless real, symbolic order operating to provide confirmation and represent the underlying order of things within society (ibid.). Research has focused particularly on the role of national news representations as symbolic "glue" binding and renewing bonds among members of the national community. It argues that news' fundamental role, rather than being transmission of information, is symbolic production of national people as an "imagined community" (Anderson 1983). News fulfills this role through ongoing, banal perpetuation of shared symbols and beliefs (Billig 1995), constructing and reproducing dominant narratives and a consensual national collective "we" versus "them" (Schudson 2002; Waisbord 2002), and creating a temporal framework (e.g. through broadcast television schedules) organizing national community members' everyday lives (Scannell 1996). Unlike media events, ordinariness, familiarity and the taken-for-granted character of news are key. As Billig (1995: 8) observes, "In so many little ways, the citizenry are daily reminded of their national place in a world of nations. However, this reminding is so familiar, so continual, that it is not consciously registered as reminding."

Frosh and Wolfsfeld's (2007) analysis of television news reports of a terrorist attack in Israel is a useful example of an investigation whose central motivation is sociological in the sense I have described here. The authors show how, by focusing on citizens' everyday social interactions and personal stories, these representations of terrorist attacks turn resilience of everyday interpersonal relationships into a conspicuous national value and, ultimately, into a national myth. News thus acts as affirmation of nationhood.

Despite the enduring relevance of news representations' production of national social imaginaries, the changing nature of news within the globalized mediated environment raises new concerns and questions for research. I develop some of these in the third section of this chapter, discussing avenues for future sociological analysis of representations.

Related to the concern with how media representations help to bind individuals to a community and a realm of shared values is the question of how they help to shape, enhance, and define everyday life. How do media images and stories orient individuals and help them make sense of their lives? In a crude functionalist sense, this question directs analysis toward identifying the function of representations as agents of socialization – what McQuail (1969: 14) argued was one of sociology's then main interests in mass communication. This interest reverberates in current research, e.g. in studies of lifestyle magazines, talk shows and reality television programs, showing how textual and visual representations model thought and behavior, providing audiences with vocabularies and definitions to deal with everyday situations. However, the critical interest in media representation and everyday life goes beyond this. It is the *ethical force of media representations* that animates research and has underlined sociology's interest in cultural representations since the turn of the twentieth century (Illouz 2003). At the heart of such research is the question of how images and narratives, in privileging and legitimizing particular frames of thinking and feeling, and excluding, marginalizing, and devaluing others, shape and orient people's everyday lives and society's moral fabric. This is the question underlying the second area of sociological research of media representations discussed below.

Media representations and the exercise of symbolic power

The central motivation for sociological analysis of media representations is to account for their exercise of power: how representations are embedded within and, in turn, reproduce and transform power relations and inequalities. This exploration is rooted in Marxist scholarship, which views the media as agents of social control, tied into the politically and economically dominant, whose power they help (consciously or not) to reproduce and sustain. In this view, the prime work of media representations is to "paper over the cracks of the contradictions of global capitalism in the drip feed of ideological framing and naturalization" (Silverstone 2005: 190).

Analysis has focused on the operation of ideology in representations and how it gains consent through strategies and devices such as legitimation, naturalization, identification, rationalization, universalization, and reification. It has sought to unravel the ways in which different types of media representation are involved, often in subtle, latent, and highly sophisticated ways, in reproducing domination, inequality, and injustice with regard to class, gender, race, sexuality, ethnicity, age, and other social categories and identities.

The concept of ideology, which refers to "the ways in which meaning is mobilized for the maintenance of relations of domination" (Thompson 1984: 5) and its theoretical developments (most notably by Gramsci, Althusser, Eagleton, and Thompson), propelled and informed a huge body of work on representations across media, genre, contexts, and cultures. Notwithstanding the literature's richness and diversity, a common argument is that media representations are intimately related to and contribute to maintenance and reproduction of prevailing frameworks of social understanding and power structures in society. Research has documented and theorized the range of discursive techniques and tactics through which media representations – from news to advertisements – help to embed, legitimize and naturalize certain ideologies, making them appear as "truth," as the "right," "normal," and appropriate ways of thinking and feeling.

Ideologies have tended to be associated most explicitly with informational media genres such as news and documentaries (Gitlin 1980; Tuchman 1978). However, their operation through other genres appealing to pleasure and associated with entertainment, e.g. soap operas, advertisements, and talk shows, has been recognized prominently by feminist critique of popular representations and corresponding audience responses (Macdonald 2003: 32). For example, numerous studies are dedicated to showing how popular representations are involved, often in subtle, indirect and "soft" ways, in articulating and reproducing unequal gender identities and relations (Gill 2007b; Kilbourne 1999; McRobbie 1977; Nichols 1981; Ross 2009). Race is another center of analytical attention; media texts and images – in both informational and "entertainment" genres – have been shown consistently to convey and reconfirm stereotypical views, legitimizing forms of racism (e.g. Hall 1997; Ross 1996).

Gramsci's notions of hegemony (the process through which a group or a party is able to claim social, political and cultural leadership of a society) and common sense have proved particularly powerful tools for understanding how power is exercised through media representations. Gill (2007b: 57) aptly summarizes Gramsci's contribution: "His work allows us to attend to the dynamic qualities of ideology – its mobility and fluidity; the fragmented nature of subjectivity; and the significance of winning consent for particular identities through struggle."

Gramsci's theory, especially his observation that because hegemony needs to be won and requires approval it is always temporary and contested (Gill 2007b), allows a more dynamic view of representations' exercise of symbolic power. In other words, representations are not pre-fixed, static reflections of prevailing social structures and values but rather symbolic sites of struggle over establishment of "truths."

The view of media representation as a site of contestation gained substantial force from Foucault's model of power's operation through discourse. Foucault insists that power does not, as ideological critique would have it, operate only through repression (Macdonald

2003). Power is more dispersed, and discourse is the site of struggle over power. Discourse is the product of certain social, historical, institutional, and political conditions that render certain statements truthful and meaningful and others false, marginalized, and deviant. Although Foucault refers to discourse, not representation, his theory suggests that the act of representation itself transforms power relations and subjectivities and the way we experience and define ourselves (Orgad 2012).

For Foucault, "the question is not whether discourse is truthful but 'how effects of truths are produced within discourses which in themselves are neither true nor false' (Gordon 1980: 118)" (Macdonald 2003: 18). The power of representations resides in producing certain "truth effects" and legitimizing certain discursive regimes, while rendering others illegitimate, deviant, and "false." Therefore, our analytical efforts, à la Foucault, should be directed toward identifying how certain media representations emerge from and within "regimes of truth," and how they thus establish the truth and legitimacy of certain ideas and statements, and the illegitimacy and deviance of others. For example, a Foucauldian analysis shows how a variety of representations across seemingly unrelated themes, contexts, and fields, including feminist discourses on sexual abuse, the Holocaust, discourses of health and illness, and reality television, converge to support the construction of the "survivor" as a desirable role for coping with trauma and suffering in contemporary western culture, rendering false and illegitimate the categories of victim and the dead (Orgad 2009a).

Foucault's theory[2] has been applied in a variety of ways to analysis of media texts and images, examining a vast range of discourses, e.g. risk (Macdonald 2003), childhood (Burrows and Wright 2004; Macdonald 2003), femininity (Bartky 1990), Orientalism (Said 2003 [1978]), and neoliberalism. Notwithstanding its diverse applications, common to all is interest in the processes and effects of symbolic exclusion and inclusion: how certain people, places, social entities, objects, ideas, voices, and relations are accorded visibility, authority, normality, legitimacy, and "truthfulness," while others are rendered invisible, deviant, and/or illegitimate (Orgad 2012).

A central concern within this discussion (influenced by, but certainly not confined to Foucault) is representation of the other: the ways in which images and narratives construct practices and populations that diverge from what, at a specific moment in time, is seen as central, safe, legitimate, normal, and conventional to become a source of strangeness, hostility, and danger (Pickering 2001). Hall's

(1997) writing has been foundational in spelling the significance of symbolic production of difference and otherness, developing an analytical vocabulary for the operation of "othering" in the representation of race, gender, sexuality, ethnicity, and other dimensions of difference. Said's (2003 [1978]) seminal study, *Orientalism*, in which he explored symbolic forms of knowledge that the European colonial project employed, had a major impact on this debate. Numerous studies inspired and informed by Hall and/or Said show how certain groups, people, cultures, and places are stereotyped, victimized, demonized, and invested through discourse and images with negative meanings. Fundamentally, this research underscores the moral force of media representations in providing definitions and frames orienting our relation to *the stranger*. Interest in the stranger as a social category and society's relation to the other – one of sociology's major preoccupations – appears evermore salient in today's global world, marked by the force of mass migration.

While Marxist critiques regard media representations (and media more generally) as instruments upholding the interests of the powerful, more dispersed models of power, such as Foucault's, allow for serious consideration of the capacity of media representations to foster social change. An important contribution of sociological study of media images and narratives has been the focus on the role that media representation can – and sometimes do – perform in subverting stereotypes, challenging dominant ideologies, symbolically rehabilitating others (Cottle 2006) and redressing inequalities and injustice. For example, studies document the ways in which the representation of certain groups, issues, and identities have changed over time toward greater inclusion and fairness, although the extent of these shifts' progressive and positive nature is contested (e.g. Gill 2007b in relation to gender; Cottle 2006; Liebes and Kampf 2009 in relation to ethnic minorities; Smith and Yanacopulos 2004 in relation to "faces of development"). Sociology usefully reminds us that media representations alone cannot impel change; changes must correspond with and be supported by broader social discourses and larger political, economic, and cultural structures.

Thinking sociologically about media representations: a look to the future

Discussion so far has demonstrated that sociology has inspired rich and valuable analysis, advancing understanding of media representations' social importance, role, and potential. Analysis has focused on two central areas. The first underscores the central role of media representations in creating and sustaining social integration, order, and cohesion, enabling management of social tension and continuity of society, culture, and values, and orienting and enhancing the meaning of everyday life. This literature demonstrates especially the constitutive role of media images and stories in symbolic building of national communities. The second strand documents and argues convincingly for the many subtle, latent, and highly sophisticated ways in which varied types of media representations are involved in articulating and reproducing power relations and inequalities.

The continued relevance and importance of these research areas and their underlying questions is indubitable. However, new questions, concerns, and analytical challenges are presented by the rapidly changing nature of the contemporary media environment and attendant media representations. To remain adequate and relevant, simultaneously building on the strengths and contributions of previous research, social analysis of media representations must respond to the increasingly interconnected and globalized media landscape within which representations are produced, circulated, and consumed. In what follows, I reflect on what this might entail.

Giddens's (1990) account of globalization and especially his phenomenology of modernity are especially helpful for this discussion. Giddens (1990: 137) argues that sociological literature's two dominant images of what it feels like to live in the world of modernity – namely Weber's iron cage and Marx's (and many others') image of modernity as a tamable monster – are inadequate. Giddens (1990: 139) proposes to substitute for them the image of a juggernaut: "a runaway engine of enormous power which, collectively as human beings, we can drive to some extent but which also threatens to rush out of control and which could rend itself asunder." Any attempt to capture the experience of modernity Giddens contends, must grow out of this image of the juggernaut, a "tensionful," contradictory and indeterminate engine, deriving from radical separation of time and space (ibid.).

Media representation analysis is part of the sociological endeavor to capture the experience of modern societies. Thus, if we accept Giddens's juggernaut image, our analytical efforts should be focused on exploring representations' role in "riding the juggernaut" (Giddens 1990: 151). Put differently, how do media images and narratives provide symbolic resources that enable and, in turn, are produced by dialectic frameworks of experience in modernity? How do they provide frameworks for ordering time and space, for global orientation and mobilization, while simultaneously disrupting temporal and spatial stabilities and continuities? And how do they contribute to creating and sustaining familiarity and ontological security, while at the same time exposing and cultivating insecurity, anxiety, and estrangement?

These are some of the "big" questions that media representation research should pose and address to inform relevant and valuable analyses, accounting for the contemporary global media environment and its consequences for social life. The remainder of this chapter offers further reflections on these questions, demonstrating how the two concerns that have preoccupied media sociology of representations hitherto, i.e. creating and sustaining community and social order and the exercise of symbolic power, can be developed further and redesigned to engage with and address these questions.

Dialectic of displacement and re-embedding, and intersection between estrangement and familiarity (Giddens 1990), have been central themes in the debate on media and communications and globalization (e.g. Meyrowitz 1985; Thompson 1995; Tomlinson 1999). The focus has been how *technologies* of media and communications have radically altered spatial experience, conjoining proximity and distance, consequently transforming social experience and interaction in unparalleled ways. More recently, empirical attention has turned to the role of texts and images in this dialectics, and their concurrent articulation of local and global, continuity and disruption, familiarity and estrangement.

Creating and sustaining community and social order in a global age

Recent study of *media events* is an important area of this development in the sociological analysis of media representation. Couldry et al. (2010) revisit the theory of media events in an attempt to establish a basis for researching them in a global age. Their project argues that the national framing in Dayan and Katz's original argument and their understanding of societies as marked by a shared set of values are highly problematic as we move to an examination of media events within a global perspective. In particular, the authors argue that "understanding media events on a global scale as the genre of integrative ritual they were originally thought to be" (Couldry et al. 2010: 10) is limited. Their character is potentially more contradictory and dialectical than Dayan and Katz's original theory assumes: rather than a singular power-center (the nation-state in former analyses), a variety of interest groups and discourses, exercised across multiple channels, are related to performance of these events (Couldry et al. 2010: 11); rather than their (Durkheimian) cohesive function and their symbolic capacity to erase differences and bind dispersed individuals in a realm of imagined shared values, media events' relevance and significance may reside in their capacity to allow "for the constructions of a common 'we', and of many varied national, ethnic, religious, subcultural and other voicings of that 'we'" (Couldry et al. 2010: 12). Indeed, Dayan's (2010) account of the 2008 Beijing Olympics revisits his and Katz's original formulation of media events, observing that, in the current hyper-mediated global age, exclusive focus on a single event has become scarce and dominant events have now come to serve "as the contested ground for a multiplicity of media voices" (Dayan 2010: 29). Similarly, Katz and Liebes (2007) observe that the importance of integrative, ceremonial media events is receding, while live broadcasting of disruptive events such as disaster, terror and war take center-stage. Other studies (e.g. DeLisle 2008; Latham 2009) develop these observations, establishing that media events in the global new media age constitute a battleground for competing voices and narratives, in tension with their cohesive, integrative role.

Similarly, current study of *news* representations highlights the increasing complexity and contradiction in news and its social role. For example, research shows that images produced by national media broadcasts may still fulfill an important function, portraying the nation as a coherent stable construct, providing its members reassurance and sustaining social order, but these images increasingly compete with and are contested by other images and accounts of the nation articulated by news and other genres of representations in the current mediated space. My analyses (Orgad 2008, 2009b, 2011, 2012) of various examples of national and international media representations of national conflicts (e.g. the 2005 French riots, 2005 Madrid terror attacks, and 2008/9 Gaza war) reveal how media representations, from news reports to citizens' online content (e.g. blogs, YouTube, etc.) may trigger simultaneously symbolic distancing and estrangement, feelings of self-doubt, disturbance, reassurance, and reaffirmation of national narratives and the social order. Thus, the news, I argue (Orgad 2011), acts simultaneously as symbolic "glue" binding together members of the nation and as the "horse" (drawing on Shklovsky's analysis of Tolstoy) fostering self-estrangement and disrupting national narratives. This dialectical work of media representations relating to national identity is not exclusive to news; other genres and media participate in ongoing interjections of displacement and re-embedding, familiarity and estrangement. Gilroy's (2004) analysis of the satirical television series, *Da Ali G Show*, is a useful example of how popular satire distances viewers from entrenched notions of nationalism (Britishness), offering different ways to imagine identities and culture.

Today's global context, "the collage of images we have of the social totality [of the 'nation'] and our relationship with it" that Frosh and Wolfsfeld (2007: 109) and many others have described in their media representation analyses, is increasingly vulnerable and potentially less coherent, consistent, and homogenous than in the past (Orgad 2012). One important task for media sociology is to account for this changing relationship between media representations (which are themselves changing dramatically), such as news, and the nation and to capture and explain the consequences for our sense of belonging and ontological security of the growing visibility of different, contesting voices and accounts in media space.

Gilroy's (2004) *Da Ali G Show* analysis also throws into relief the centrality and importance of concern with the construction of the "other" in contemporary media. We live in a world in which we are continuously introduced, through narrative and image, to others who are *not* like us. But it is also a world in which it is precisely the commonality of difference that is shared (Silverstone 2007): "The mediated globe involves lifting the veil on difference. . . . The problem is that while globalized media have lifted the veil, they have provided few or no resources to understand and respond to that difference, nor do they necessarily represent it adequately. And the consequences of that representation have tended to produce either worldly indifference or hostility" (Silverstone 2007: 28).

We ought not to be satisfied with the media's limitations, narrowness, and intransigence, Silverstone warns. A crucial task for media sociology is to study representations of "others" in contemporary mediated space – e.g. terrorists, migrants, asylum seekers, refugees, victims of natural disasters, atrocities, and wars – and account for the questions: do they extend understanding and moral judgment? How can they perform this moral role better?

Exercise of symbolic power in the contemporary media environment

Analysis that stresses the conservative role of media representations and shows how certain frames for thinking and explaining the world that sustain inequalities are articulated, legitimized, and perpetuated continues to be salient in accounting for why and how media representations matter. However, Giddens's juggernaut image invites exploration of directions that are also less predictable, and recognition that media representations are less controllable than in the past. New media are particularly (but not exclusively) central in disrupting and challenging prevailing structures of power and inequality in the public sphere. The field of media representations, which now includes numerous narratives and images produced and disseminated by ordinary people – on Twitter, Facebook, YouTube, blogs, etc. – can trouble dominant power structures and inequalities. For example, Tyler and Gill (in press) show how British media representations of Gamu Nhengu, a Zimbabwean teenager ejected from a popular British reality television show, including a Facebook campaign supported by a quarter of a million people, offer new forms of "post-colonial migrant audibility" that trouble racial discourses and "the deep inequalities which underpin and sustain British national life" (ibid.).

This is not to argue for what may seem to be a celebratory view of the current media environment as an open, inclusive and necessarily transformative space, in which media representations always challenge existing social structures and inequalities. Much research shows how current representations in both "old" and "new" media mirror and reproduce old structures, upholding unequal power relations. Rather, my argument is that sociological analysis must account for *contestation* and consequently *decreasing controllability and predictability* as key features of media representation in the contemporary globalized environment. This is what Thompson (2005) refers to in his description of today's mediated environment as an age of new visibility. Sociology of media representation in the age of new visibility is interested in how contestation is articulated and exercised, what possibilities it creates, and what challenges it poses and addresses. It does not deny that material, structural, and historical power relations of inequalities matter but insists that *how* they matter cannot be simply mapped through fixed categories (Orgad 2012) and that our analysis "must go beyond the repeated discovery of domination and the romanticization/fetishization of resistance in global contexts" (Shome and Hegde 2002a: 186).

Emphasis on situating the study of media representations in the current media environment, in which anyone potentially can express opinions and produce representations, may lead to an unhelpful focus on individual representations (e.g. bloggers' accounts, Facebook personal pages, etc.), with little or no consideration of relations to collective narratives and discourses or broader social significance.

Couldry (2010b: 128) warns that "[a] sociology that stays at the level of *individual* narrative resources cannot be adequate." For example, studies of patients' online representations of their experiences of illness are limited (as sociological analyses) if they fail to situate these representations within broader narratives available in society (e.g. health and illness, therapeutic, consumerist) on which patients draw and which, in turn, they help transform and/or reproduce. Sociological inquiry should seek to forge the connection between personal and collective discourses, and to ask how proliferation of personal narratives online relates to the collective narratives formulated, uttered, valued, and promoted in the public sphere, and to types of narratives sustainable (or not) under certain social, historical and political conditions. As Foucault would remind us, the analysis of particular media images and narratives should be situated always in broader historical, social, cultural, political, and institutional contexts within which they are produced, disseminated, and consumed, and which in turn they shape.

The sociological analysis proposed above has several methodological implications, two of which I now discuss briefly.

First, following Beck's (2003) broader critique of social sciences' "methodological nationalism," analysis of media representations would also benefit from moving beyond the nation as its privileged reference point. In an age of accelerating globalization, driven by economic, political, cultural, and technological forces, the national is no longer the only nor necessarily dominant context in which representations are produced, disseminated, and consumed, and within which they acquire meaning. Thus, analysis must account for the complexity and consequences of interactions and communication in the context of globalization. Of course, some research is and will continue to be interested explicitly in national media representations. However, it should be wary of making universalist claims with no appropriate acknowledgment of the specificity of its analytical concepts and the national frameworks of representations examined. Even when interest is in the national media, it may be adequate to ask whether and how such representations are shaped by and/or shape categories outside the nation. Furthermore, representations increasingly cross cultural and national boundaries, endowing them with different meanings. It is important for sociological research to trace this journey and its consequences; think, for example, of the controversy around the Muhammad cartoons, first published in September 2005 by Danish newspaper *Jyllands-Posten* before being reproduced by many European and international media outlets.

Second, analysis must respond to the increasingly converged, interconnected, and networked media landscape within which representations are produced, circulated, and consumed. The compartmentalization characteristic of much media representations research, e.g. the institutionalized split between film studies and other areas of research on media representations (e.g. television, newspapers) and separation of theoretical paradigms, and thematic and methodological orientations (Macdonald 2003), seems ill-equipped to address the changing, twenty-first-century media environment (Orgad 2012). Research must examine media representations and the meanings they produce *across* technologies, genres, contexts, discourses, modes of address, and forms. Specifically, analysis should allow for a better understanding of how ideas and frames for understanding emerge and are accumulated across different texts and realms, and how different fields of discourse and action give rise to and, through a variety of representations (e.g. personal and collective, informational and entertainment, textual and visual, etc.), support some statements and ideas while delegitimizing others.

Sociology of media representations is far from being methodologically and analytically "neat." It demands examination across sites and contexts and a search for tensions, contradictory processes, and meanings in order to account for the extreme dynamism and globalizing scope of contemporary media and our modern world.

Notes

1 In Dayan and Katz's (1992) original analysis: contests, conquests and coronations.
2 Foucault's approach has several shortcomings that are beyond the scope of this chapter. For discussion of these, see Orgad (2012).

8

Too Little But Not Too Late: Sociological Contributions to Feminist Media Studies

Laura Grindstaff and Andrea Press

At the turn of the nineteenth century, Jane Austen described history as all about men who were "good for nothing, and hardly any women at all" (Austen and Fraiman 1994: 86). Indeed, history, literature, and the classics had, for centuries, focused on men's experiences from a male perspective. Other disciplines followed suit. This androcentrism was challenged in the 1970s by second-wave feminism and its transformation of American universities. As a social movement and theory of power, feminism has influenced scholarly thought and study, particularly in the humanities and humanistic social sciences where interpretive approaches to understanding social life create space for rethinking relations between power and knowledge-production. Although the establishment of women's studies departments is a clear legacy of this influence, feminist inquiry has been "mainstreamed" to some degree. In sociology, gender is a topic of analysis in its own right (consider the large body of literature on "doing gender," for example) and a dimension of analysis within other substantive areas – e.g. work, occupations, organizations, health, immigration, education. From a feminist perspective, all social institutions can be understood as being constituted by, and vehicles for sustaining, gendered ideologies and practices in tandem with other axes of stratification such as race, class, and sexuality. Feminist inquiry is not simply about adding women to research agendas from which they have been excluded, but also understanding gender as an organizing principle of the social order. In the younger field of communications, feminist influence takes multiple forms, but is especially evident in media representation analyses. The phrase "feminist media studies" typically refers to work primarily (but not exclusively) focused on readings of visual texts, from film and television to magazines and music videos, with an eye to unpacking gendered meanings and implications.

So far so obvious, perhaps. But if feminist scholarship has transformed sociology to the point where the sex and gender section is among the largest of the profession, and transformed communications such that "feminist media studies" is now a well-known subfield, there is a different but related issue that pertains to how the two disciplines intersect. How and to what degree has sociology influenced media studies? More specifically, how and to what degree has feminist sociology influenced feminist media studies? In this chapter, we argue that feminist inquiry can and should be a major point of articulation for bringing sociology and media studies together, but that, as yet, feminist media studies has tended to marginalize what is distinctly sociological about the study of media (in particular, its methods), just as feminist sociology has tended to ignore the media. Consequently, the two arenas of scholarship seem to run on parallel rather than intersecting tracks. Almost thirty years ago, Stacey and Thorne (1985) wrote about the "missing feminist revolution in sociology," referring to the relative ghettoization of gender concerns in sociology at the time in comparison to history, literature, and anthropology. Playing off that theme, we posit there is a missing sociological revolution in feminist media studies, a revolution that is partly methodological insofar as the field of feminist media studies prioritizes textual analysis over ethnographic and other social science approaches. At the same time, media revolution is missing in sociology (feminist and otherwise); sociology seems to have virtually relinquished study of the media to scholars working in communications and media studies departments. Even cursory perusal of key journals in the respective disciplines and subfields will reveal these gaps and disjunctures (*Gender & Society* compared to *Feminist Media Studies*, for example, or the *American Journal of Sociology* compared to the *Journal of Communication*).

Drifting apart: brief histories

To begin, then, there are two interrelated questions to unpack. Why has sociology, including feminist sociology, largely abdicated the study of media to other disciplines, and why has feminist media studies marginalized sociological methods and practices?

The first question has much to do with the rise of communications as a distinct field of inquiry. A relative newcomer in the map of disciplines characterizing western universities, communications emerged in the postwar period as an interdisciplinary endeavor focused on processes mediating communication in western cultures and societies. Although it was often positioned as social science, drawing on sociology, anthropology, and psychology to focus on communicative processes (Delia 1987), communications also had strong influences from humanities. Rhetoric – the study of language and its processes, as influenced by classics and literary analysis – was an important antecedent and respected subfield from the beginning. Unsurprisingly, interdisciplinarity resulted in an often fragmented (and sometimes polarized) field with both substantive and methodological differences; offshoots such as film studies and various strands of cultural studies emerged, cultivating distinctively humanistic, interpretive approaches as alternatives to the perceived scientism of mainstream dimensions of the communications canon.

Second-wave feminism influenced both social-scientific and humanistic media scholarship, more so the latter. At the social science end were studies of women's presence and participation (or lack thereof) in media industries (M. Cantor 1977; Isber and M. Cantor 1975), gender stereotyping in advertising and media programming (Bretl and J. Cantor 1988; Dominick and Rauch 1972; Lichter, Lichter, and Rothman 1994), and the impact of media on women (Harrison and J. Cantor 1997; Hoffner and J. Cantor 1991; Stice and Shaw 1994). At the humanities end, the greatest transformation came via study of film. Haskell (1974 [1987]) and Rosen (1974) were among the first to apply feminist critique to the portrayal of women in film, although critical attention to this had begun earlier (see Bell 2011). By the mid-1970s, the key theoretical paradigm that would shape film studies for decades to come was Freudian psychoanalysis (in concert with Lacanian psycholinguistics), as developed by scholars such as Laura Mulvey (1975) and Christian Metz (1975, 1986). Mulvey famously applied a psychoanalytic framework to critique the patriarchal nature of Hollywood cinema in her classic 1975 essay "Visual Pleasure and Narrative Cinema." She argued that classical Hollywood cinema constructed a "male gaze" for spectators by positioning women on-screen as objects of sexual difference in relation to male protagonists; women characters are defined by their "to-be-looked-at-ness," subject to and object of voyeuristic and fetishistic desires, while the male protagonist is "bearer of the look," relay for the camera and spectatorial privilege of the (implied male) viewer.

Mulvey's theory of patriarchal spectatorship – which she argued could best be disrupted by alternative, feminist methods of film-making – was widely debated into the 1980s and 1990s. Articles responding and alluding to her work flooded film, media, and feminist journals, such that "action" in feminist media studies became firmly centered within the psychoanalytic paradigm that Mulvey had spawned (key volumes and collections include Carson, Welsch, and Ditmar 1994; Cook with Dodd 1993; de Lauretis 1984; Doane 1987; Doane, Mellencamp, and Williams 1984; Erens 1990; Gledhill 1978; Kaplan 1978, 1983; Kuhn 1982; Mayne 1990, 1993; Penley 1988, 1989; Silverman 1988; Thornham 1999). Her influence ensured that the new and growing field of feminist media studies would be identified primarily with humanities rather than social sciences, although not all feminist media scholars focused on film, of course, and not all feminist film scholars employed psychoanalytic frameworks (e.g. see Mellancamp 1995). Like Mulvey, most feminist film scholars were located initially in literature or language departments, later in film studies departments and programs. This is unsurprising, given the absence of a textual analysis and/or psycholinguistic tradition within sociology and mainstream communications research. In many universities, film studies became a discipline distinct from other humanities and from communications departments, reflecting methodological as well as substantive specialization. The psychoanalytic paradigm gradually lost its stronghold within film studies, due in part to challenges to its ahistoricism, ethnocentrism, and white, western biases (see Hansen 1994).

Perhaps the strongest competitor as an early US feminist media studies "trendsetter" was Janice Radway. A professor of literature and American Studies, Radway published *Reading the Romance* in 1984. It was remarkable at the time for using methods of interpretive social science – including depth interviews, participant observation, institutional production analysis, and detailed textual analysis – to explore the significance of romance novels for female readers in a small Midwestern town. Radway examined the generic structure and ideological meaning of romance novels in relation to the reading practices of women themselves within the broader context of marriage and domesticity. Incorporating a small number of interviews and reader surveys by social science standards, *Reading the Romance* nevertheless represented a less text-centered and more ethnographic feminist media analysis than was then common in the United States.

Like Mulvey, Radway was widely read while feminist media studies gained traction. Her ethnographic approach was compatible with existing strands of communication scholarship and new cultural studies developments (see her introduction to the new edition written in 2002), and some scholars emulated her (e.g. Press 1991). But the persistence of critical textual analysis within feminist circles limited her influence: in sheer numerical terms, many more studies published in the 1980s and 1990s drew on psychoanalysis than reader-response theory. Consequently, sociological themes emphasized in reader-response tradition – e.g. attention to lived experience, social, and institutional context – remained recessive. In contrast, early British feminist cultural analysis was more self-consciously sociological, associated primarily with Angela McRobbie and colleagues at the University of Birmingham's Centre for Contemporary Cultural Studies. British feminist scholars, such as McRobbie, Rosalind Gill, Ann Gray, Bev Skeggs, and Helen Wood, engage a wide range of social and cultural theory while adhering to methods of interpretive social science.

Within the US discipline of sociology, feminist scholars were much more likely to focus on gender in contexts of work and family life than on media or popular culture. There are notable exceptions. Muriel Cantor wrote about gender and soap opera (Cantor and Pingree 1983), publishing a series of policy reports in the 1970s on sex discrimination and gender stereotyping in the media.[1] Gaye Tuchman also conducted research on gender and media. Her edited volume, *Hearth and Home: Images of Women in the Mass Media* (Tuchman, Daniels, and Benet 1978), focused on gender stereotyping in television, newspapers, and women's magazines. Her *Making News* (1978) contained an important critique of gender inequality in news production, and *Edging Women Out: Victorian Novelists, Publishers, and Social Change* (Tuchman with Fortin 1989) documents women novelists' historic marginalization in the publishing industry. Andrea Press, partly influenced by the reader-response tradition developed by Radway, explored the cultural impact of television drama on women of different classes and generations (Press 1991) and women's reactions to television narratives about abortion (Press and Cole 1999). During roughly the same period, Denise Bielby co-wrote what is now one of the go-to books in qualitative fan studies on the gendered identities and practices of women soap fans (Harrington and Bielby 1995). Some of her quantitative labor-market studies of film and television industries also focused on gender, specifically gender inequities in numerical representation and pay (Bielby and Bielby 1992, 1996). And then there is Patricia Hill Collins's analysis of "controlling images" in media discourse as part of her larger focus on black female sexuality and black feminist thought (Hill Collins 1986, 2000).

There was marginal attention to gender in research associated with the "production of culture" tradition that dominated the field of cultural sociology in the 1970s and 1980s, of which Tuchman was part, although, with her exception and that of Crane (2000), little of it focused on gender or employed feminist perspectives. Studies of news-making associated with this tradition arguably represented the strongest and most coherent corpus focused on the media within sociology's history, making significant contributions to both cultural sociology and the sociology of knowledge (see Altheide 1976; Epstein 1973; Fishman 1980; Gans 1979; Gitlin 1980; Kannis 1991; Molotch and Lester 1974; Sigal 1973; Tuchman 1978). Generally speaking, this work seeks to understand media institutions as a set of formal and informal conventions that frame reality in ways that reproduce established power relations. The main concern is with the nature of "reality" constructed and disseminated by media: who has access to making media; who/what shapes professional media practices and values; and how/why do these practices and values promote certain versions of reality over others? Little of this research considered entertainment, as sociologists and other academics tended to view it as less relevant than the news agenda to democratic citizenship. This may partly explain gender's exclusion as an analytical topic. Male scholars – who are less likely to "see" and/or have an interest in gender than female counterparts – predominate in the production-of-culture tradition, and news itself carries masculine valence ("hard" and "serious") compared to "softer" qualities of entertainment and is therefore seen as a more "legitimate" concern for sociologists.

Although individual sociologists in the years since have focused on media and media processes (those not already mentioned would include the authors represented in the present volume, as well as Herman Gray, William Hoynes, Darnell Hunt, Eric Klinenberg, Ron Lembo, and Tom Streeter), the only coherent corpus to consistently incorporate interest in media, other than production-of-culture research on news-making, is social movements literature, specifically "framing" studies. Framing refers to the social construction of issues and events by media sources, journalists, political leaders and/or social movement actors to encourage certain interpretations and discourage others. Frames are fundamental to constructing meaning and media are fundamental to projecting this meaning to publics. Social movements are "successful" when rhetorical frameworks deployed by movement participants align or resonate with constituencies they seek to influence (for an overview, see Benford and Snow 2000; see also Bateson 1972; Gitlin 1980; Goffman 1974).

In sum, there is a history of feminist theory and research in sociology, but feminism made the strongest inroads in sociological subfields that had little to do with the media. This was partly because sociological research on media prioritized news and politics (where gender concerns remained backgrounded) but mostly because study of media itself was already relatively marginal in the discipline as the "feminist turn" was happening. We find the general lack of attention to media by sociologists regrettable and short-sighted. Sociology emerged out of concern to theorize and understand the industrial revolution and the massive social changes it engendered; here we are amidst another, media-technology revolution, and sociologists as a group have very little to say about it.

Coming together (sort of): recent developments

In recent years, feminist media studies at home and abroad has grown to encompass historicized studies of production, spectatorship, genre, and reception/use, often in the context of television and new media. This complicates any simple binary between humanistic and social science methods, even as the latter remain underrepresented (more on this later). The field is enormous, of course, covering many different types of media and addressing popular as well as academic audiences (for books with popular appeal, see Douglas 1994, 2010; Rapping 1994; E. Taylor 1989). In the discussion below, we emphasize trends in scholarship most familiar to us (admittedly biased toward television) circulating within academic contexts.

Since the heyday of feminist film theory, new literatures have developed around feminist approaches to melodrama and soap opera (Ang 1985; Brunsdon 1991, 2000; Byars 1991; Gledhill 1992; Harrington and Bielby 1995; Modleski 1990), daytime talk-shows (Gamson 1998; Grindstaff 2002; Illouz 2003; Livingstone and Lunt 1994; Lowney 1999; Manga 2003; Peck 2008; Shattuc 1997; Wood 2011), prime-time drama (D'Acci 1994; Dow 1992, 1996; Lotz 2006; Probyn 1990), and the medium of television more generally (see especially Brunsdon et al. 1997; Haralovich and Rabinovitz 1999; Spigel 1992). While some scholars have focused on the meanings and uses of television in domestic contexts (Gray 1992; Hoover et al. 2004; Morley 1986; Spigel 1992; Spigel and Mann 1992), others have explored new conceptualizations of "the audience" (Ang

1991, 1996; Bird 2003; Meehan 2002; Seiter 1999), the meaning and reception of media in everyday life (Banet-Weiser 2007; Bird 1992a, 2003; Hains 2012; Parameswaran 1999, 2002; Press 1991; Press and Cole 1999; Schofield Clark 2003; Seiter 1999; Shively 1990), the activities and practices of fan cultures (Bacon-Smith 1992; Bielby, Harrington, and Bielby 1999; Harrington and Bielby 1995; Leblanc 1999; Schippers 2002), and the rise of indigenous and community media (Ginsburg, Abu-Lughod, and Larkin 2002; Mayer 2003; Wilson and Stewart 2008). Feminist scholars have recently devoted attention to postcolonial media analyses (Benwell 2012; Gajjala 2002, 2012; Parameswaran 2002, 2004; Shohat and Stam 2003), reality programming (see especially Hill 2005; Holmes and Jermyn 2004; Murray and Ouellette 2009; Ouellette and Hay 2008; Sender 2012; Wood and Skeggs 2011), and the significance of "postfeminist" media representations (Benwell 2003; Gamble 2001; Douglas 2010; Genz and Brabon 2009; Gill 2003, 2007a; Hollows and Moseley 2006; Lotz 2001; McRobbie 2004, 2009; Pitcher 2006; Projansky 2001; Tasker and Negra 2007),[2] including the related concepts of "commodity feminism" (Goldman, Heath, and Smith 1991) and "girl power" (Banet-Weiser 2004; Hains 2009, 2012).

With apologies for the inevitably partial listing above, we reiterate that feminist media studies is amazingly vibrant and diverse. A good portion of feminist research is sociological, if by "sociological" we mean attending to the people, practices, and institutional contexts at stake in the production and consumption of media texts in addition to the texts themselves; indeed, as with other interdisciplinary fields, feminist media studies is a place where we can find sociology without sociologists per se.

Where is feminist media studies heading? What new areas are emerging? In the 10th Anniversary issue of the journal *Feminist Media Studies*, published in March 2011, long-time editors Cynthia Carter and Lisa McLaughlin asked seventeen scholars to reflect on the state of the field (in and outside the United States) and suggest areas for future research; the editors summarized six recurrent themes or subject areas. We share them here as they resonate with our assessment. The first theme is an upsurge in interest in political-economy of media in the neoliberal context. As both a suite of political-economic policies and their ideological underpinning, neoliberalism has provided a rich context for feminist exploration of how markets and consumer culture reshape gender relations via new trends in media content, practices, industries, and the formation of mediated subjectivities. Such feminist research tends to reflect the same developments in social theory influencing the rest of media studies (see Barry, Osborne, and Rose 1996; Beck 1992; Beck, Giddens, and Lash 1994; Ong 2006; J. Rose 2003; N. Rose 2006) and more readily links individual and social/structural concerns than earlier work emphasizing psychoanalysis and psycholinguistics.

A second theme relates to cyberculture, ICTs (information and communication technologies), and digital media practices. As Carter and McLaughlin note (2011), many topics fall under this rubric, including the relationship between new ICTs and women's overall social and economic development, the digital divide and its implications for women and families, the gendered character and impact of contemporary digital and online communities, and potential for development of transnational social movements and virtual connections – at least some of which may be amenable to progressive feminist politics.

A third theme is "media and identity," which refers broadly to the ways in which gendered media identities "register" on body and self in an era of seemingly limitless virtuality. Memory, emotion, affect, desire, voice, hybridity, and notions of "difference" (sexual, racial/ethnic, national, cultural, etc.) are the grounds on which embodied subjectivities are mobilized and deployed in and around media discourses. Although much work related to this theme is text-based, broader political and sociocultural forces figure prominently.[3]

A fourth theme, "sexuality and sexualization," is concerned with increasing sexualization and objectification of women and girls across media outlets and platforms. Following second-wave feminism and in the context of important gains in gender equality overall, media representations appear to be taking us back to the future, prompting renewed interest among feminist scholars in resurrecting attention to sexism and media stereotypes. Questions of agency and complicity are particularly important: why do girls and women go along with what appears (from a second-wave perspective) to be blatant sexism, even to the point of participating in their own apparent objectification? What is the nature of young women's "choice" to embrace hypersexualized femininities? What if young women themselves do not see their cultural participation in these terms?

Closely related to sexualization is the fifth theme, "postfeminism." There is indeed a large, growing postfeminist literature extending beyond communication and media studies. Its key issues include postfeminism's definition and periodization, its relationship to second- and third-wave women's movements, generational tensions between scholars with different understandings and attachments to postfeminist ideas and practices, and postfeminism's association with neoliberalism. We will return to postfeminism later.

The final theme discussed by Carter and McLaughlin (2011: 4) is near and dear to our hearts: "the need to broaden and deepen both the theoretical frameworks and methodologies that feminist scholarship now employ so as to provide a better sense of the conceptual complexities and empirical realities of contemporary media forms, practices, and audiences." This translates to a call for more participatory action research (working with community members as collaborators rather than studying them as research subjects) and more empirically based research vis-à-vis production and reception: studying production of media texts rather than analyzing meaning of texts isolated from production context, and focusing on how audiences make sense of and use media.

Put differently, feminist media studies needs more ethnographically informed and sociologically relevant research. The contribution of ethnographic approaches to media studies differs from more purely humanistic traditions in focusing on lived experience – against a backdrop of specific organizational, institutional, and/or structural forces and constraints. Such work exists in feminist media studies by non-sociologists (see Abu-Lughod 2004; Banet-Weiser 2007; Bird 1992a; Hains 2012; Mayer 2003, 2011; Parameswaran 2001; Seiter 1999; Sender 2012) but is still exceptional, reflecting (we suspect) the tendency of humanities-based feminist media scholars to see all social science research, regardless of type, as inevitably positivist. Social science is perceived by its humanities critics as framing knowledge in abstract, universal terms, making truth-claims based on assumptions of "objectivity," unrelated to perspective or standpoint. This critique is important; many feminist scholars in the social sciences share it. It was this very view of social science that led to feminist interventions within sociology and other social science disciplines in the early years of second-wave feminism.

That this view reflects a certain truth about some traditions of social science research is why inroads made by feminist theory and research were uneven: as Stacey and Thorne (1985) noted, feminist thinking was more warmly welcomed in fields where traditions of interpretive inquiry were already primary (history, cultural anthropology, literature) compared to fields more deeply anchored in positivist epistemologies (psychology, sociology, political science) because the former are more reflexive about the circumstances and politics of knowledge-production. Feminist scholars then and now generally concur with Habermas (1971) that the attitude of technical and instrumental rationality, historically embedded in positivist social science, has served dominant (patriarchal) interests. Feminist scholars tend to reject this attitude because, to paraphrase Audre Lorde (1984), the master's tools cannot dismantle the master's house.

At the same time, sociology is broad and eclectic, with deep roots in interpretive, phenomenological, and ethnographic traditions. Over time, these roots gave rise to a "cultural turn" consistent with (and partly responding to) feminist calls for knowledge, that is reflexive, historically situated, and mindful of ethical dilemmas. Consequently, although typically classified as social science, sociology encompasses modes of inquiry that are not social scientific in a positivist sense. At the same time, since social inequality is a – perhaps the – central disciplinary preoccupation, much sociology is "critical" in stance and orientation, regardless of method. So when humanistic media scholars question the fit between social science research and feminist principles and ideals, the distinction between critical/interpretive and mainstream/positivist approaches may reflect divisions within the discipline of communications that translate less well to sociology; it may also overlook the degree to which even mainstream, quantitative research in either discipline can have feminist implications and further feminist aims (survey research that shows the numerical underrepresentation of women and people of color in top positions in media industries, for example). Perhaps, too, the unquestioned dominance of social science in so many subfields of media and mass communication research *other* than feminist media studies leads feminist media studies to defend itself as a safe space for specifically humanistic inquiry. This is entirely understandable and would go unremarked if a robust body of critical, feminist social science research on media was currently happening within sociology instead.

The study of audiences is one place to turn for illustration of the debate over what counts as "legitimate" feminist media analysis. Although reader-response theory as taken up by Radway was used early on to study aspects of media reception, focus-group and interview-based social science research were later criticized for hypostatizing demographic categories like class and for treating reception as a discrete process rather than as fluid, mobile, and (geographically and psychically) dispersed. To quote Ang (1996: 68): "the activity so often simplistically described as 'watching TV' only takes shape within the broader textual horizon of heterogeneous and indefinite range of domestic [and increasingly, public] practices." Radway herself, shortly after the publication of *Reading the Romance*, called for a rethinking of the premises of reception study in light of the complexity of interaction between media use in everyday life and the diffuse modalities of subject-formation espoused within the feminist media studies mainstream (Radway 1988). (A decade earlier in a different context, Gitlin [1978] came to a similar conclusion, noting the impossibility of isolating and measuring the central importance of media to culture and society.)

This challenge has only intensified with the rise of new communication technologies, media platforms, and environments which together have transformed media "audience" research into media "user" research and made more urgent questions of media impact (Livingstone and Press 2006). What we now term the "new media environment" expands the role of media in our lives exponentially; some argue that our culture has become indistinguishable from its media representation and that mediated communication processes have infiltrated almost every crevice of our lives (Livingstone 2009). In light of this, Radway (2008: 342) suggests that "what are needed are ways of identifying, understanding, and talking about the social practices of cultural use that refuse reification and the teleology of assumed closure . . . [we need] some way of conceptualizing social process and its messy vagaries in a more fluid, less discrete, less body-bound way."

That being said, Radway (2008) makes clear that she is not seeking to specify a universally "correct" method for studying the reception/use of media; rather, her aim is to flag and problematize the theoretical assumptions embedded in all of the disciplinary approaches that have tackled the vexed subject of reception. Certainly, ditching social science and returning to the study of texts makes little sense. Elizabeth Bird (1992b: 250) speaks to this point in relation to ethnographic inquiry. Although rethinking ethnography's use in reception studies "has been necessary and useful," Bird writes, "it also has the potential to paralyze research of this sort and to continue building an evermore abstract theoretical narcissism." The way out, she says, is not to eschew ethnography but to improve ethnographic practice through constructive feminist dialogue. As people and media become more interdependent and entwined, ethnographic practice must continue to innovate and adjust. What also makes sense – as proposed by Radway (2008), and we concur – is to encourage greater collaboration between and cross-fertilization among disciplinary traditions. We need multiple scholars, employing multiple methodologies in multiple sites, all contributing (individually or in collaborative research clusters) to collective bodies of knowledge under the ecumenical rubric of feminist media studies. Such an instantiation of feminist media studies is all the more urgent in an historical moment in which critical research of all kinds is under concerted attack, a targeted casualty of higher education's relentless marketization.

Back to the future: postfeminism in the media

As we have seen, "postfeminism" is well suited to interdisciplinarity and is of considerable interest to feminist media scholars. In this final section, we elaborate on postfeminism's meaning and briefly discuss our current research on the subject. In the process, we hope to demonstrate the intellectual purchase of a sociologically informed feminist approach to media.

Although postfeminism has no one meaning or definition, in the US context it most often refers to contemporary orientation toward, or expression of, gender, owing its existence to feminism but eschewing explicit feminist politics. Often assumed to come after second-wave feminism, postfeminism sidelines or minimizes second-wave feminism by positioning it as a past social movement, largely irrelevant or unnecessary to the present. To quote McRobbie (2004: 255), "[in postfeminist discourse and practice] feminism is cast into the shadows, where at best it can expect to have some afterlife, where it might be regarded ambivalently by those young women who must in more public venues stake a distance from it, for the sake of social and sexual recognition."

Gill (2003, 2007a) and Douglas (2010) focus on the specifically sexual dimension of postfeminism, with the latter coining the term "enlightened sexism" to characterize it. Douglas argues that enlightened sexism helps deflect and contain the threat posed by feminist challenges to structural gender inequality; it does this by framing certain patriarchal practices – e.g. production of sexist media imagery – as harmless and irreproachable because of presumed gender equality. "Post-feminism insists that women have made plenty of progress – indeed, full equality has allegedly been achieved – so now it's okay, even amusing, to resurrect sexist stereotypes of girls and women" (Douglas 2010: 9). Indeed, for Douglas, the willingness of women and girls to embrace these stereotypes is offered as proof of their empowerment. Related to and coincident with the rise of postfeminism is the concept of "girl power," a commoditized, sanitized version of Riot Grrrl culture now manifest in popular groups such as the Spice Girls and more empowering representations of girls on television (Banet-Weiser 2007; Hains 2009, 2012). Girl power is consistent with – is perhaps a facet of – postfeminism, insofar as it takes for granted feminist gains and uses feminist imagery to advance commercial interests through commodification. As such, girl power is also a component of what some scholars call "commodity feminism": the co-optation of feminist ideals by marketers in the interests of capital with no concern for the implications (positive or negative) on gender relations or gender equality (Goldman, Heath, and Smith 1991).

Reading across the variety of analyses that identify media representations as postfeminist, common themes emerge, despite scholars' failure to agree a single definition. One such theme revolves around "femininity" and its relation to "feminism." Key here is the effort to bring expressions of emphasized femininity into the fold of feminist politics, with traditional feminine characteristics such as sexual attractiveness repackaged and revalued as expressions of freedom and choice. Other themes include marginalization of collective action as a response to structural conditions of patriarchy in favor of a focus on individuals, incorporation of sexual and racial difference with respect to gender representations, but in ways that leave heterosexual and white privilege essentially unquestioned, and use of humor and irony to acknowledge feminist critique while simultaneously minimizing its importance.

Unsurprisingly, the media have been generally unkind to feminism (see R. Rosen 2000 for an historical perspective); it remains to be clarified whether postfeminist media representations are out of synch with how young women think about gender and feminism today. At least one study suggests that they are, revealing a clear gap between the (remarkably stable) measures of support for feminism in public opinion data over a twenty-year time span and the various forms of backlash against feminism identified in postfeminist media texts (E. Hall and Rodriguez 2003). Aronson (2003) found support for feminist goals among young women, coupled with ambiguity about the concept of feminism, while Scharff (2011) argues that popular support for feminism as an identity has eroded. The potential misalignment between media-ready labels and reported opinions about feminism implies that a key function of media discourse is to promote and "sell" postfeminism to audiences, who may or may not be thinking and acting in postfeminist terms as defined by scholars, or whose understandings of gender and feminism may not be entirely legible in the media text discourse.

The relationship between mediated and lived experience partly informs our own postfeminist research interests. Andrea's latest project, *Feminism LOL: Media Culture and "Feminism on the Ground" in a Postfeminist Age* (Press in press), uses interpretive methods of media and discourse analysis to analyze second-wave feminism's successes and failures. First, it identifies key issues addressed by the feminist movement – women's body image, sexual freedom, reproductive rights, work–family balance, and so on – and charts the success of a feminist perspective by examining a variety of currently popular media representations expressing and reflecting this perspective in relation to the key issues identified. It discusses the limits of societal transformations that have occurred, noting the unfinished dimensions of feminist reforms. Finally, I interview a variety of men and women across lines of age, ethnicity, and socioeconomic background, and use interpretive analysis to see how viewers and users of new media make sense of and reconcile the chasm between a media system alleging feminist reforms are completed and a social reality in need of further transformation. The resulting discussion serves as commentary on both the relationship between popular media representations and popular opinion about social issues, and the relationship between popular media representations and social movements (for a preliminary discussion of findings, see Press 2010, 2011, 2012, in press; Press and Tripodi, in press).

This work represents a clear attempt to develop an integrated methodology drawing from both social science and humanistic methods to cogently articulate the media's cultural effects. My (Laura's) goal is related but different: to use ethnographic research as a springboard to explore the postfeminist concept in and beyond the media.

I am specifically interested in tensions and correspondences between "feminism" and "femininity," because this particular dimension of postfeminism has surfaced repeatedly in my ethnographic research, undertaken with my colleague Emily West, on American cheerleading. Female cheerleaders are, arguably, the quintessential embodiment of postfeminist sensibility. Cheerleading lost status in the wake of Title IX with the rise of second-wave feminism and women's sports. Among other changes, cultural scripts about femininity expanded during this period to incorporate notions of toughness and physical strength. The cheerleading industry responded by bringing cheerleading up-to-date, incorporating legitimizing traits once associated primarily with masculinity – competitiveness, assertiveness, and athleticism – while retaining key elements of emphasized femininity – supportiveness, attractiveness, and sex appeal (Adams and Bettis 2003; Grindstaff and West 2006, 2010).

The media were slow to reflect this shift because cheerleaders occupied an iconic status in American culture: icons are difficult to retool. Gradually, however, new iconic images emerged of cheerleaders as "sexyfit" athletes – in news, film (consider, especially, *Bring It On* and its four sequels), and television (including ESPN coverage, dramas, animated series, and a wide array of reality shows). Emily and I use ethnographic research to inform our analysis of these representations, not to determine how they differ from or fail to measure up to "reality" but to guide our selection and analysis of texts. Which images matter to those actually involved in cheerleading, in what ways, and why? We are interested in what images say to us, as scholars informed by feminist theory, and the way images create a parallel reality that cheerleaders of different ages, genders, sexualities, and ethnicities must negotiate in their quest for legitimacy and respect. Like women generally, cheerleaders are exalted and reviled. The media help shape this polarity in ways that simultaneously challenge and sustain current theorizing about gender, femininity and post-feminism in the culture at large (Grindstaff and West 2011, 2012).

Conclusion

The new media environment is pervasive, complex and ever-changing. For better and worse, it is transforming how people live in the most public and private ways – unevenly, sometimes unexpectedly and often reproducing inequalities. Scholars in communication and media studies are studying at the crest of this wave; sociologists, as a whole, are not. This is puzzling and disappointing for a discipline so deeply concerned with macro- and micro-processes of social transformation, to which media have become increasingly central. This is the "missing media revolution in sociology" of which we spoke at the outset. Sociologists must reengage with media. In the study of media production, distribution, reception, and representation, there are enduring issues of political, economic, and cultural power, as well as emerging issues requiring new theories and methodological competencies.

Feminist scholarship can develop a more intersectional relationship between sociology and media studies by forging interdisciplinary connections and collaborations along substantive and methodological grounds. Feminism by definition traverses disciplinary boundaries because it provides a dynamic framework for analyzing power and inequality (a key preoccupation of sociologists), not merely a set of topics or a recipe for conducting research. Feminist inquiry has already transformed sociology and the academy at large, although this transformation has been uneven and is incomplete (see Lorber 2006). Given the current US political climate (most notably the current "war on women" and a popular press privileging biological explanations for virtually anything and everything gender-related), feminist inquiry is well positioned to impress upon wider publics the critical importance of sociological knowledge to social justice agendas. To accomplish this, however, feminist media scholars must continue on their current course of methodological diversification, distinguishing interpretive (useful) from positivist (less useful) social science approaches and embracing the strategic possibilities of grounded and empirical, yet reflexive and critical, social science. This is the aforementioned "missing sociological revolution in feminist media studies." Happily, unlike the missing media revolution in sociology, it is well under way.

Notes

1 These reports, important interventions at the time, are little known today. They include "Women in the wasteland fight back: a report on the image of women portrayed in TV programming," published in 1972 in association with the National Organization of Women (NOW); "Report of the Task Force on women in public broadcasting," published in 1975 with Caroline Isber; "Differential effects of television violence on girls and boys," published in 1977 with Jack Orwant; and "Sex and sexual violence in fiction: content and control," published in 1983 with Eileen Zeitz.

2 In 2002, *The Communication Review* devoted issue 4 of volume 5 to the topic of postfeminism in the US TV drama *Ally McBeal*. Contributors include Bonnie Dow (2002), Rachel Dubrofsky (2002), Susan Mckenna (2002), and Laurie Ouellette (2002). Mosley and Read (2002) also published an essay the same year, using *Ally McBeal* as a springboard to discuss the concept of postfeminism.

3 Salam Al-Mahadin's analysis of the media presence of the Arab/Muslim woman provides a good illustration for readers unfamiliar with critical analyses of this type. Noting that the Arab/Muslim woman is depicted in radically divergent ways in Arab versus western media – bikini-clad in the former, burqa-clad in the latter – Al-Mahadin argues that this dichotomous positioning situates the woman as a signifier par excellence of contested ideologies about gender, race, and nation in both intra-Arab contexts and between Arab and western worlds. Constructions of western and Arab masculinity are shaped by and through their relation – politically, culturally, and socially – to an Arab/Muslim female body always already mediated and animated by patriarchal structures and ideologies (Al-Mahadin 2011).

9

Media Sociology and the Study of Race

Ronald N. Jacobs

With the success of *The Cosby Show*, as well as events like the Rodney King beating, the Los Angeles uprisings, and the O. J. Simpson trial, race was a prominent topic in the US media during the 1980s and 1990s. Unsurprisingly, media sociologists turned to the topic of race with renewed urgency during this period, producing important books and articles that reshaped our dominant understandings of racial representations, media organizations, and public life.

Some things have changed dramatically since those turbulent times; others have not. There are still racial crises that occupy public attention; most of these still involve the police. But the election of Barack Obama as the first African-American president has led to a protracted debate about whether the US has entered a "post-racial" age (Smith 2012; Sugrue 2010; Tesler and Sears 2010). At the very least, the media embrace of Obama suggested that there might have been important changes in mediated racial discourses.

With Obama's election as a backdrop, this chapter revisits key sociological studies of race and the media from the 1980s and 1990s. Identifying the central questions that sociologists asked about media and race, I consider whether research findings from that period still hold up today. I pay particular attention to two big events that have dominated the public agenda in recent years: the terrorist attacks of September 11, 2001; and the 2008 Obama election. While the events of September 11 shifted the media discourse about race in important and complicated ways, the Obama election has largely served to return media narratives about race to overall patterns discernible during the 1980s and 1990s.

The primary focus of this chapter is media representations of African Americans and the history of scholarship by media sociologists on this topic. While this is a relatively narrow focus, it reflects the central concerns of sociological thinking about race, media, and public life, particularly in the United States and the United Kingdom. As Young (2012: 344) has argued, "throughout much of the history of American sociology, the urban street corner was a mere structural backdrop for cultural sociological assessments of the behavior of these [African-American] men." The situation was similar in England, where the major sociological theorists of race (e.g. Hall, Gilroy, Rex) were concerned primarily with racial prejudice, particularly as expressed against black urban residents. Media discourses about black men and urban life have an obvious connection to these theoretical concerns, which helps to explain the connections that exist between mainstream sociology and a specific type of research agenda in the media sociology of race.

There are indeed other issues related to race explored by media sociologists. For example, Rodriguez (1997, 2004) has examined media representations of Latinos in the United States, while Kim and Chung (2005) explored images of Asian-American women in magazine advertising. Scholars in media studies have explored a host of important issues related to race, including the social history of Latino newspapers (Rodriguez 1999); media discourse about interethnic conflict (Shah and Thornton 2004); and the industry forces that prevent Asian filmmakers and media executives from producing non-reductive racial representations (Saha 2012). But overall, media sociologists interested in race have been much slower to adopt this more expansive research agenda. I address the implications of this at the end of the chapter.

Media sociology and race before 1990

In the aftermath of the 1960s, urban upheavals, surprisingly, US sociologists did not expend much energy studying mediated racial representations. The most important research study of the early 1970s, written by three psychologists but published in the *American Journal of Sociology*, found that press attention to African Americans had not increased significantly in the aftermath of the urban uprisings (Johnson, Sears, and McConahay 1971). Most sociologists interested in race were primarily concerned with social factors that shaped "race consciousness" and mostly ignored the possibility that media representations were an important and necessary factor to consider.

An interesting contrast to the US case can be found in the United

Kingdom, where Stuart Hall and his colleagues developed the approach that became known as British cultural studies.[1] Influenced by Gramscian notions of hegemony, Hall emphasized struggle over public meaning in which dominant and oppositional groups are perpetually engaged. This battle for cultural influence takes place on an unequal playing field in which the creative personnel and "organic intellectuals" who articulate the dominant worldview have better credentials and control over the means of public communication, particularly in the mass media era. This makes it easier for dominant groups to use media to create moral panics, scandals, and other public events that tip the balance of influence in favor of their own interests. Audiences may have the power to resist these ideological readings in the way they decode the media text, but the text itself is encoded in a way that reinforces the ideological assumptions and privileges of dominant groups (S. Hall 1973).

For Hall and his colleagues, much of what one could find in official media discourse involved conflation of race and class, organized in a way that privileged dominant class interest. For example, in *Policing the Crisis*, Hall and his colleagues explored the British media's growing obsession during the 1970s with the "mugging crisis" (Hall et al. 1978). The term "mugging" was neither a legal concept nor a descriptive term that had much of a history in Britain. Rather, it was a term imported from the United States, where it had been used by politicians and journalists to describe urban crime in a context where cities were becoming racial ghettos, and where drugs were increasingly a part of the urban landscape. British journalists initially used the concept in stories about American crime waves, but eventually began to apply it to Britain, doing so before any concrete instances of "mugging" ever appeared in the United Kingdom (Hall et al. 1978: 23).

Hall and his colleagues argued that the introduction of these mugging stories served to naturalize racial fears, creating a moral panic about urban crime that had significant political consequences. In the press, attention paid to dramatic and violent events focused lots of attention on the most extreme cases of urban crime. At the same time, the news practices of privileging official voices allowed police, judges, politicians, and crime experts to define what the events meant. Emphasis on the urban ghetto as a space of inadequate socialization encouraged moral condemnation equating "black" with "insufficiently British." This cultural achievement prevented cross-racial, working-class alliances from forming to tackle the common problem of unemployment. Resulting racialization of urban crime and poverty created a hegemonic situation, which naturalized middle-class sensibilities as the best way to confront the contemporary economic and political challenges facing England. In other words, the mugging crisis allowed dominant groups in England to shift attention away from the failure of the British state to protect its citizens from economic crisis to focus instead on the moral threat posed by racial minorities in poor neighborhoods.

The influence of British Cultural Studies was increasingly felt by media sociologists throughout the 1980s, coinciding with the introduction of a new television program, *The Cosby Show*, which raised important questions about mediated racial representations. First airing in 1984, *The Cosby Show* was the most popular television program in the United States during the second half of the 1980s. It was a huge global success, quickly becoming the most important asset in Viacom's international syndication business (Havens 2000). *The Cosby Show* almost single-handedly revived situation comedy, a television genre that many critics had pronounced dead several years earlier (McNeill 1996: 180). Earlier global television hits, e.g. *Dallas*, had relied on universalistic themes and characters to be more easily accessible to a wide range of audiences (Liebes and Katz 1993). *The Cosby Show* differed from these earlier shows in important ways, particularly concerning its relevance for racial representation.

The Cosby Show was the first top-rated television show in the United States to center on the lives of an African-American family. It was notable for resisting some simplistic, racial stereotypes that could be found in earlier popular sitcoms, e.g. *The Jeffersons* or *Sanford and Son*. Anti-apartheid posters adorned the walls of the family home, along with photographs of Martin Luther King, Jr and Frederick Douglass. Historically-black colleges featured prominently in the show's story line. Many cultural critics praised the show and its success, suggesting that it represented a turning point in race relations and racial discourse (Tucker 1997). Others were more cautious in their public interpretations. For example, African-American public intellectuals, such as Henry Louis Gates and Michael Eric Dyson, praised the show but also criticized its portrayal of a very narrow, wealthy slice of African-American family life, and its failure to address structural impediments facing most African-American families. *The Cosby Show* became a touchstone for thinking about mediated racial representations and media sociologists contributed important insights to the debate.

Among academic studies exploring *The Cosby Show*'s social significance, the most clearly indebted to Hall's approach was Jhally and Lewis's (1992) *Enlightened Racism*. Their central argument was that *The Cosby Show* displayed two hegemonic tendencies: it reinforced bourgeois sensibilities and the American ideology of upward mobility and self-reliance. These features of the television text were hegemonic because they reinforced Reagan's neoconservative vision for America, combining "feel-good individualism" with a sharp attack on government interventions to alleviate structural inequalities (1992: 71–5). By naturalizing the upper-middle class lifestyle occupied by the Huxtable family, it encouraged viewers – particularly white viewers – to blame the less fortunate for their own problems. Thus, despite the fact that Cosby explicitly created the program to "humanize" African Americans and counter prevailing stereotypes, viewers interpreted the program in reactionary and hegemonic ways. "For many white respondents," Jhally and Lewis argued, "the Huxtables' class position distinguishes them from other black people, making it possible for white audiences to disentangle them from preconceived (white) notions of black culture . . . They will, at the same time, distinguish between the Huxtables and most other black people, and their welcome is only extended as far as the Huxtables" (1992: 109–10).

Gray's research on race and media in 1980s' television shared these concerns about ideology and hegemony but focused more closely on the existence of plural discourses and counter-hegemonic challenges. Gray argued that the ideological effect of *The Cosby Show* was connected to the larger public field of representations. On the one hand, the Reagan administration had racialized welfare and social disadvantage as part of its larger attack on the the welfare state in a manner that championed individual achievement and blamed the less fortunate for putative laziness and irresponsibility (Gray 2004). In this respect, *The Cosby Show* operated intertextually and semiotically, with the success of the fictional Huxtable family made meaningful through contrast with images of black urban poverty and crime appearing every day on television's evening news (Gray 1989).

Gray was not content to identify the existence of a putatively monolithic, omnipotent racial media ideology. He criticized Jhally and Lewis for overestimating the degree of ideological uniformity one could find in media representations of race. Gray also suggested that they underestimated the audience's ability to resist and challenge the circulating ideological messages. "Ironically", Gray (1993: 470) wrote in a review of *Enlightened Racism*, "their evidence demonstrates that the show's meanings are open, negotiated, and contingent. . . . as demonstrated by rap music and other forms of contemporary commercial culture, commercial network television is more porous and ambivalent in the effects it produces and the meanings and uses to which audience members put those effects." In fact, in Gray's own research on mediated racial representations during the 1980s, he found that there was more than one style of racial representation on television, and that most programs offered multiple interpretive pathways. Furthermore, Gray (2004) argued, African-American voices were actively challenging Reagan's racialized critique of the welfare state; they were doing this as audience members and also as creative personnel with access to the means of symbolic communication.

Timothy Havens's (2000) research on international reception of *The Cosby Show* also challenged assumptions about ideological uniformity, showing how media representations of race acquire a complicated, often contradictory, set of meanings when considered in a transnational context. Viacom, believing that American television comedy was fairly unpopular among international audiences, initially provided limited global marketing for *Cosby*. It was quite surprised at *Cosby*'s global success (Havens 2000: 379–80). The reasons for *The Cosby Show*'s success were complicated, involving "multiple articulations and dislocations between the show's racialized representations and the audiences' understandings of race, both in their own countries and beyond national borders" (Havens 2000: 377). Black audiences worldwide responded positively to the show's representations of a "dignified blackness," in a global context where they could be certain that white audiences were also watching these same racial representations (Havens 2000: 384). Black audiences outside of the United States recognized the Huxtable family's privileged class background, but their positive response to this was filtered through cultural environments in their own country where white politicians refused to acknowledge the possibility of black success (Havens 2000: 385). Viewers in the Middle East liked the fact that the Huxtables had managed to be successful "without having sold out to white culture" (quoted in Havens 2000: 385). As Havens's research suggests, understanding global audience interpretations of *The Cosby Show* requires a theoretical lens moving beyond singular concern with state hegemony.

Cumulatively, several key points emerged from *The Cosby Show* research, as well as from the Birmingham School studies that preceded and often informed them. First, as Gray's (1989) research demonstrated, racialized representations derive meanings from intertextual circulation of factual and fictional media. Consequently, it is important for media sociologists to study the full range of mediated representations. Second, media representations of race are connected to the larger field of political and social representations. Third, while media representations have clear ideological tendencies, they are also multivalent and polysemic texts, offering a variety of interpretive paths. Because of this fact, it is important to study racial representations as part of a larger struggle over meaning, in public as well as private communicative spaces. We cannot only study texts themselves; we must also explore how media texts become objects of commentary and critique in a variety of multiple yet overlapping publics.

Perhaps ironically, the series finale of *The Cosby Show* was broadcast during the 1992 Los Angeles uprisings: Los Angeles Mayor Tom Bradley urged residents of the city to observe the curfew, stay home, and watch *The Cosby Show*. The local NBC affiliate interrupted its live coverage of the uprisings to show the series finale. But events taking place on the streets of Los Angeles quickly overran events taking place in the Huxtable home. Media narratives about race shifted accordingly, as did media sociology of race that sought to map the contours of racialized media discourse.

Media sociology of race after Rodney King: a focus on the public sphere

In the early 1990s, US media discourse about race focused heavily on Rodney King, before becoming obsessed with the O. J. Simpson trial in 1994 and 1995. These events (and research into them) suggested a poignant social fact: African Americans had sharply different interpretations of racial crises and African-American media relied on noticeably different narratives in their reports about racial crisis.

Borrowing heavily from earlier Birmingham School work on hegemony and resistance, Hunt's *Screening the Los Angeles "Riots"* compared African-American, white, and Latino interpretations of television news coverage of the 1992 Los Angeles uprisings. Hunt (1997: 35–50) began by identifying the ideological features of the television text, which emphasized and criticized the "chaos" and violence; deployed racialized representations highlighting the activities of African Americans, and searched for similarities with earlier race "riots" that might help to explain what was happening. To assess how much ideological power these media texts actually had and the different strategies audiences used to resist ideological messages, Hunt organized focus groups and showed them one of the key television broadcasts from the early days of the uprisings.

Focus group discussions allowed Hunt to identify clearly differentiated and "raced" ways of seeing between different groups.[2] White focus groups tended to define violence and property destruction as "crime" and were generally critical of the uprising. Voicing little criticism of the coverage itself, these groups treated news narratives "as a clear window into events gone by" (Hunt 1997: 122), i.e. white focus group respondents largely accepted the dominant reading offered by the text. In contrast, African-American focus groups were more sympathetic toward the individuals depicted on the television screen and were more likely to discuss structural racism as an important, contributory factor in the events. They were also much more likely to challenge the ideological encoding of the text, relying for support on their own experiences in the city. These groups offered more oppositional interpretations, resisting many ideological tendencies in the text. Hunt (1997: 162) celebrates these acts of textual resistance – which were much more common among African-American audiences but were also present among white and Latino focus groups – "as either constituting meaningful acts of resistance in their own right, or contributing to a consciousness necessary for meaningful social action at some later moment in time."

Just as African-American audiences rejected and criticized mainstream media narratives about the uprisings, so too did Korean-American audiences. According to Lie and Abelmann (1999: 76), most Korean Americans rejected the idea that simmering conflict existed between Korean shop-owners and African-American residents in South Central Los Angeles, arguing that the black–Korean conflict was media-constructed and had little or no basis in reality. Ultimately, Lie and Abelmann (1999: 79–80) argue, the power of the media narrative about black–Korean conflict was connected to the larger ideological environment, "which pit[s] Asian Americans, as a model minority, against African-Americans, as an urban underclass." Most Korean Americans resisted reified images of inter-ethnic conflict, emphasizing instead structural problems afflicting inner-city Los Angeles, and trying to place these structural problems against their own desires to realize the American dream of social mobility. Despite the fact that rejection of the dominant media narrative was widespread among Korean-American audiences, there was great frustration among Korean-American leaders, whose attempts to steer the mainstream media narrative toward greater nuanced and interpretive complexity were almost entirely unsuccessful.

In fact, the significant gap between everyday interpretive resistance and the larger environment of public discourse pointed to several shortcomings that media sociologists were coming to identify with the Birmingham-inspired model. The most important of these limitations was the failure to think about the relationship between media power, resistance, and the *public sphere*. The idea of the public sphere points to a model of media power that moves beyond a consideration of the text's ideological power or the audience's powers of interpretive resistance. Rather, media are important because they provide spaces of deliberation in which citizens and state officials meet to (a) make arguments about matters of common concern; (b) make those arguments in public; (c) support their arguments with good reasons; and (d) defend their arguments against criticisms and alternative positions (Habermas 1989; Jacobs and Townsley 2011). Importantly, from this perspective, potential power of oppositional interpretation must be judged in light of its success in gaining visibility and influencing the public sphere itself. Circumstances in which individuals and focus groups make alternative reading of television texts do not constitute "meaningful acts of resistance in their own right," Hunt's suggestions notwithstanding. Opinion formation of a certain type does occur in informal publics such as these but, without media access, "the signals they send out and the impulses they give are generally too weak to initiate learning processes or redirect decision making in the political system in the short run" (Habermas 1996: 373).

Drawing inspiration from this public sphere media power model, Jacobs (2000) explored the role that different kinds of media play in the public contest to define the meaning of racial crisis. Tracing the history of African-American newspapers in New York, Chicago, and Los Angeles, he compared African-American and "mainstream" media coverage of the 1965 Watts riot, the 1991 Rodney King beating, the 1992 Los Angeles uprisings, and the 1995 O. J. Simpson verdict, finding that African-American newspapers continued to provide a perspective on public issues distinct from the majority media.

Lending support to Fraser's (1992) arguments about the importance of "oppositional publics," Jacobs argued that a distinctive African-American press filled three important needs in American civil society. First, the black press provided a forum for debate, free from surveillance and the discipline of the mainstream, "official" public sphere. Newspapers such as the *Chicago Defender* were critically important in shaping distinctively African-American narratives about inclusion, democracy, and community. Second, African-American newspapers actively monitored and criticized mainstream news narratives, reminding African-American readers that they needed to read mainstream newspapers oppositionally and in dialogue with the African-American press. Finally, albeit with decidedly limited success, publishers of African-American newspapers hoped to increase black visibility in white civil society by circulating alternative voices and perspectives in public conversation about matters of common concern.

Comparing news stories about racial crisis, Jacobs found that the African-American press offered a distinct perspective on public issues that was missing in the majority media. The black press consistently refused to label rioters and protesters as irrational or to dehumanize them as "thugs" or "animals." Its journalists were much more likely to characterize African Americans heroically, encouraging collective mobilization around black leaders. African-American news stories about racial crisis involved more historical context and narratives emphasizing continuity of racial crisis and oppression. These discursive features of the African-American press encouraged critical reflexivity toward racial representations circulating in the mainstream press.

While the black press has introduced new narratives and new points of difference to the interpretation and discussion of public events, there have been structural constraints that consistently limited its broader influence. The most important of these constraints was racial stratification of the public sphere. In a civil society consisting of multiple publics, the possibility of inter-public communication is essential for expansion of solidarity; emergence of critical discourse from alternative publics can influence the larger public conversation. But only the largest news publics have sufficient resources for regular intercommunication. The largest daily newspapers share the same wire services, enjoy large readerships, and operate regularly as public forums for intellectuals and politicians to discuss matters of common concern. Intercommunication also operates between major daily newspapers and television news: through concentration of ownership, reliance on "mainstream" newspapers by television journalists, and orientation to the same stock of speakers and sources.

By comparison, major African-American newspapers such as the *Chicago Defender*, *Los Angeles Sentinel*, and *New York Amsterdam News* do not share wire services; all suffer ever-shrinking circulations. From 1965 to 1992, the *New York Amsterdam News* lost 49.7% of its circulation, and the *Chicago Defender* lost 17.1%. The *Los Angeles Sentinel* actually gained 7.6% in circulation, but this gain was due to increased attention regarding the Rodney King crisis. Between

1965 and 1990, before Rodney King, the *Sentinel* lost 26.6% of its circulation. Furthermore, with the notable exception of the *Chicago Defender* which had both a daily and a weekly edition, almost all black newspapers were published weekly, limiting ability to provide a daily public forum for discussing matters of common concern. These infrastructural imbalances made the *practice* of intercommunication between African-American and "mainstream" public spheres increasingly difficult.

Jacobs argued that racial stratification of the public sphere was actually becoming worse with the introduction of new communication technologies and digital archiving practices. Digital archiving of the African-American press was spotty and incomplete, generally housed in different archives to the mainstream press. The most important digital news archive, Lexis-Nexis, maintained records for more than 2,300 different news sources but no African-American papers. While all but two of the hundred-largest daily US papers had established an online edition by 1999 (Boczkowski 2005: 8), none of the major African-American papers had an online edition at that time. While digital media made major media increasingly easy to access, they rendered the African-American press virtually invisible to the general population.

In addition to infrastructural stratification, there were other imbalances of perception weakening the potential influence of the African-American press. Until the 1960s, African Americans were virtually invisible in the "mainstream" press; African-American *newspapers* continue to be mostly invisible. By contrast, one of the primary functions of the black press historically has been to monitor the mainstream media. The effect of this rather one-sided intercommunication between African-American and mainstream press is reinforcement, in the black public sphere, of the sense of white indifference, reinforcement suggesting a more tragic genre for understanding racial crisis, reducing the likelihood of building trust and solidarity across racial lines.

The larger point is that mere existence of oppositional or critical discourse does not constitute effective resistance. For resistance to have any significant steering influence, it must become part of the intertextual, nested environment of discussion and commentaries taking place within the larger, "official" public sphere. This is more likely to occur during crises, as Habermas (1996) recognized, but even during crises there must be feedback mechanisms flowing from oppositional discourses circulating in smaller publics up to agenda-setting discourses circulating in major media. Jacobs suggested several practices that might make this more likely, at least for mediated racial discourse. "Mainstream" journalists could monitor the African-American press, particularly during moments of racial crisis. Journalists from the major media could insist that Lexis-Nexis add African-American newspapers to its otherwise comprehensive news archive. Well-resourced tech organizations could help to ensure that African-American papers had effective websites and blogs, making it easier for major media organizations to provide hyperlinks to the African-American press during racial crises. These steps would make it easier to expand public conversation about race in the media, rather than isolating oppositional discourse within informal publics and specialized publications.

While Jacobs and Hunt focused primarily on news media representations of race, public meanings about Rodney King and O. J. Simpson were also shaped by the intertextual relationship between factual and fictional media. For example, Williams (2001) has argued that US public understandings of race have been shaped by two competing versions of melodrama, which were established within fictional media but transposed onto real-world debates. First, and initially established by Beecher Stowe's *Uncle Tom's Cabin*, is the portrayal of African-American suffering as virtuous and deserving of white sympathy. Second, embodied in D. W. Griffith's *Birth of a Nation*, is the portrayal of white women's virtuous suffering as a sign of African-American evil and depravity. Williams shows how these two melodramas have been repeatedly re-elaborated in Hollywood cinema and ultimately institutionalized in American public culture. They have become so routinized that they form dominant tropes for representing racial crisis in the news media. Rodney King was a sympathetic figure because he signaled the melodrama of Uncle Tom. O. J. Simpson was hated because he provoked Griffith's melodrama of the black beast stalking white women. In the end, as Williams so convincingly demonstrates, our ability to talk seriously about race has been shaped fundamentally by our participation in popular culture and fictional media.

Identifying central questions and perspectives from the media sociology of race

Before considering the prospects for a media sociology of race today, I want to summarize the key issues and questions identified by the Cosby and Rodney King studies. These include the following:

- What is the larger intertextual environment that shapes media discourse about race? Does this cultural environment present monolithic ideological unity or an ambiguous patchwork of competing and contradictory meanings? At a minimum, attending to these questions includes a consideration of (a) different narratives about mobility and disadvantage that are circulating in the political public sphere; (b) different news narratives about poverty and criminality; and (c) different fictional narratives about race, family life, and current social issues.
- To what extent do media narratives about race operate from assumptions about racial marginality and inter-ethnic competition?
- How do the racial representations produced by US media organizations change when they are filtered through a global and transnational context?
- To what extent do media representations about race become objects of commentary and criticism in themselves? Which representations provoke the most critical commentary? This can include a focus on audiences, their abilities to read the texts oppositionally, and their successes and failures in decoding the ideological intent of media discourse. But it should also include a focus on the critical commentaries that take place in the multiple and overlapping publics that constitute civil society. Of particular interest is the ability of narratives developed in informal or alternative publics to gain visibility and influence in the larger media spaces of the official public sphere.
- How do new communications technologies change the racial stratification of the public sphere? To what extent are alternative publics included in the new media environment?

These are general questions and issues that can be extended into broad media sociology of race extending beyond focus on media discourses about African Americans. Fresh consideration of these questions is important as there have been a number of significant contemporary developments that would appear to be relevant for the larger US cultural environment of media and race. The two most important are (1) the events of September 11, 2001; and (2) the 2008 election of Barack Obama as president of the United States (POTUS). The remainder of the chapter considers the impact that these two events have had on media representations of race and the challenges and opportunities presented for contemporary media sociology of race. The discussion is necessarily preliminary and provisional; future research must more fully determine what the consequences of these events have been for mediated racial representations.

September 11 and the media sociology of race

The events of September 11, 2001 presented a significant challenge to the journalistic field, and especially to its professed stance of detachment (J. Rosen 2002). As Waisbord (2002) has argued, US journalism is poorly equipped to serve the needs of democracy during times of global crisis because of its sensationalism and inability to talk about structural issues without relying on "news hooks." Waisbord argues that journalists turn to narratives of patriotism because ideals of objectivity and detachment do not provide the resources to respond effectively to large-scale trauma. Despite the temporary nature of the move away from detachment, there has been growing confusion and contestation about what counts as authentic journalistic practice, and an increasing quantity and influence of opinion media (Jacobs and Townsley 2011). Importantly for the purposes of this chapter, September 11 also dislodged African Americans from the center of larger public discourses of otherness and marginality. In place of these well-established discourses, new narratives arose about Islamic fundamentalism and "clash of civilizations" (e.g. Huntington 2011; Lewis 2003).

Media narratives about race, developed after September 11, were shaped by this changed cultural environment. This could be seen most clearly, perhaps, by the immense popularity and critical acclaim for the television drama *24*, whose protagonist was a counterterrorism agent working in Los Angeles. The changed racial environment was signaled by its casting of an African American as POTUS, and by its reliance on negative representations of Muslims as actual and potential terrorists. Discourse of Muslim threat circulated consistently in the political public sphere, though some attempts were made to distinguish between Muslim citizens and Islamic fundamentalists. Overall, shows like *24* were part of a larger shift toward new assumptions and narratives about inter-ethnic competition, racial threat, and criminality.

24 was not an outlier. Other critically acclaimed programs, e.g. *Lost* and *Battlestar Galactica*, signaled a new threat environment differing markedly from racially charged urban scenes in previous crime procedurals such as *Law and Order* or *NYPD Blue*. Both in the United States and abroad, critical commentaries emphasized these new programs' allegorical power, in the sense that a battle between good and evil clearly referenced real-world connections to the "war on terror" (Jacobs 2012; Jacobs and McKernan unpublished).

These new shows' success made African Americans less central to dominant threat narratives in fictional media and enabled emergence of more nuanced racial representations. Most notably, the critically acclaimed television series *The Wire* was much less likely than previous shows to rely on simplistic moral distinctions about "the street" and was quite powerful in its ability to undermine racial and urban stereotypes. As sociologist William Julius Wilson wrote in a *Washington Post* op-ed,

> *The Wire*, which depicted inner-city Baltimore over five seasons on HBO, shows ordinary people making sense of their world. Its complex characters on both sides of the law defy simplistic moral distinctions .... Through its scrupulous exploration of drug-dealing gangs, the police, politicians, unions, public schools and the print media, viewers see that an individual's decisions and behavior are often shaped by – and indeed limited by – forces beyond his or her control.[3]

Shifting patterns of racial representation on such programs was a frequent topic of aesthetic public sphere debate in the United States and abroad (Jacobs 2012; Jacobs and McKernan unpublished). More research is needed to determine how these meanings were connected to audience interpretations and informal public discussions, but it seems clear that, in the post-9/11 context, fictional, mediated racial narratives were changing.

Mainstream news narratives post-9/11 changed in a similar manner, focusing more on Islamic threat, less on African-American criminality. From earlier news coverage about the headscarf debate in France, there was already a narrative portraying "Islamic fundamentalism" as fundamentally anti-secular and anti-modern. This narrative was easily appropriated for a vigorous, symbolic pollution campaign against the putatively undifferentiated global Muslim community (Karim 2002). Debates about how to modernize the Middle East dominated the pages of the *New York Times*, most columnists emphasizing the need to understand how to address "angry young Muslims" who hated modernity (Jacobs and Townsley 2011: 203–5). Relying on Orientalist narratives, these media representations pushed aside many racial stereotypes and urban threat narratives, so prevalent during the days of Rodney King and O. J. Simpson, which had been a target of critique and counter-mobilization in African-American mediated publics.

This changed symbolic environment influenced African-American newspaper reporting about 9/11 and its aftermath. Mukherjee (2003) has argued that black press coverage was characterized by "complex ambivalence," combining patriotic and critical discourse. African-American news narratives about the attack on the World Trade Center activated strong commitments to an American identity and equally strong rejections of Islamic fundamentalism in a manner very similar to mainstream media coverage. And yet a more critical discourse emerged, expressing wariness about how easily an "Islamic threat" narrative could become a general attack on racial otherness, and thereby jeopardize important civil rights gains since the 1960s (Mukherjee 2003: 45). Cautioning readers not to forget the long US history of "oppressions, brutalities, and terrorism," this more critical discourse complicated what was otherwise a uniformly ideological media narrative of Islamic otherness (Mukherjee 2003: 39). Just like the 1990s, African-American media provided useful critique and narrative complexity but were largely ignored by mainstream media. The events of 9/11 and the rise of new communication technologies thus failed to alter the racially stratified public sphere, even as they changed larger patterns of racial representation.

Barack Obama and the media sociology of race

If 9/11 helped displace some of the old media discourses about race, Obama's election promised and suggested that the United States might be entering a "post-racial age." As columnists in *The New Republic, New York Times,* and *Los Angeles Times* wrote, it drew on the idealistic hopes of many Americans that the country was finally ready to move beyond racism (Crowley 2008; Steele 2008; Tierney 2008). Impromptu celebrations were held throughout the world when it was announced that Obama had won (Townsley 2012). Foreign newspapers declared the event the dawning of a new era, the realization of a dream articulated forty-five years earlier by Martin Luther King, Jr. How did this event change the cultural environment of mediated racial representations? Future media sociology research will doubtless provide answers to this question, but for the moment it is possible to make a few observations and propose a few hypotheses.

One narrative seeks to connect Obama and *The Cosby Show,* portraying the Obama family as a real-life, twenty-first-century version of the Huxtables. This narrative has circulated consistently in various formats. In the immediate aftermath of the election, a *New*

York Times article explored the possibility that *The Cosby Show* "had succeeded in changing racial attitudes enough to make an Obama candidacy possible."[4] Less seriously, perhaps, *The Daily Show with Jon Stewart* produced a segment "Barack Obama is Cliff Huxtable," in 2009, while *Saturday Night Live* produced a skit in 2012, "The Obama Show," which was a direct parody of *The Cosby Show*.

Just like during the 1980s and 1990s, the "Cosby" trope was the subject of critical commentary, particularly in more specialized and alternative media publics. Writing in *The Atlantic* in 2009, Ta Nehisi-Coates noted that "nothing says more about the gap between black America, and the people who write about black American, than the fact that, when looking for a precedent for Barack and Michelle, what we get – quite literally – is fiction." Coates argued that a more effective way to combat the 1990s' media obsession with "the black poor" was not to contrast them with a fictional African-American family, but with real people: "Because the true precedent – from the perspective of race – for the Obamas are Michelle Obama's parents, and Corey Booker's parents who were execs at IBM. It's Colin and Alma Powell. It's the engineering majors I knew at Howard, busting their asses in Founders Library during exams. It's dudes working construction, working plumbing, driving buses" (Coates 2009).

The African-American press explored the relationship between Obama's election and *The Cosby Show*, paying special attention to mainstream press interpretation of this relationship. Columnist Clarence Page wrote an article for the *Philadelphia Tribune* arguing that Obama owed a cultural debt to the fictional Huxtable family, also noting how African-American audiences had a much deeper historical connection to the show's representation of black culture, which linked back to a specific kind of social conservatism that had been an important part of the African-American community since the time of Marcus Garvey.[5] Making a different kind of argument, a column in the *Los Angeles Sentinel* explicitly rejected the proposition that *The Cosby Show* changed racial attitudes enough to make an Obama victory possible, arguing instead that Obama won despite continuing racism.[6] Similar to the 1990s, the African-American press continued to provide alternative perspectives and critique about the mainstream press. These alternatives were, as in the 1990s, largely ignored by mainstream media, continuing racial stratification of the public sphere.

In fact, continued racial stratification of the public sphere has been a topic of frequent commentary and disappointment within the African-American press during the Obama administration. There has been a recognition and tragic acceptance of the fact that "the nation's first Black president is constrained in discussing those lingering biases because he has to prove to skeptical whites that he isn't consumed by racial issues or attempting to pass special favors to Black constituents."[7] In other words, racism's persistence prevents Obama from responding effectively to institutional racism. Yet there has also been a strong criticism of Obama's mostly distant relationship with the African-American press, an overriding sense of disappointment that he did not seem interested in moving the black press more forcefully into the "official" public sphere.[8]

Despite talk of a post-racial era, Obama's era has actually been marked by return to patterns of racial representation that characterized pre-9/11 media discourse. A series of racial crises hastened this return to the old patterns. The first clue of such a return could be found during the election campaign itself, when a crisis emerged over comments made by the pastor at Obama's church, Jeremiah Wright. Next, shortly after Obama's inauguration, one of the most well-known African-American academics – Henry Louis Gates, Jr – was arrested while trying to enter his own home. The most significant event came in 2012, with the killing of Trayvon Martin in Florida. In each instance (fueled in large part by arguments being made on cable television), descriptive news coverage quickly degenerated into rancorous debate about the African-American threat. African-American media offered criticism throughout of shallow and racist tendencies in mainstream media coverage, though again their contribution was largely invisible in the larger public debate. When more systematic research about African-American and mainstream media coverage of these events is published, it will almost certainly document strong continuities with the news narratives of the 1990s.

Conclusion

Media sociologists have made important contributions to our understanding of racial representation. They have explored ideological structures and multivalent discourses of race in factual and fictional media, and have considered the intertextual relationships between different media formats. They have examined ways that individuals can resist media ideology, and studied ways in which mediated racial discourses become the object of public commentary and critique. They have examined how different racial meanings are filtered through national, transnational and minority media. They have considered how racial stratification of the public sphere marginalizes oppositional voices and minority media spaces. Cumulatively, the last thirty years of media sociology chart a clear research agenda for studying mediated racial representations.

What distinguishes media sociology of racial representations is a focus on the relational and public quality of discourse and power: meaning involves more than the interaction between text and reader. A variety of public processes and institutions are inserted between text and reader. These include communities of critics and other expert interpreters, whose evaluations are published in high-profile media, shaping public reception of any given text; alternative publics and media, offering alternative interpretations and critiques about dominant media discourses; creative personnel, whose fictional texts provide interpretive resources for thinking about real-world events, and communities of citizen-users participating in internet forums, blogs, and other communicative spaces of collective discussion about the meaning of these texts and "official" commentaries.

Moving forward, it will be necessary to expand this research agenda to incorporate important developments in the media landscape. There has been a vast proliferation of media technologies and formats over the last twenty years. This proliferation appears to be accelerating. As the boundaries between news and entertainment increasingly blur, several important new media formats arise within genres such as opinion media and political comedy (Delli Carpini and Williams 2011; Jacobs and Townsley 2011; Jacobs and Wild forthcoming). New political blogs and other social media occupy an ever-larger portion of the public (and private) attention space (Boczkowski 2005; Wallstein 2007). Further research is needed to determine how these changes have altered the dynamics of racial representation. A pressing question, in this context, concerns the extent to which these changes have altered the racial stratification of the public sphere.

Media sociology of race also needs to develop a more expansive research agenda, moving beyond focus on representations about African Americans. While some sociological work does already exist, it has not tended to be published in high-visibility sociological outlets and has not therefore exerted influence on the field. There are, however, reasons to believe that the dynamics of media, power, and resistance might be different for other racial groups. There is evidence that Latino media use is different from African-American media use (Hargittai and Litt 2011). Furthermore, the Latino press has a different history and institutional position to the

African-American press. There are also differences in the racial composition of media production, although all racial minorities remain significantly underrepresented (Weaver and Wilhoit 1996: 196). Future research should try to chart the extent to which these different circumstances change the dynamics of interpretive resistance or the ability of alternative interpretations to gain visibility in mainstream media. A more nuanced media sociology of race would result, building on the accomplishments of existing work while pushing it in important new directions.

Notes

1 For a more extended discussion of the relationship between sociology and British cultural studies, see Chaney (1994) and Alexander and Smith (2006).
2 Hunt's focus groups were composed almost entirely of college-aged respondents which makes it somewhat more difficult to generalize from his findings. Nevertheless, the patterns he reveals are interesting, if not altogether surprising.
3 Anmol Chaddha and William Julius Wilson, "Why We're Teaching *The Wire* at Harvard", *Washington Post*, September 12, 2010.
4 Tim Arango, "Before Obama, there was Bill Cosby", *New York Times*, November 7, 2008.
5 *Philadelphia Tribune,* September 27, 2009, p. A4.
6 *Los Angeles Sentinel,* February 3, 2009, p. A6.
7 *Philadelphia Tribune,* October 2, 2011, p. A11.
8 See for example a recent article in the *Chicago Defender,* which opened with the following criticism of Obama: "A panel discussion Thursday at the National Newspaper Publishers Association annual convention titled 'Get Out the Vote' should have been renamed 'Get Out the Anger' as black newspaper owners expressed their strong displeasure over the Obama administration's failure to accommodate the needs of the Black Press." (*Chicago Defender,* June 27, 2012, p. A6)

PART IV
Digital Technologies, Self, and Society

10

Digital Media Technology and the Spirit of the New Capitalism: What Future for "Aesthetic Critique"?

Graeme Kirkpatrick

Introduction

Digital technology is often cast as the causal agent that explains the sweeping social changes of the last forty years: the economy has been informationalized (Castells 1996); global corporations operate in "virtual" spaces beyond the reach of regulators (Sassen 2006), and these developments go along with a "new spirit" of capitalism (Boltanski and Chiapello 2005) that is more individualistic and competitive than ever. This chapter[1] presents a sociological perspective on contemporary media technologies in which they appear as entangled in and shaped by the historical developments they explain. The argument highlights the contingency of designs that tend to be taken for granted by media theorists on social antagonisms. Investigating the shaping of digital artifacts by ideas and processes that are connected to wider social transformations also has implications for social thought itself. This is not simply a matter of where we place technology in our social topography but concerns the investments that social critique has in questions of technology design and, in particular, critical theory's historic attachment to the aesthetic as a neglected yet potent dimension of social existence. In conclusion, this chapter raises the question of the implications of digital technology for this aspect of critical theory.

The chapter makes three central arguments. First, digital media technology has been shaped by socioeconomic developments of the last forty years as much as it has facilitated them. This can be shown with reference to the origins of modern computing in the 1960s and 1970s and to the transformation of the technology in the 1990s. These decisive moments in the social shaping of computer technology are also turning points in the development of "informational capitalism" and the rise of what Boltanski and Chiapello (2005) call the "new spirit" of the capitalist economy. Secondly, the traditional hegemonic alignment of capital with "technological rationality," expressed in technology designs that reflect a narrow concern with instrumental efficiency, seems to have come undone. In the industrial era of capitalism, critical theorists argued that capitalist technological rationality suppressed the aesthetic dimension (Marcuse 1978). Because of this, the aesthetic became a fundamental reference point for critique and was mooted as a privileged point of connection between theory and human reality. Engaging the ideas of the leading contemporary exponent of this view, Andrew Feenberg, my third argument is that the new spirit of capitalism has involved opening up and exploiting the energies of the aesthetic in ways that force a change on this perspective.

I begin by describing the social and economic transformations associated with the digital revolution, especially as they have been understood by Boltanski and Chiapello (2005). While much sociological literature elaborates on the social impacts of networked, universally accessible computing, and with good reason, the question of the qualitative, aesthetic character of this technology has tended to be overlooked. Boltanski and Chiapello's (2005) study links the changed ethos of capitalism in the networked era to what they call the "artistic critique" associated with the uprisings of 1968. I extend the logic of their argument to include contemporary capitalism's technical infrastructure, which embodies this new ethos.

The second section below discusses the origins of personal and home computing in the 1960s' US counterculture to explore the relationship between the "artistic critique" and technology. This section also makes the link to critical theories of technology, which at this time advanced the idea of a new, emancipatory technology that would break qualitatively with industrial capitalism just as surely as socialist economics would abolish capitalism. Introducing critical theory in this way, I hope to demonstrate the continuing interest of classical sociological ideas, especially ideas from the critical theory of Herbert Marcuse (1964) and Andrew Feenberg (2002), to discussions of contemporary digital media.

We then turn, in the third section, to the aestheticization of computers in the mid-1990s through which, I submit, capitalism's absorption of the artistic critique was, in significant part, made feasible. Drawing on social constructionist ideas, especially the notion of "relevant social actors" bringing competing claims and priorities to the scene of design, this section describes how human–machine interfaces were redesigned in line with new, aesthetic standards in a process that created digital media technologies as we know them today. The academic subdiscipline of human–computer interaction (HCI), which originates from this time, and the aesthetic standards it promulgated constitute a radical departure within the history of capitalist technology. This raises an obvious problem for critical theory, which is that capitalist technology has changed without any corresponding reduction in the exploitative nature of the system. Work activity tends to be organized less under the rubric of overtly technical imperatives and more in accordance with a framework of metaphors that guide us to completion of our tasks, but it is still exploited labor.

The chapter's last section focuses on how the qualitative transformation of computer technology relates to discussions of digital media in contemporary theory. Here we find that contemporary media theory deepens and extends critical social theory. In works by Scott Lash and Celia Lury (2007) and others (e.g. Poster 1995, 2006), the point is made that digital media replace the work of interpreting texts and of operating or guiding machines with novel forms of engagement characteristic of "interaction" with digital computers. Rather than standing between us and the world, including the substantive social world, digital media present us with objects that tend to constitute, if not worlds, environments in which to work. Rather than interpreting, we navigate and play our way through. In contemporary business studies' boosterism of this idea we find the notion that contemporary work processes can be "gamified," or made to resemble a computer game. This literature in some ways updates the management science materials studied by Boltanski and Chiapello (2005) and, in a manner that is consistent with their analysis, I argue in this section that, understood sociologically, gamification is a profoundly ambivalent concept. I offer the distinction between ludification and "ludefaction" to clarify the ambivalence of the play element in contemporary capitalism.

In conclusion, I suggest that the changes to technology described here subvert some of critical theory's preferred ways of understanding the articulation of technology to social domination. The problematic of societal rationalization, expressed in ethical and aesthetic values present in increasingly neutral technical codes (Feenberg 2002, 2010), no longer seems appropriate to grasp this relationship or to mount a practically workable critique. Rather, as I have argued elsewhere (Kirkpatrick 2004, 2008, 2011), critical theory has to open up a new front, in which technical knowledge takes on some of the functions previously accorded to conceptual, or reflective, understanding.

I argue here that we are forced to acknowledge that the aesthetic is not alien to capitalist technical infrastructure and that "re-aestheticization" strategies are not necessarily calibrated to the goals of progressive social change in a wider sense. Indeed, friendly communicative technology may not be inherently better for those who have to work with it than ugly, demanding machines. Rather, the aesthetic appears here as an autonomous dimension in which conflicts and tensions are played out according to their own logics and whose wider significance can only be assessed in context, not read off from the ideological positionings of individual movements within the arts; the statements of prominent designers, or even the presumptions of a critical theory that somehow lays exclusive claim to that aesthetic.

Computers and the new spirit of capitalism

As Manuel Castells puts it, technology was essential to the creation of "an economy with the capacity to work as a unit in real time on a planetary scale" (Castells 1996: 92). Digital technologies have changed our ways of creating and communicating so that scientific practices, the arts, and entertainment media all now move to a different rhythm than before. Networked computing has reconfigured our understanding of society and our understanding of our own contribution to social life. Social media like Facebook are a clear illustration of how the very practices of social interaction have been altered by the salience of digital devices and the reality of digital connection. The internet has made it possible for corporations to relocate many of their processes to digital space, rendering their geographical location increasingly notional. The technology that underlies globalization has its origins in the activities of a generation of computer "whizz kids" who came to maturity in the 1980s (Sassen 2006: 363), many of them having spent their childhoods playing games on home computers like the Commodore 64 or Spectrum ZX. The key global networks were initially formed around a fateful "triangle of wealth, power and technology" (Castells 1996: 163) in Japan, the United States and the European Union, and these areas were also the strategic centers for new media industries like computer gaming (Johns 2006).

In perhaps the most sociologically interesting appraisal of the way that capitalism has responded to computers and computerization,

Luc Boltanski and Eve Chiapello (2005) invoke the idea of a new "capitalist spirit" or ethos. They trace the origins of this new spirit to the revolutionary upheavals which took place in France and around the developed world in 1968 and to the way that management in particular responded, over the course of the subsequent three decades, to the specific sources of discontentment expressed by those events. This new spirit, they argue, explains the character of the contemporary workplace. It also facilitates a contextual, situated understanding of how digital media technologies have been used to transform the world of work. We may add that their account also furnishes us with a context for the sociological interpretation of the shaping of computer technologies. In particular, the dominant ideas in contemporary technology design have been heavily informed by what they call the "artistic critique" of capitalism and its assimilation.

Boltanski and Chiapello distinguish between a social and economic critique of capitalism, which is historically associated with the labor movement and focused on issues of social security and remuneration for work, and what they call the artistic critique. The latter was associated with nineteenth-century bohemia, various kinds of dandyism and the ethos of artists and intellectuals. These groups are normally . economically marginal and their critique of capitalism focused more on its hierarchical, bureaucratic, and ordered character than on its exploitative foundations. The artistic critique of capitalism:

> stresses the objective impulse of capitalism and bourgeois society to regiment and dominate human beings, and subject them to work that it prescribes for the purpose of profit, while hypocritically invoking morality. To this it counterposes the freedom of artists, their rejection of any contamination of aesthetics by ethics, their refusal of any form of subjection in time and space and, in its extreme forms, of any kind of work. (Boltanski and Chiapello 2005: 38)

In the revolutions that started on university campuses in Europe in 1968 and quickly spread to include workers, nearly toppling the French government in the process, the two kinds of critique came together. Workers and students opposed capitalism on two fronts, as unfair economically and as a restrictive and oppressive "system."

The convergence of the two kinds of critique is unusual in historical terms and 1968 represents a kind of high watermark for those who would like to see the overthrow of capitalism. The wider 1960s movement was predominantly critical of, and on occasion just opposed to, technology. Its motivational basis lay in disaffection with the kinds of social organization associated with industrial society.

People were suspicious of technology's role in forms of domination associated with "the system": at this time computers were strongly identified with corporations and "big government" (Agar 2003; Burnham 1984). Much counter-cultural writing of the period identifies industrial and computer technology with bureaucracy and hierarchy and seems motivated by the idea of a romantically inspired return to nature. Theoretical sources important to the movement targeted "technocracy," an organizing principle in which experts and the perceived requirements of technical systems hold sway over important social decisions. The role of human beings and of deliberative communicative processes seemed to be increasingly effaced in a culture that prioritized economic and administrative efficiency to the exclusion of other values. The clearest exponents of this view were critical social theorists like Herbert Marcuse who flew to Paris in May 1968 to address students involved in the uprising, many of whom had been inspired by his ideas (Feenberg and Freedman 2001).

Technology was clearly a big part of the imagined future that the students and young workers of 1968 did not want for themselves. They feared a life of repetitive drudgery under the command of austere machines programmed by others. They rejected the hierarchical organization of work that might place them in a management role where they imposed such a life on others. Above all, perhaps, they craved a life that would involve more humane values, including ethical ones of self-determination but also aesthetic notions of play and adventure. Although the movement became exhausted in a relatively brief period, some of its ethos persisted and this can be observed in a range of effects that continue to reverberate down to the present. Boltanski and Chiapello describe a "great refusal" on the part of the generation of 1968, which meant that French industry in particular struggled to recruit young managers in the 1970s.[2] As late as 1980, Andre Gorz's analysis of the crisis of that era reflected the persistence of the 1968 perspective in the following terms:

> Mechanisation has given rise to the fragmentation and dequalification of work and made it possible to measure work according to purely quantitative standards. You can do your job and not bother about what happens, since the quality of your work and of the finished product depends on the machines, not on you . . . (1980: 38) Work no longer signifies an activity or even a major occupation; it is merely a blank interval on the margins of life, to be endured in order to earn a little money. (Gorz 1980: 70)

The people Gorz calls the "non-class of post-industrial proletarians," then, do not share the Marxist vision of appropriating the technical infrastructure of capitalism and creating a super-efficient society of abundance:

> Technological development does not point towards a possible appropriation of social production by the producers. Instead it indicates further elimination of the social producer, and continuing marginalization of socially necessary labour as a result of the computer revolution. (Gorz 1980: 72)

> What matters instead is to appropriate areas of autonomy outside of, and in opposition to, the logic of society, so as to allow the unobstructed realisation of individual development *alongside* and *over* that machine-like structure. (Gorz 1980: 73)

However, in the rich countries at least, Gorz's vision has not been realized.[3] The resistance and withdrawal movements of the 1970s and 1980s have largely dissipated. Few now dream of an alternative social reality, apart from those who project those dreams, usually in the guise of money-making schemes, onto cyberspace.[4] The key change has been in the organization of the workplace and of the experience of work, associated with informationalization.

In their study of management science literature in the 1990s, Boltanski and Chiapello argue that the artistic critique has been incorporated into the operation of the capitalist system. Basing their thesis on an extensive content analysis of 1990s management science literature, they find that from the late 1980s there is a new awareness on the part of those charged with organizing and managing production processes that work has to be made more attractive (2005: 191). Management no longer seeks to motivate employees through monetary rewards or the threat of unemployment, but rather to structure the labor process in such a way that worker motivations are "bound up with a desire to perform the work and the pleasure of doing it" (2005: 80). This "involves transferring constraints from external organizational mechanisms to people's internal dispositions" so that workers are viewed as sources of "feeling[s], emotion and creativity" (2005: 87). Work is now infused with the values of play (2005: 97), which is used for its capacity to unlock creative energies, and with a sense of adventure to be found through engagement with diverse projects, which workers manage for themselves (2005: 90). The new spirit of capitalism involves a workplace that is transformed by these ethical and aesthetic values. As I have pointed out in previous work (Kirkpatrick 2004), this aestheticization extends to technology design so that the values of the artistic critique are also imprinted on the technical infrastructure of digital capitalism.

Critical theory and digital media

There is irony in the way the content of the artistic critique has transformed the ethos of capitalism and been used to intensify the hold the system has over most people's lives. Critical theory has, in the main, been wrong-footed by these changes largely because, as Jacques Rancière points out (2009), the very idea of a critique is essentially romantic in the sense that it depends upon the notion of an untapped "other" to the system; a source of difference that cannot be assimilated but whose roots also resist elucidation in rational discourse. As such it is inherently and often counterproductively suspicious of technology. While Marcuse, for example, was not "anti-technology," he was critical of modern society's "construction of techniques" aimed at dominating nature and controlling human beings. He believed that modern technology had the capacity to assign "a directing function to the free play of thought and imagination," but achieving this would require an aesthetic reform of machines to translate "the adventures of the mind into the adventures of technology" (Marcuse 1964: 234).

The leading contemporary exponent of critical theory, Andrew Feenberg, has added interest to Marcuse's ideas and developed them into a full-blown theory of the "re-aestheticization" of technology, which he conceives as an essential part of any meaningful social transformation. According to Feenberg, technology's appearance of neutrality – the way it presents itself as sets of tools with prescribed functions that enhance our leverage over the world – is an effect of what he calls the "technical code." In any society, the technical code condenses values and technical reason to produce artifacts that, on one side, act on the world to bring about predetermined effects and, on the other, present this facility as an affordance to putative users. Historically, this meant that part of being a good tool pertained to its efficiency, while another equally integral dimension in which it ought to be esteemed concerned its appearance and the ethical values associated with the services it provided to a given community. Hammers and forges, for example, give rise to horseshoes and nails but also to blacksmiths, and the meanings of all these objects are relative, or contingent upon the ways in which they are tied into networks of other humans, things, and practices. These networks confer value and meaning on technology and the pre-capitalist technical code condensed these values with the functionality or technical reason they embodied. Tools were then defined as part of the "mechanical arts" and this context positioned them in the prevailing cultural system of perceptions.

For traditional critical theorists, what seems to define capitalist technology is that it focuses exclusively on the functional or technical dimension related to efficiency to the exclusion of other ethical and aesthetic values. Feenberg points out that in fact, and contrary to the arguments of earlier critical theorists, this cannot be the case. In the absence of a "human" dimension, technical objects would be unusable because they would present no meaningful aspect that humans could respond to. The idea of a technology that has not been in some way "recontextualized," as Feenberg puts it (2010: 73), is therefore unthinkable. All technology involves what Feenberg calls "primary instrumentalization," in which objects are "de-worlded" by being torn from their natural locations and reduced to their fundamental properties, as understood in the perspective of physical science. Equally, however, it is part of the meaning of technology that it should also be "re-worlded" through a "secondary instrumentalization," which articulates the artifact to a system in which it functions and presents it to human users in what Feenberg calls a "valuative mediation" (2010: 73), where it appears as meaningful and as something a human being might use. Even under capitalism, secondary instrumentalization is necessary for technology to make sense to people and appear to them as something they can include in their lives.

What changes with modern, capitalist technology is that the networks in which technologies are embedded grow larger, with the result that their technical codification alters its evaluative dimension: "Modern societies emphasise systematization and build long networks through tightly coupling links over huge distances between very different types of thing and people" (2010: 76). Technology then has to appear as neutral in order that it can become culturally universal. What really distinguishes capitalist technology and the capitalist technical code from non- or pre-capitalist variants, therefore, is not the absence of values but rather their null or mute character. As Boltanski and Chiapello also point out, capitalism is the first historical society to understand itself in amoral terms: it rationalizes its systems dimension in terms of survival and a narrow conception of efficiency, and projects these as universal. Capitalist technology is therefore not free of values; rather, it is imprinted and identified with the value of having no *particular* ethical or aesthetic values – a peculiar situation indeed. Feenberg argues that any meaningful break with capitalism will require a change to this capitalist technical code: "An alternative modernity . . . would recover the mediating power of ethics and aesthetics" (Feenberg 2010: 77).

Feenberg's instrumentalization theory offers a normative basis for the sociological study of media technology. It posits a quasi-transcendental framework within which all technology design takes place and offers its terms (de- and recontextualization; aestheticization) as a serviceable vocabulary within which designs can be assessed, contrasted, and criticized for how well they serve human interests. At the same time, the theory is sensitive to sociological context. Feenberg insists that communicative and aesthetics principles are involved in all technology design without falling into the trap that ensnares Marcuse when he seems to envisage a utopia based on tools that persuade nature to behave the way we want it to (Habermas 1987a: 88).

Applying his ideas to computer technology, Feenberg proposes that a progressive re-aestheticization should involve a naturalistic aesthetic, perhaps influenced by Frank Lloyd Wright. Technology designs would be attentive to how technical and natural elements combine to produce habitable environments for humans to work in. Insisting that Marcuse's position "makes intuitive sense," Feenberg advocates designs whose "structures harmonise with nature and seek to integrate human beings with their environment" (2002: 155). He emphasizes that the choice in computer systems design is between "rationalistic" principles "designed for hierarchical control" (2002: 107) and those that promote use of the computer as a "communications medium," in which case the computer is presented as "an environment for an increasing share of daily life" (2002: 106). Such design strategies, he suggests, will facilitate a fuller integration of technology into the value basis of a better way of life. However, the re-aestheticization of technology represented by the design of personal computers (and subsequent generations of digital devices) has proceeded in such a way as to trouble some of Feenberg's core assumptions, especially the notion he inherits from Marcuse of the aesthetic as a linchpin for progressive social transformation.

The social shaping of digital technology

Part of the importance of Feenberg's contribution is that it highlights the fact that technology is contested terrain rather than a monolithic element that acts on society as if from outside. Social and political struggles can be identified within technology design. The goal of making computers that are pleasing and easy to use, which is now an accepted principle relating to most if not all technology design, was by no means obvious when it was first formulated and its current hegemony reflects the outcome of a series of such struggles. Social constructionist principles applied to the history of computers and computer interface design provide valuable insights here, filling out the history that has shaped digital infrastructures. Computer technology was shaped by a number of relevant social groups (Bijker, Hughes and Pinch 1989; Edwards 1995) and the designs we take for granted are the outcome of contingent social struggles.

In the US context it was "hippy hackers" who first developed the idea, at the time radical, of computers for everyone. As Freiberger and Swain (1984) point out, it took several years for any of the established computer manufacturers to realize the potential of microcomputers as the kind of thing that ordinary people might want to own and use themselves. The first computer that might fit under a desk, the PDP-8, was made by Digital Equipment Corporation in 1965 (Freiberger and Swain 1984: 20), but there were no plans to market it outside of the scientific research community: "Without exception, the existing computer companies passed up the chance to bring computers into the home and onto the desk . . . . the microcomputer was created entirely by individual entrepreneurs working outside the established corporations" (Freiberger and Swain 1984: 17–18). In the midst of "women's lib," the hacker Ted Nelson wrote a book called "computer lib," which was a manifesto for those elements of the counter-culture who believed that computers could change people's lives for the better. They wanted to create a new kind of technology that could serve human beings and communities rather than control them, perhaps realizing Marcuse's vision of an alternative technology designed by a new, benign social elite and modifying what Feenberg calls the technical code in such a way that it seems completely normal for technology to be appealing, playful, and communicative.

Fred Turner (2006) argues that this culture around small computers was not really influenced by the New Left political movement, which was concerned primarily with economic and other injustices arising out of the capitalist economic system, but was more concerned with what we would now call "lifestyle" issues. In other words, computer technology was being shaped by the artistic critique. The first computer "hackers" (Levy 1984) were playful experimenters and in computers they identified a counter-technology – one that could make work feel more like play. For Richard Neville, editor of one of the counter-cultural magazines of the time and prominent spokesperson for what was then called the "underground," the driving force of the counter-culture was "playpower," a form of work that was "done only for fun; as a pastime, obsession, hobby or art-form and thus is not work in the accepted sense" (Neville 1971: 213). The playfulness of the computer movement is evident in the names they chose for their associations, which included: Golemics Inc; Loving Grace Cybernetics; Itty Bitty Computer Company; Chicken Delight Computer Consultants, and Kentucky Fried Computers from North Carolina (Turner 2006). These kinds of slightly zany business names are perhaps commonplace now but, in the bureaucratic and hierarchical world of 1960s commerce, they stood out. The public rhetoric around computing signaled the presence of what Freiberger and Swain describe as an "amorphous subculture of technofreaks, hobbyists and hackers, people untrained in business skills and more interested in exploring the potential of the microcomputer than in making money" (1984: 59).

By the late 1980s, we can see some of the ideas of this movement being incorporated into mainstream technical and commercial practices. Boltanski and Chiapello do not mention that the management science literature in their study was developing a concern specifically with the design of "Management Information Systems."[5] This literature was concerned with "business process restructuring," which involved using digital networks to reconfigure organizations as flat rather than hierarchical, and with how to manage firms in which, in principle, everyone has access to broadly the same information. This concern to use computers to fashion a new kind of working environment, structured around ideas of connection and communication as integral to performance, runs in tandem with a transformation of the computer itself, especially its human interface. New design principles were formulated that drew heavily on cognitive psychology and were codified in a new subdiscipline in computer science, human–computer interaction (HCI). The declared goal of HCI was to create interfaces that relieved users of the "cognitive burdens" of technology use (Schneiderman 1997). HCI transformed computers toward the end of the 1980s, reorganizing computing under metaphors like the "desktop," or the "environment," and structuring HCI with narrative orderings familiar to users from other, "natural" contexts of action.

As late as the mid-1990s, it was not immediately obvious to all the relevant social actors that computers should be designed in this way. Within computer science, for example, papers like those by R. S. Nickerson (1976), who expressed concern that the interface should not deceive users by misrepresenting what was going on in the machine, or M. Fitter (1979), who recommended design in which "as the user becomes more proficient he should be allowed to see more of the system" (1979: 344), expressed alternative visions of the way forward. For them, technical designs should take integrity and transparency as key values, resulting in machines that make demands on users while at the same time educating them about the techno-logical realities. They were opposed by advocates of the burgeoning discipline of HCI who emphasized the power of the interface to "support" users in their pursuit of non-technical objectives. For the latter group, the communicative capacities of computers needed to be amplified so that people could use their machines simply by oper-ating in environments that simulated natural and familiar contexts of action and interaction and required no specialist knowledge or technical understanding.

HCI pioneers had to struggle to secure preeminence. Brenda Laurel (1993), Nicholas Negroponte (1995) and other visionaries of the friendly human interface refer bitterly to a "technical priest-hood" that seemed to them to be withholding computer power from the people. As usual, this genuflection to the popular conceals as much as it proclaims in terms of the actual democratic impact of the recommended technical changes. Friendly user interfaces steer sub-ordinate users into prescribed routines with their machines, closing off unanticipated explorations of the computer's potential. As Laurel writes, a good interface should constrain the user but not in such a way that they are aware of it: "Constraints should be applied without shrinking our perceived range of freedom of action: Constraints should limit, not what we can do, but what we are likely to think of doing. Such *implicit* constraints, when successful, eliminate the need for explicit limitations on our behavior" (Laurel 1993: 105). The easy-to-use interface is one that feels nice to use but it also saves companies money in terms of training employees to understand the tools they are operating and solves the problem of limiting specific users' access to functions and information within a system that, in its fundamental architecture, is open to anyone with a connected machine. A critical sociological perspective, therefore, reveals that seemingly benign and "pleasing" designs may actually be ambiva-lent when placed in social contexts shaped by power. An adequate aesthetic appraisal of technology designs has to position judgment in social context: what is attractive and benign in one context may be manipulative and form part of a strategy of domination in another. Similarly, the instrumental reasoning that menaces one generation in the guise of industrial machines may become an attractive route to empowerment for the next – and there is a range of ambiguous positions in between. It is in light of such a reflexive sociological approach to media aesthetics that I have argued that technical reason is an essential dimension of critical thinking today (Kirkpatrick 2004).

To say this is not to argue against usable interfaces, but rather to open up a margin within contemporary technical politics: how "friendly" you want a software interface to be, as against being open to user experimentation and the costs necessarily associated with this, ought to be part of the pragmatic judgment that is made each time a new program is introduced in a workplace setting. What is interesting and important in this, from the standpoint of critical theory, is that the negative aspects of capitalist technology in this context cannot be understood in terms of a failure of the technical code to imprint technology with positive values, especially aesthetic ones. The capitalist technical code does not here consist in a lack of mediation or a failure to translate values into design and sediment them in the machine. Rather, and contrary to what even Feenberg's theory leads us to expect, capitalist computer technology tends to be heavily and positively loaded with aesthetic principles and values.

The widespread acceptance of aesthetic design principles for work (and all) machines is of vital importance for critical theorists hoping to rethink the relation of technology to social power. It is largely through the implementation of these design values that the labor process has changed to become more playful and engaging, within a social context of less security and, as Boltanski and Chiapello point out (see also Sennett 2006), more precariousness for employees. Machines with seductive interfaces (Turkle 1995), running routines that present only moderate challenges to users, integrated within representations that have narrative coherence and perhaps even include positive aesthetic "pay-offs," are all fundamental to contemporary workplace technology design. This transformation of technology adds a new dimension to Boltanski and Chiapello's account of capitalism's "adaptation" to the pressures for change that came from the artistic critique. They identify the anti-technological orientation of that critique, highlighting the dominant tendency within the counterculture, which, as we have seen, was anti-technocratic and focused on technology's social control functions (Boltanski and Chiapello 2005: 440). In arguing that capitalism "internalizes" this critique, however, they neglect to deal with the resulting transformation of its technical infrastructure.

Like most authors on informationalization and the networked economy, Boltanski and Chiapello tend to evaluate technology only in economic terms, that is, according to whether it contributes to improvements in economic performance. It is evident, however, that the aesthetic transformation of computer technology confirms the central thrust of their argument and extends the reach of their critique. In technology as in other dimensions of society, the artistic critique's fulfillment of its aims has been bought at the price of an evasion on the part of the system and a series of displacements. In place of hard industrial technology that could quite easily be criticized for its inhuman effects, we now have glossy, colorful tools that demand a different kind of engagement from workers. The aestheticization of contemporary technology is powerfully suffused by the idea of play and this is allied to the new emphasis placed on individual creativity and flexibility in the "new spirit of capitalism." Power is then displaced away from management control at the point of production to self-management through the intense, playful labor of scrutinizing and controlling variables often pertaining to one's own performance. Work and life are a game, with all the ambiguity that term brings to any situation.

What future for aesthetic critique?

The capitalist assimilation of the 1960s' aesthetic critique has resulted in interface design principles that are largely consistent with the recommendations of critical theorists. The tools most people now use at work offer "environments" in which communication (essential to "networking") is central and much of what is done has strong affinities with play. We have also seen a proliferation of new digital media technologies that promote these values even more overtly and which further efface the distinction between work and play. Aestheticized computer technology has transformed the cultural landscape and in the process the link between technology and a rationalistic oppressive social system has been broken. Viewed in terms of Feenberg's theory, it is clear that Gorz's prediction that people will disengage with the economy fails in large part because he was unable to foresee that the technical code, which condenses values and technical imperatives at the scene of technology design, would itself change, resulting in computers that offer people (or appear to) work experiences that are much more than a "blank interval on the margins of life."

However, this has not led to a straightforwardly more benign situation for capitalism's human subjects. In Scott Lash and Celia Lury's (2007) study of the contemporary culture industry, they argue that the situation is both worse and better than the one described by previous generations of critical theorists. It is worse because now individuals are far more dependent on the objects they are involved in. We define ourselves more than ever through our consumption and increasingly the new commodities, which they call "virtuals,"[6] demand non-remunerated labor to instantiate them and bring them to life. As Robert Heilbroner puts it (in Boltanski and Chiapello 2005: 476), these commodities represent an "expansion of capital within the interstices of social life." At the same time, things are better because through those objects we reflexively co-participate in the production of new experiences. Lash and Lury argue that a defining feature of contemporary commodities is that they involve a "provocation to play"; they "tantalize" their consumers and "ensnare" them in surprising processes, diversifying what is meant by "consumption" and creating possibilities for active "fun." This constitutes a revival of play and presents novel possibilities of being "drawn outside the frame of purposive, communicative rationality to out-do ourselves and be out-done" (Lash and Lury 2007: 207). In other words, a reflexive approach to media sociology reveals that the aesthetic dimension of play has now assumed a prominent role in the circulation of commodities.

Computerization has not only involved reorganization of social functions and practices on the network metaphor, it has also seen play and gameness come to the fore as organizing principles. The computer game is exemplary in relation to these developments, especially in its agonistic structure. The activity of playing computer games is in many ways consonant with the experience of work in the networked society. The effects of this are not straightforwardly pleasant. Carstens and Beck (2005), for example, argue that the generation of people who grew up playing computer games, often continuing the practice into mid-life, have a distinctively competitive, even ruthless attitude at work. Gamers, they write, "will not learn for learning's sake" alone (2005: 24), confirming the idea that no work is undertaken in consideration of the longer-term edification of the self. Rather, work is about performing well in the present and being seen to perform well by relevant others: it has become gamelike. In this context, some authors in business and management studies have written of a pervasive "gamification," or ludification of economic and social life.

Ludification is the notion that playful behavior with computer technology is reconfiguring an increasing array of social domains, mainly with beneficial consequences. Recent management literature urges managers to design tasks in such a way that they appear game-like to putative employees. In the words of the *Economist* magazine, this strategy "inverts completely" the notion that people have to be paid to do work, especially repetitive tasks. Instead, "players will happily fork out good money for the privilege of being allowed to attempt arbitrary jobs. What if, say the gamifiers, it were possible to identify the 'special sauce' responsible for this strange effect, extract it and then slather it onto business problems? Can the compulsive power of video games be harnessed to motivate workers?" (*Economist* 2012: 72).[7]

This kind of promotion of game play as a way to reconfigure the labor process offers a perspective on the contemporary capitalist mediation of technology and shows how far we are from an industrial "null" aesthetic in technology design. Contemporary work and technology are playful and framed by a perspective of levity, which gives them a kind of weightlessness. Work no longer determines identity because people no longer expect to have one definitive career and because what is done there is not completely serious (cf. Sennett 2006). The criteria for success are those of playing the game well, with the undertow of cynicism this attitude usually connotes. Jobs are no longer secure, still less "for life", but rather employment is increasingly disparate: people pick up the threads of a project here or there and move on to the next one when they run out. This is all made acceptable by the feeling that it is only a game: working life has been ludified. Here the nihilistic aspect of play with computer games is paradigmatic. Activities like "gold-farming," in which players "grind" out repetitive in-game routines in order to mechanically produce game items that can be sold on real-world markets, illustrate the ambivalence of the contemporary experience of play. It can be creative and exciting but it also has a nihilistic strain (G. Kirkpatrick 2011), which comports with Boltanski and Chiapello's observation of a widespread disorientation, in which no one really knows any more what the purpose of life is (2005: 424).

As these comments imply, ludification is only half of the picture here. Drawing on an adaptation of geological metaphors, I would like to contrast ludification with "ludefaction," in the way that geologists speak not of "liquification" but of the more hazardous liquefaction.

Liquefaction involves dry structures turning fluid as the result of a kind of internal collapse at the granular level and is associated with the reverberations caused by earthquakes or hazardous mining activities. Liquefaction can cause subsidence and damage to surface structures. Ludefaction may pose a similar threat via the psychic and cultural substructures that are necessary for human creativity and cultural life. The proliferation of playful yet manipulative technologies, interfaces that are pleasing and charming yet ultimately just making us work in accordance with other-imposed norms, corrode our sense of self and of purpose. Ludefaction gives rise to work processes which "demand greater commitment and rely on a more sophisticated ergonomics . . . [they] penetrate more deeply into people's inner selves – people are expected to 'give' themselves to their work – and facilitate an instrumentalisation of human beings in their most specifically human dimensions" (Boltanski and Chiapello 2005: 98). Fracking the aesthetic in this way means that capitalism threatens the substrata of culture. We see this in pathological forms of play identified by many scholars of the computer game. In his study of the online massive multiplayer game (MMPG) *World of Warcraft*, for example, David Golumbia (2009) describes how the kind of repetitive "grinding" players engage in reacts back onto play itself, rendering it empty and pathologically addictive as it loses all connection with meaning.[8]

Viewing this employment of play in social context, we see similar processes of ludification/ludefaction elsewhere in contemporary digital media culture. Facebook and other new social media, for example, have been hailed as tools of social connection. Through them people reconnect with long lost friends and relatives and establish connections with others who share the same interests. For some, this represents a new public sphere replete with democratic potentials. Facebook is also playful, not only in the sense that it includes a multitude of mini games, of which Farmville is perhaps the best known, but also in its core dynamic. Each account holder has an advertised number of "friends" and the game is on to win and maintain a positive profile. Here friendship and connection are not "instrumentalized" (the bugbear of old-style critical theory and substantivist critiques of technology[9]) but ludified. Playing this game tends to involve a constant struggle to be interesting, to come up with new posts and to present oneself in a way that maintains one's "score." This impels the endless cycles of self-disclosure that give rise to the "ambient intimacy" (Kirkpatrick 2010) characteristic of new social media – the feeling of being personally involved in the lives of people we have often never met. It is here that self-disclosure is also an opening to commerce and capital. As David Kirkpatrick (2010) points out, Facebook monetizes by selling data aggregates based on its records of all this activity. Other firms gain free advertising by encouraging users to "like" them – an operation that is seen by all their "friends," with each resulting "impression" working as something bordering on personal recommendation.

In these circumstances, it seems that no private, inner recess of the subject is left untouched by capital. Play and games are openings to greater areas of subjective life than could ever be accessed using discipline and rationality alone. And, as the case of *World of Warcraft* indicates, play itself, the fount of human creativity, is here distorted into one of its more pathological variants.[10] A social system that toys with this is both curiously triumphant and, one suspects, utterly exhausted – where else is there to go?

Rather than merely facilitating the transformation of work into an "adventure," computer interface design principles are themselves informed by the strategic necessity of fashioning environments to accommodate and displace critique. The salience of easy-to-use, friendly devices often tailored to the "needs" of individuals seems like a fulfillment of Herbert Marcuse's vision of a humanized technical practice. Yet at the same time it is consistent with intensified exploitation and a deeper insinuation of the demands of work into the lives of human beings. The terms of technology's alignment with power have changed. We are no longer dealing with a bureaucratized, rationalized social system that is organized on the model of machines. Rather, technology is part of a fluid, viscous social background that inhibits the development of categorical distinctions essential to critique (Boltanski 2011). The metaphor used above of "fracking" the aesthetic is appropriate, then, because in unlocking the energies of the aesthetic we also unleash new risks: the ambiguities of play enter the finance system, to name but one obvious example, and the system becomes more difficult to regulate and control through public mechanisms based on deliberation and democratic debate.

In previous decades it seemed as if a revival of play as a positive force in human behavior was incompatible with capitalism and the modern institution of work. However, the changes described here, which have been made possible by the spread of digital technologies with "friendly" and ludic interfaces, have undermined this idea. No one could now decry contemporary work for its lack of a playful dimension. This raises questions for the very idea of aesthetic critique. The transformation of technology described here is also a transformation of technical politics. When contesting current designs it will not suffice to ask that artifacts be more pleasing to use, that they make life more comfortable for the worker, or even that they facilitate creativity and free expression. Capitalism has all these things covered but it has not ceased to be exploitative, to threaten the natural environment, or to impose relations based on domination on its subjects. Aesthetic critique in these circumstances will need to abandon its romantic inheritance and reposition itself in relation to power.

Notes

1 My thanks to Sarah Carling for extensive discussion of ideas in this chapter, especially the distinction between ludification and ludefaction. I'm also grateful to Andrew Feenberg, Silvio Waisbord, Cheryl Martens and an anonymous reader for their comments and suggestions on earlier drafts.
2 This was also a problem elsewhere. See Hardt and Negri (2000) and Virno (2004).
3 It could be argued that some of Gorz's ideas have gained practical expression in 1990s' social movements of the global South, especially Latin America; see Petras and Veltmeyer (2011); Stahler-Sholk, Vanden, and Kuecker (2008).
4 An interesting study could be made of the conversion of various radical visionary projects of this time into internet businesses. Ivan Illich's (1971) idea of abolishing schools, for instance, gets recycled into various "online learning" schemes, while communitarian utopias and protests against social atomization are transmuted into the rhetoric of building "personal networks," "finding friends" on Facebook, or joining "guilds" in the fantasy worlds of massive multiplayer games.
5 Zwass (1992) and Robson (1998) are good examples of the genre.
6 Lash and Lury define "virtuals" as objects that lack physical extension and so are not "real" but get "actualized" in the course of their consumption.
7 The article is a review of Werbach and Hunter (2012), a contemporary management science text.
8 Golumbia finds that play in online games "demand[s] intimate and profound engagement from individual users" (2009: 196) and so resembles contemporary work. Both are addictive. Sociological studies of MMPGs like *World of Warcraft* have aligned them with neoliberal, undemocratic governance strategies that use this ambivalent kind of play as part of an armory of social control (Humphreys 2008; Ruch 2009).
9 Feenberg and Grimes (2009), for instance, argue that play is "rationalized" by games, but there is no promotion of efficiency here. Rather, play, in all its purposelessness, is being turned against itself.

10 The idea that play might be pathological has always been well understood by psychologists, for example, Donald Winnicott associated
playing "joyless, obsessive games" (1971: 29) with an excess of fantasy
blocking personal growth.

11

Mobile Communication and Mediated Interpersonal Communication

Rich Ling

Introduction

It is perhaps fair to say that media sociology has often been concerned with the interaction between mass media and various publics. The analysis has often assumed the "mass" in mass media and has not focused on other constellations where mediated communication takes place (Gitlin 1978). Mediated interpersonal interaction is another important issue in society. Complementing the one-to-many metaphor of earlier work is the development of one-to-one and one-to-some forms of mediated interaction. Castells (2009) calls the latter of these two "mass self-communication." Sociology has something to say, however, about the use of mobile communication. It gives us an excellent lens (indeed several lenses) through which we can better understand the way that mobile communication plays into our social lives. Application of sociological insights to mobile communication helps elucidate the state of social cohesion: how membership in social groups plays out and how technology helps us in everyday life.

Mobile communication is a fundamentally social technology. Mobile devices afford individual functionality but also tie us securely into social networks. Sociology therefore has something to offer. Examining mobile communication illuminates classical sociological issues of autonomy, social network analysis, cohesion, and solidarity. Furthermore, sociological analyses and theoretical lenses facilitate approaches to these issues. Rather than focusing on individual experience, the sociology legacy compels understanding of how an implicitly social technology functions in the context of social life.

Mobile communication is the most broadly distributed form of electronically mediated interaction. According to the International

Telecommunication Union (ITU), as of 2011 there were almost 6 billion mobile phone subscriptions. The global population is about 7 billion people. By contrast, there were about 1.1 billion landline subscriptions and 2.4 billion internet users (of whom about 1.2 billion used mobile internet).[1] Thus, mobile phones' affordability, ease of use, and functionality secure wide adoption. High-flying socialites in New York, busy sales personnel in Hamburg, and impoverished farmers in Cote d'Ivoire all use mobile phones, each for their own purposes. As pointed out by Jensen (2007), this spreading is not so much consequent on planned governmental programs but grew organically through technical developments and social demand.

Adoption of mobile phone networks is, in many ways, simpler than diffusion of the PC-based internet and landline phones. In the case of landlines, diffusion relies on an extensive network of copper wires connecting different phone terminals. This is a resource-intensive enterprise.[2] Once installed, wires in the "local loop" are in use only when the particular subscriber uses his/her phone. This commits significant resources for very little use. Radio-based mobile telephony, by contrast, does not demand the same physical resources. It requires base-stations and accompanying data control systems. There is, however, no need for the "last mile" cabling of landline telephony. Radio frequencies can be reused by many people, making them more resource-efficient. From the user-perspective, mobile communication is also simpler than the PC-based internet. Mobile phones are small, relatively intuitive devices that mostly come ready for use. There is no need, in contrast to PC/internet setup, for the installation of different programs, wiring to modems, configuring Wi-Fi access, and so on.[3]

Given its wide diffusion and the way it is changing daily life, it is unsurprising that a research community exists examining the social consequences of mobile communication. The literature is presently sparse on one-to-one interaction mediated via landline phones. Most notably, de Sola Pool (1971) engaged in this type of analysis. And yet the development of widely accessible mobile telephones has energized analysis of mediated interpersonal communication. Mobile usage raises fundamental social questions regarding the way that we enact sociation and how we develop and maintain social structures. The development of mobile internet also promises innovative forms of information retrieval (location-based services, "just-in-time" scheduling, new uses of photography) and social interaction based on social networking. Mobile communication has also been used to reduce the ravages of disease (Piette and Kerr 2006), facilitate transportation logistics (Ling 2012a), and support entrepreneurs of various types (both legitimate and more dubious) in both the global North and global South (Donner 2009; Ito 2005; Jensen 2007). The mobile phone has been used to disrupt gender roles (Chib and Chen 2011), coordinate the comings and goings of our daily life, and provide digital traces of our mobility (Licoppe 2007) that can be used to follow the diffusion of disease and/or our social interaction (Robertson et al. 2010). The mobile phone has changed the way teenagers interact with one another and their parents (Ling 2008a); it has been the cause of crashes and accidents because of distracted driving (Strayer, Drews, and Crouch 2006); and it has challenged our notions of privacy via the same digital traces previously noted (Eagle, Pentland, and Lazer 2009). Mobile communication will affect the provision of health across the globe, change the financial industry via development of mobile payment and machination of credit ratings (Hughes and Lonie 2007); it will change our coordination of the transportation system and be integral in the growth of the "internet of things."

This chapter will examine some of the social consequences of mobile communication. These will include the social effect of individual addressability, the effect of mobile phones on social cohesion, and how mobile communication progressively structures social interaction. It will also consider future developments and trends in social effects.

Individual addressability

The diffusion of mobile communication devices into society has fundamentally changed the way that we can interact with others via mediated communication. It means that we are individually accessible to one another in new ways. With mobile phones, we call individuals, not places.[4] In landline-based communication, we called a specific location in the hope that the person to whom we wished to speak was there. In the early days of landline telephony, there could have been a single phone for many users. A whole office or dormitory floor might have one phone that was shared by many people. In small Norwegian villages in the period before World War II, only some families had a phone. They were in some cases (e.g. emergencies or special occasions) expected to share this service with others in the village. Rather than being a simple technical inconvenience, these arrangements were coded into social (and status) interactions. Goffman described a situation where a single phone was used by many residents in a college dorm (1959: 4). Presumably someone of lower status had to answer the phone and then call out for the person being called. Goffman described how students who wished to enhance the sense that they were socially popular would wait to be called several times to multiply the effect of having their name shouted out among peers.

Mobile phones subvert such systems and replace them with direct, interpersonal communication. We call directly to one another, regardless of where we and they might be and of what is happening. We are individually addressable.[5] This seemingly small change has had a range of social consequences. It has changed the organization of social interaction in several subtle but important ways. It has changed the way we stay in contact and how we arrange our calling. It has changed the way we experience and operationalize security and safety; how we coordinate interaction, and challenges our sense of etiquette and courtesy. Finally, it has disrupted pre-existing notions of how we engaged in co-present interaction (Ling 2004).

Safety and security

Individual addressability changes how we view safety and security. Mobile communication gives us a safety link. With this link we can mobilize help in emergencies, either from the emergency services or those closest to us. Mobile phones can be used in major emergencies, e.g. 9/11 (Dutton and Naiona 2003; Katz and Rice 2002), the Virginia Tech shootings (Figley and Jones 2008; Vieweg et al. 2008), suicide bombings in Israel (Cohen and Lemish 2005), and the July 22, 2011 Oslo bombing (Sundsøy et al. 2012). In all the above, there were not only major logistical communication tasks but also a need for people to confirm the status of those closest to them. Individual accessibility, afforded by mobile phones, was invaluable.

Mobile phones are also useful in smaller-scale emergencies (Wellman and Rainie 2012: 98–9). For example, if a family member suffers a sudden medical emergency, we use mobile phones to organize other members of the family as they react to the situation. Mobile devices facilitate easier mobilization of resources in unforeseen situations.

In each case, we reach out to our nearest to help us through the situation, drawing on the interpersonal social capital (accumulated in a range of previous interactions) which defines tightly knit groups. And the response of different close ties becomes part of our group's lore.[6]

Micro-coordination

Another consequence of mobile phones is our discovery of new ways of coordinating interaction. We take for granted the very large degree in which we use time to synchronize everyday life (Elias 1992; Eriksen 2001; Glennie and Thrift 2009; Landes 1983; Levine 1998; Mumford 1934; Thompson 1967; Vilhelmson 1999; Zerubavel 1979, 1985). Mobile phones challenge the time/place system of coordinating interaction by adding flexibility to the planning of meetings and events with colleagues. They help us to resolve the mundane logistics of our interaction with partners, children, friends, and parents.

Before mobile phones, we relied on clock-time when agreeing to meet. Clock-time, of course, is a social construction based on the development of reliably mechanical clocks, first in the fourteenth century.[7] Clock-time replaced a variety of other timekeeping, signaling, and coordinating systems with a single metric, easily adoptable by different groups to fit their respective needs. It is said that in cities such as Florence, there were as many as eighty different, bell-based timing systems, each with its own cycle and system of bell-ringing. Rather than bell-ringing to mark the start of town council meetings, points of a prayer cycle or the opening of a market, the clock now provides a common standard. Time-based coordination is now at the core of many large-scale organizations (Dohrn-van Rossum 1992).

Mobile phone-based coordination has on occasion challenged the hegemony of time-based coordination. While time-based coordination is essential when thinking about large organizations (Mumford 1934; Thompson 1967), when considering small groups it can be inflexible. This is particularly the case when a small group, such as a family, needs to move about a large suburban landscape. For many of us, our jobs are commonly distant from our homes. Our children are schooled in one direction, their after-school events are in another, and our social lives are in yet a new urban quadrant. In the pre-mobile era, the geographical reach of the urban/suburban landscape made it difficult to coordinate with others as we moved. If we were delayed by traffic, we could not send messages unless we found a phone booth. And if our intended meeting partners were not near a phone or were themselves in transit, we were both incommunicado.

Mobile communication changes this, allowing us flexibility in our interactions. We shuffle and rearrange meetings as needed (so long as our meeting partners are also similarly disposed). If we find that locations for ad hoc get-togethers are unacceptable, e.g. an intended restaurant is full, then we call those coming and organize an alternative. Instead of stipulating a particular meeting time and place, we indicate to one another our intention to meet and then, nearer the time, we finalize details in a series of progressively refined coordinates.[8] Using group applications, e.g. mobile Facebook, also facilitates coordinated interaction since they replace a long series of one-to-one interactions with a log of all partners' comments (Ling 2012a: 126). When there are more than a handful of participants, however, the total weight of interactions becomes unmanageably complex.

Thus, mobile communication is becoming an expected part of interpersonal coordination. Mobile communication adds flexibility to our interactions with others, particularly in the face of the need to coordinate in the vast suburban landscape.[9]

Challenges to co-present interaction

Mobile phones provide a way to deal with emergencies and to synchronize our lives, but they also distract us from co-located friends and activities. Mobile internet has recently allowed us to pass time by playing small games, reading the news, and so on, when we perhaps should have been more attentive to our immediate surroundings, e.g. smelling flowers or enjoying the weather.

Unhindered access to one another comes at the cost of being reachable. Sometimes, receiving calls enhances our day. Other times, unexpected calls disrupt our activities and disturb those who are with us. Indeed, one of the commonest complaints about mobile communication – and the subject of some of the earliest research – was that it forces people listen to others' trivial mobile phone conversations (Ling 1997). Later work has shown that we are even sensitive to other co-present people who are involved in "half" conversations over the mobile phone (Monk, et al. 2004). Our notions of courtesy and etiquette are largely based on face-to-face situations. We are therefore scrambling to find an appropriate way to understand and acknowledge one another when we often have to divide our attention between different publics within (local or mediated) earshot.

Social cohesion

With the development of individual addressability we might think that there is increased atomization in society. This is classic sociological turf.

Some have suggested that increasing use of media in society is a dangerous direction (Turkle 2011). While there are changes in the way that sociation is taking place, research shows that social bonding is still secure (Boase and Kobayashi 2012; Hampton, Sessions, and Her 2011; Ishii 2006). Indeed, mobile communication and the ability to reach out to our closest sphere of friends as needed changes the nature of interpersonal interaction by supplanting co-present interaction with people to whom we are less connected (e.g. vague acquaintances we have met at the bus stop) with mediated interaction with our closest sphere of friends or family. In so doing, we shuffle the social cards and sociate in new ways. Beyond the more instrumental forms of coordination and insuring one another's safety, we are using mobile communication for expressive interaction and thereby tightening bonds with our closest circle.

Christian Licoppe (2004) describes this as "connected presence," i.e. we use mobile phones to engage in relatively ongoing interaction within our closest sphere. We can call and text one another throughout the day as need or whim dictates. Similarly, Barry Wellman has developed the idea of networked individualism where "people remain connected, but as individuals, rather than being rooted in the home bases of work unit and household. Individuals switch rapidly between their social networks. Each person separately operates his networks to obtain information, collaboration, orders, support, sociability, and a sense of belonging" (2002: 16). I have contributed the idea of bounded solidarity whereby our unimpeded, mediated access to one another via mobile communication strengthens interpersonal bonds of small groups of intimates (Ling 2008b) containing only a handful of people (Ling, Bertel, and Sundsøy 2012).

To understand how mobile communication contributes to our sense of social cohesion among our closest social circle, it is useful to consider some of the ideas of classical sociology, specifically the work of Durkheim (1995), Goffman (1967) and Collins (2004) on ritual interaction. They suggest that it is possible to see how we create and maintain a legacy of social cohesion within various groups. Perhaps the most intense group in which this takes place is that of our closest social group.

According to the Durkheimian/Goffmanian approach, cohesion is built and maintained through ritual interaction. Ritual is a mutually focused activity engendering a common mood in a bounded group. For Durkheim, this was often a larger-scale affair, perhaps including a patterned liturgy and a formal institution. Goffman scaled this down to more mundane types of interaction in daily life. In both cases, there is mutual reflexivity. The focused activity may be rooting for the team, sharing a joke over beer, participating in a religious ceremony, or any number of other social situations where we share a common focus and maintain a common mood. By engendering a common mood, we set aside to some degree boundary awareness and become more amenable to bonding with one another. Furthermore, shared experience gives us a common point of reference in our otherwise individual biographies. It is the weight of many such encounters that allows us to develop trust in one another and this is the core of social cohesion. Durkheim notes:

> By themselves, individual consciousnesses are actually closed to one another, and they can communicate only by means of signs in which their inner states come to express themselves. For the communication that is opening up between them to end in a communion – that is, in the fusion of all the individual feelings into a common one – the signs that express those feelings must come together in one single resultant. The appearance of this resultant notifies individuals that they are in unison and brings home to them their moral unity. It is by shouting the same cry, saying the same words, and performing the same action in regard to the same object that they arrive at and experience agreement. (Durkheim 1995: 231–2)

Taking this into the realm of mobile communication (or for that matter chatting on social network sites, etc.), we can see how we enact social cohesion rituals through these personalized technologies (Ling 2008b). In this way, mobile communication helps to maintain what Tönnies saw as the *gemeinschaft*, albeit via mediated interaction (Ling 2012a, 2012b).

The structuring of social interaction

The result of individual accessibility and mediated cohesion afforded by mobile phones is that they are increasingly structured into our social interaction. Mobile communication is progressively becoming a part of the way that we collectively carry out our daily lives. Indeed, we increasingly rely on direct access and negotiated coordination. In some ways, it is taking on characteristics of what Durkheim would call a social fact and Weber would see as an "iron cage."

The mobile phone is becoming a taken for granted part of how we coordinate interaction. In the phrase "taken for granted," there is the idea that we have grown to expect mobile communication of one another. This is a critical transition. Until we can make the assumption that others are accessible via mobile phones – that is when there is the common *perception* of a critical mass of users – we will not rely on mobile communication as an ordinary means of interaction. After this common perception has formed, there is a shift in the position of mobile communication's status. After general adoption of this mediation technology, if we lack a mobile phone we are not full social participants. In practical terms, if we do not have a mobile phone or if our phone is inoperative or inaccessible, we cannot engage in mobile micro-coordination or respond effectively to the large and small emergencies of others. Indeed, many teenagers see it as an unmitigated tragedy if they are without a mobile phone. One focus-group teen described the period without his broken mobile phone as "the boringest week of my life." He noted that, "The first day without my phone, like, I didn't text anybody. I felt like 'Where did all my friends go?' like I moved or something, because no one knew my house number. So I just sat there, and it was during summer break too!" This teen clearly lived by the logic of mobile coordination. When that was removed, no substitute was readily available for his social interaction.

When the system is operative, when people in our social circle have mobile phones, an efficiency is afforded to the group. We can assume that others are available for talking, texting, social networking and, in a broad sense, sociation.[10] When all the members of, for example, a family have mobile phones, they are freed from the stiffness associated with strict time-/place-based coordination. They can recipocally assume that other family members are immediately available via mobile phones. As this understanding becomes taken for granted in group interaction, there can be increasing reliance on mobile-based coordination to the degree that it becomes mutually expected. Other methods of, for example, coordinating meetings fall into disuse. As this happens, mobile-only coordination becomes structured into their interaction.

As with Durkheim's social facts and Weber's iron cage, there is a coercive element in all this. The system functions only as long as all participants possess mobile phones. However, as the teen cited above discovered, if we cannot use our phone, we are excluded. Group efficiency presumes, for example that each individual must subscribe to a mobile phone provider, and must keep their (sufficiently charged) mobile phone with them. Moreover, if a particular individual cannot be reached, then they are the cause of difficulty for others in their circle of friends. In a lightweight version of Durkheim's social facts, mobile phones are, to some degree, "imbued with a compelling coercive power by virtue of which, whether he wishes it or not, they impose themselves upon him" (Durkheim 1938: 31).

This illustrates how mobile communication is becoming a social technology. Individuals benefit from mobile phones but mobile phones are also increasingly integral in group interaction. As individuals, we choose at some level to possess mobile phones but there also significant social forces pushing and cajoling us to participate.

Other themes

Other common themes in mobile communication research include investigation of negative effects, for example sexting (Lenhart 2009), bullying (Smith et al. 2008), mobile fraud, and use of mobile phones while driving (Strayer et al. 2006). An intense, if inconclusive, discussion is also current regarding the effect of electromagnetic radiation generated by mobile phones.

Beyond studies of the dark side of mobile communication, there is a long tradition of studying the situation of mobile phones among particular populations. These include teens (Lenhart et al. 2010; Ling et al. 2010), developing countries (Donner 2008) and the effect of mobile communication on gender roles. Some of the first work on the social consequences of mobile communication was done by Rakow and Navarro (1993). Their study addressed the question of whether mobile phones would empower or enslave women. The broad conclusion was that, above all, mobile phones would reinforce existing power relations. The study asserted that mobile phones would extend gendered parenting responsibilities and provide a new channel through which men could surveil women. Subsequent work has supported the first element in this equation and also explored how children call their mothers at work more often than they call their fathers (Chesley 2005).

Technology is, of course, not static. Mobile device functionality has expanded beyond voice and texting. Smartphone development and mobile internet change the functionality of mobile devices: we now use social networking and location-based services on our mobile devices (Gordon and Silva 2011). The development of tablets and pads is also changing the way that we consume different types of information and news. In turn, this affects news-gathering and the very structure of news organizations (Westlund 2011).

Mobile communication also presents researchers with new data collection opportunities. Since mobile phones are usually with individuals, they can be used in an advanced version of experience sampling (Csikszentmihalyi, Larson, and Prescott 1977). This approach is being used by researchers to understand the smartphone usage and cross-media communication (Boase and Kobayashi 2012).

Conclusion

The general "plotline" for mobile communication outlined here is that this development has given us conditional autonomy, just as it has tied us more thoroughly into our close social networks. Technology, at least in the phase of mobile voice and texting, made us individually available while freeing us from the geographical constraints of the landline era. This might ultimately, at first thought, cause us to think that society has been atomized. Yet the opposite seems to be the case. We can roam while retaining contact with our core social network. Rather than freeing us into an anomic void, mobile phones enhance our ability to contact our nearest friends and family and thereby maintain (and even create) social cohesion. This connects to well-established sociological questions of autonomy, interaction with social networks, and cohesion with social groups.

This technology has become so intertwined with daily life that it is now part of the structure of sociation. We use mobile communication systems to organize our affairs and to stay in touch with each other in the name of expressive and instrumental interaction. We increasingly assume that mobile communication will be possible with our potential circle of interlocutors. Consequently, when we have forgotten our phone or it is otherwise out of service, we are a missing node in the social landscape.

Focus on mobile-based, interpersonal communication promises to enrich media sociology. It shifts our attention away from the one-to-many metaphor to the way that individuals interact with one another when not co-present. Moreover, it gives us the chance to study how the cascade of information provided by mobile internet will filter into daily life in the "here and now."

Notes

1 See http://www.itu.int/en/ITU-D/Statistics/Pages/stat/default.aspx.
2 In many places, the copper in the wires is worth so much on the salvage market that they are not left in place for long. Indeed, this is not only a

phenomenon in the developing world, but also in many industrialized countries (Bennett 2008).

3 It is clear that some of this is changing with the development of smart-phones and tablets which increasingly resemble pocket-sized computers.

4 It is true that we call individuals but we also use mobile phones to call institutions, e.g. the doctor's office, our child's school, or a local pizza outlet. Furthermore, we increasingly use mobile phones to retrieve infor-mation via mobile internet.

5 This is not a universal truth: mobile phones are proxies for individuals but this is truer in developed than developing countries. In both cases, there are people without phones, e.g. children, the elderly, and in many cases women and the poor.

6 We also use mobile phones as links to others when we feel insecure. Teenage girls often call friends when they are walking through dicey parts of town in order to deter potential attackers. In some cases, teenag-ers admit to faking calls to effect the appearance of such contact (Baron and Ling 2007).

7 With the addition of the pendulum in the sixteenth century, they gained accuracy as they diffused in society.

8 It should be noted that the temptation to operate a car, while simultane-ously renegotiating our affairs on mobile devices, is an unfortunate and dangerous side effect of this new capability (Strayer, Drews, and Crouch 2006; David L. Strayer and Johnston 2001).

9 On a larger scale, there is the question of organizing protest actions and more fanciful "flash mobs" (Rheingold 2002). This is a different type of coordination than the localized, micro-coordination of families and smaller groups.

10 The same perception of critical mass also pertains to office calendar systems and pertained, in their day, to fax machines (Ling 2012a, 2012c).

12

Sociology and the Socially Mediated Self

Jeff Pooley

The rapid ascent of social networking sites (SNSs) like Facebook is a gigantic, but largely untapped, opportunity for media sociology. So far, sociologists' contributions have been modest, especially compared to work with a psychological cast. Consequently, a major role for sociological studies of social media is to bring the discipline's core intellectual commitments to bear on a research area that is now largely ahistorical and individualist. Cumulatively, a handful of rich sociological studies have begun to chart a more interactional, institutional, and historical approach to social media questions. A foundation is, therefore, in place, but SNS merit greater attention from sociologists and sociology-oriented communication scholars.

Explicitly mindful of the relative prominence of psychology vis-à-vis sociology, this chapter reviews a rapidly growing body of research: work centered on social media and the self. Facebook's swift rise and its fascinating implications for self-presentation have set off a predictable mushroom-burst of scholarship: 179 articles, books, and chapters, half of which were published in the last two years.

Research on SNSs and the performance of self is well suited for a probe on the relative contributions of psychology and sociology. After all, there is some evidence that sociologists have taken a renewed interest in media questions recently, drawn by the patently disruptive internet (Jurgenson and Ritzer 2012). There is, too, a rich tradition of sociological work on the social self, with obvious relevance to Facebook self-fashioning. Psychologists, of course, have their own sophisticated theories of identity and selfhood. The social-media-and-the-self research context consequently makes a kind of natural experiment possible. Under favorable conditions, will sociologists contribute to a media-research literature? And will communication scholars adopt sociological perspectives to any significant degree?

The answer, based on this review, is a qualified "no" on both counts. Sociologists remain marginal, markedly outnumbered by psychologists and especially communication scholars. More important, most of the SNS-and-identity work produced by communication researchers bears the intellectual and methodological imprint of psychology. Judging by this small island of research, communication remains psychologized.

The reason this matters has nothing to do with disciplinary score-keeping. The issue instead is the lens through which scholars are making sense of the new social media landscape. In line with assumptions of mainstream psychology, the great bulk of studies under review (1) assume a pre-social subjectivity. That is, many researchers begin with pre-formed individuals, endowed with traits like extraversion or high public self-consciousness. Likewise, the typical approach is (2) ahistorical, implying (without intending to) that modern western individualism is timelessly universal. In this literature (3) difference is tracked mainly at the psychological-trait level: class, race, and gender inequalities are mostly neglected, as are the wider economic and social contexts. Facebook and its competitors are treated as (4) a bundle of technological affordances, and not as profit-seeking corporations with a major economic stake in a sharing self.

The point is not to dismiss research with a psychological inflection. Some of this work is brilliant, with counterintuitive findings and a rich theoretical yield. Yet the literature is partial in patterned ways that sociologists are sensitive to; media sociology can thus serve as a corrective. Though greatly outnumbered, the few sociological studies of the SNS self can be read to suggest an alternative approach. The self, these scholars agree, is irreducibly social – even the individualist self of the modern West, which denies its own embeddedness. The identities that get performed on Facebook, they argue, are bound up in a mix of interrelated shifts associated with modernity: market relations, urbanization, consumer culture, and the rise of mass-produced imagery. As subjects, we are shaped by these developments even as our actions help reconstitute them. Sociological studies insist that the complex societies we are born into are already stratified along axes of difference – economic, cultural, racial, etc. – with cross-cutting power and resource inequalities. Even the technological edifices we confront, sociologists argue, are products of a related mix of culture, market, and human purpose – including our own, as we interact over time with technologies and each other. This nascent sociological approach repositions the intellectual stakes: If we "brand" ourselves on Facebook – and Facebook is a platform well-matched to self-branding – then we cannot ignore the constellation of historical developments that brought to the fore calculated self-performance and Facebook.

This presents a messy object of study – one that the ahistorical, individualist orientation suggested by mainstream psychology is ill-equipped to address. A sociological alternative is already emerging.

Social media and the self: the review

To generate a picture of research on social media and the self, I read and coded all the published work on the topic that I could locate. The idea was that the research area, new and fast-developing, would provide a snapshot of the disciplinary mix contributing to contemporary media research. My intention was not to supply a traditional literature review, but instead to filter the historical relations between psychology, sociology, and communication research through a current research lens.

To locate relevant works, I used a mix of Google Scholar, Google Books, and citation chains from already-identified work to build up a bibliography, which I continued to supplement until the results were written up in early 2013. One hundred and seventy-nine articles, books, and book chapters were collected in the resulting corpus.

Four criteria were used for inclusion. First, works must be "academic" studies, excluding media accounts and public intellectual essays (like C. Rosen 2007). Second, items must focus on SNSs. I relied on boyd and Ellison's (2007: 211) tripartite definition of SNS: web-based services involving (1) at least a semi-public profile; (2) a list of connected users; and (3) the ability to observe (at least some of the) profiles and connections made by others. Work centered on, for example, Facebook, Myspace, and Twitter meets these criteria, but studies of online dating sites and personal homepages would not. Third, only published works in journals and books were included. Theses and conference papers (even those published in proceedings) were excluded. Fourth, items must "substantially" focus on aspects of self and identity. Studies focused exclusively on relationship-maintenance, for example, were not included in the bibliography.

Each criterion entails an obvious cost. Academic work is not (or at least should not be) separated from other discourses, nor are boundaries always clear. Online dating and personal website research, moreover, is often suffused with the same themes and questions taken up by scholars studying "genuine" SNSs. Excluding conference proceedings and theses was particularly painful, in part because these works are frequently cited in the fast-evolving quasi-field. The question of what counts as a "substantial" engagement with self-related questions was inevitably subjective and required a series of tough judgment calls. The criteria are nonetheless justified, given feasibility requirements, as well as the need for full-text searching of the works under review.

Given these criteria, I attempted to collect an exhaustive body of works, with the knowledge that many eligible items would inevitably be excluded. In particular, books and chapters centered on the self/social media theme were probably missed, given search limitations. Even if the unattainable ideal of full inclusivity were achieved, the corpus is already out of date: based on the current publishing growth curve, more than forty new items will have appeared by the time this chapter is published. Because of the flood of social media posts advertised in the job market of recent years, publications on this and other SNS topics are sure to follow.

Even with these limitations, the 179-count corpus of published works analyzed here provides a snapshot of the literature.[1] Each work was read, annotated, and extensively coded for a number of attributes, including the disciplinary orientation of the journal (if applicable, as described in journals' "aims and scope" self-descriptions). Data on the first author of each item was also collected, including training (university, discipline, and location) and current post (university/organization, discipline, and location), based upon public websites, posted curricula vitae and dissertation databases. Citation data were collected based on selective full-text author and title searches. (Books and book chapters were scanned and run through optical-character recognition software.) The included works were also tagged for methodology and "key" themes, based on close readings.

Content analysis like this has many obvious limitations, including the reliance for some attributes on my value-laden judgments. Still, the approach is arguably preferable to a traditional literature review, which on its own is far more susceptible to cherry-picking and proof-texting. I rather interweave findings from the bibliographic coding with interpretations and quotations from selected works exemplifying a particular pattern observed in the data.

Overview of findings

As expected, the review revealed an interdisciplinary blend of work, with contributions ranging from literature to computer science. Scholars with formal psychological training were prominent, though outnumbered by researchers trained in one or another communication program. Still, many of the communication scholars approached the topic with assumptions rooted in mainstream psychology.

Based on disciplinary training, communication scholars were far more prominent in the literature than any other field, accounting for nearly half (eighty-two) of the items. ("Communication" is a big-tent designation, referring to training or employment in a department with "communication" or "media" in its name and not linked to another recognized discipline.) Psychology-trained first authors were also plentiful, accounting for over a fifth (thirty-seven) of published works. Just seventeen articles or chapters – less than 10 percent – were authored by trained sociologists.

A number of other disciplines contributed to the SNS/self literature, including scholars trained in library/iSchool programs (nine items), literary studies (seven), education (six), anthropology (five), business (five) and computer science (four). Psychiatry, theater, gender studies, philosophy, and geography each registered a single study.

Among journals, the basic pattern held, though with notable shifts. More than one-third (38%) of articles appeared in psychology journals, slightly edging out communication journals (34%). Interdisciplinary publications accounted for 16%. Computer science journals placed fourth with less than 4%. Significantly, only two articles – about 1% – were published in sociology journals.

In geographical terms, more than half (56%) of first authors were trained in the United States. Also prominently represented are scholars trained in the United Kingdom (11%), Australia (8%), Canada (8%), and Germany (5%). Three other countries – the Netherlands, Norway, and Estonia – registered four studies each, with one or two studies from scholars trained in other European countries, East Asia, and Israel. The geographic spread, lopsided as it is, reflects the overall pattern of English-language research output on media topics.

A majority of included studies employed quantitative methods, though qualitative methods were also well represented. Excluding essays and other studies without empirical data (accounting for 30 studies, or 17% of the total), over half (57%) of the items were quantitative, with an additional 8% opting for a mixed quantitative/

qualitative approach. The remainder – just over a third (35%) – drew on qualitative data, e.g. semi-structured interviews and ethnography.

The most common method by far was the quantitative survey of SNS users, employed by almost half (46%) of studies. Quantitative content analyses of SNS profiles and wall posts were also relatively common, appearing in nearly a fifth (19%) of works. Eleven studies (7%) were centered on controlled experiments.

Of the qualitative approaches, semi-structured interviews (11%) and ethnographies (11%) were most frequently employed. What counts as "ethnography" is fuzzy, of course, but most authors self-identified their work as ethnographic if it included a mix of participant observation, interviews, textual readings of profiles and status updates, and "guided tours" (users taking the researcher through their SNS profile and activity). Focus groups of users (7%) and qualitative textual analysis of SNS content (7%) were also relatively common. Three papers relied on a case study approach, and three others used open-ended surveys. A number of other methods – including usage diaries, historical analysis, usability tests, and participant observation – were each used by a single study.

Psychology and sociology in SNS/self research

The influence of psychology is far more prevalent than the disciplinary training data suggest. The main reason is that psychological approaches have long been well represented within US communication research. In the SNS/self literature, communication scholars with a background in interpersonal and computer-mediated communication (CMC) traditions are especially common.

In addition to the thirty-seven studies authored by psychology-trained scholars, forty-one communication-authored items – half of the communication total – were classified as "psychology-influenced." No single trait determined the "psychology-influenced" label; instead, a mix of factors – including the psychological background of cited studies, theories, and journals, the use of standard psychological scales, and publication in a psychology journal – were considered. While these forty-one studies do not exhibit each and every trait, they do share "family resemblances" in Wittgenstein's sense.

Fourteen communication papers were judged "sociology-influenced" using similar, if more liberal, criteria – since no communication studies were published in sociology journals and few cited any. Together, the seventy-eight psychology and psychology-influenced communication studies made up a plurality (44%) of the corpus. Psychological research was two and a half times more numerous than the thirty-one sociology and sociology-influenced studies (17% of the total).

The imbalance is far more pronounced in journal-publishing terms. A plurality of articles (38%) appeared in psychology journals, including twenty papers authored by communication-trained scholars. Indeed, psychology-influenced communication scholars published more often in psychology journals (eighteen studies) than communication outlets (sixteen studies). Overall, more studies appeared in psychology journals (sixty-one) than communication journals, despite the relative prominence of communication scholars in the corpus as a whole. By contrast, just two studies ran in sociology journals.

Unmistakable here is the residue of American sociology's decades-old neglect of media research. Psychology supports at least five media- or web-oriented journals, including the top two journals in the SNS/self literature, *Computers in Human Behavior* (twenty-three studies) and *Cyberpsychology, Behavior, and Social Networking* (sixteen studies). Psychology-influenced communication scholars are clearly comfortable publishing in these outlets.

In contrast, not a single sociology journal centers on media or internet topics, forcing sociologists to publish in communication (six articles), interdisciplinary (four) and even psychology (four) titles. Likewise, no communication scholar – sociology-influenced or otherwise – published in a sociology journal.

Citation patterns provide another telling reflection of psychology's relative dominance. It is true that sociologist Erving Goffman is cited in seventy-six studies, placing him among the most-mentioned figures. In particular, Goffman's (1959) *The Presentation of Self in Everyday Life* gets a frequent nod, even among psychologists and psychology-influenced communication scholars. Still, in the vast majority of instances, the engagement with Goffman is perfunctory. These passing references come off as symbolic and half-obligatory, prompted by the iconic stature of Goffman's (1959) work (Allen 1997). Psychology's in-text American Psychological Association (APA) citation style – which most communication scholars and journals use too – makes serial, decontextualized referencing especially easy (Bazerman 1988; Madigan, Johnson and Linton 1995). There are studies in the corpus that grapple seriously with Goffman's dramaturgical approach (e.g. Hogan 2010), but none of these were authored by psychologists or psychology-influenced communication scholars.

Consider the parallel case of comparably prominent scholars in the self-oriented literatures of sociology and psychology, respectively. Mark Leary and Roy Baumeister, major figures in the psychology of self and identity, are cited frequently: Leary in twenty-five studies and Leary and Baumeister in twenty-one. Peter Burke and Sheldon Stryker – arguably the most prominent sociology-of-self scholars working in the symbolic interactionist tradition – are nearly invisible. Burke is referenced in just five studies, while Stryker appears only twice.

Morris Rosenberg, another important sociologist of the self, does appear frequently in the SNS/self studies – but almost always for his widely used Rosenberg Self-Esteem Scale, deployed in thirteen articles. His major work on the self-concept, *Conceiving the Self* (1979), is mentioned just three times in the entire corpus.

Psychologists of self working outside the mainstream are mostly ignored, too. Kenneth Gergen, an important critic of the discipline's scientism (Gergen 1973), has written insightfully for decades on the self in a media-saturated culture (Gergen 1992, 2009). Yet he was cited just once in the entire psychology and psychology-influenced body of studies, by a self-proclaimed "discursive psychologist" whose work is also unusual for its engagement with sociological theory (Goodings 2011).

One plausible explanation for the psychology–sociology discrepancy is the disparity in size between the two disciplines, at least in the United States. In 2011, over five times as many doctorates were awarded in psychology (3,594) as in sociology (656). Still, sociology doctorates are far more likely to plan an academic career (85%) than those in psychology (48%), largely due to doctoral requirements for clinical, nonacademic psychological practice (National Science Foundation 2011). Correcting for these academic-career plans, psychology PhDs outnumber sociology PhDs by a 3-to-1 ratio. Given this large gap, psychologists are arguably underrepresented relative to sociology in the SNS/self literature.

The two disciplines' relative size cannot, however, explain how the lopsided contributions to SNS/self research get reproduced within communication research. To account for the predominance of psychology, we need to turn to the discipline's peculiar history. As Katz and I (Pooley and Katz 2008) have argued elsewhere, American sociology effectively abandoned the study of mass communication. In the early to mid-1960s, its media research agenda was handed off to the new, would-be discipline of "communication," then establishing itself within journalism schools and speech departments. Partly owing to the individualist, social psychology-oriented "behavioral sciences" tradition from which the US communication tradition emerged, but also to a major shift in federal funding then underway (Crowther-Heyck 2006), the new field's basic mental architecture was largely appropriated from psychology. Though it is easy to point to counterexamples and pockets of intellectual resistance, US media research was in effect psychologized in concert with the emergence of "communication" as an organized academic discipline.

Psychology-oriented studies

Does it even matter that psychology-inflected work is far more plentiful than studies with a more sociological cast? Is this just an elaborate exercise in disciplinary bean-counting? After all, the differentiation of the various social science disciplines took place in the recent past. And few if any demarcation criteria, whether drawn along substantive or methodological lines, hold up under scrutiny (cf. Calhoun 1992).

Even if absolute distinctions are rare, the evidence here suggests that real differences persist in terms of what Becher (1989) has called "disciplinary cultures." Sociology, despite its smaller size, is more eclectic and open to critical, historical, and qualitative work. Psychology, especially in the United States, is more centripetal, owing in part to its long-standing aspiration to natural science status.

These differences are apparent and consequential in the SNS/self literature. It is not just that psychology-influenced studies furnish a partial picture of Facebook self-presentation. The problem is that their omissions – big omissions like culture, capitalism, and history – are not typically articulated or apologized for. Scholars and students stumbling on the literature could be forgiven for not knowing what they are missing.

Methods

Among the empirical studies authored by psychologists, the overwhelming majority (83%) turned to quantitative methods of one kind or another. Over three-fifths (68%) employed quantitative surveys, while a partially overlapping quarter (24%) used content analysis. A surprisingly small number of studies (three – 8 percent of the psychology total) conducted experiments. The numbers are similar for psychology-influenced communication scholars: most (80%) studies are quantitative, with another 10% mixing quantitative and qualitative methods. Over half (56%) used surveys, 15% employed content analysis, and a full fifth (20%) ran experiments.

Personality and disposition correlates

By far the most common approach among psychologists was to treat personality, self-esteem and other self-related disposition measures as independent variables, with various attitudes toward, and/or engagement with, SNSs as the dependent variable. Over half (57%) of psychologist-authored studies used this "personality and disposition correlates" approach, which centers on explaining aspects of the SNS self with reference to psychological traits. Many (29%) of the psychology-influenced communication studies also employed this broad approach.

Among these studies, correlation analysis of survey data was nearly universal. Very often, course-enrolled undergraduates were surveyed, and most of the time SNS behavior measures relied on survey self-reporting. The results – particularly on the personality trait predictors – have been notably weak and contradictory from study to study (Bergman et al. 2011: 707; Ross et al. 2009).

Michigan State

Another major cluster of psychology-influenced work on SNSs and the self has emerged from Michigan State's College of Communication Arts and Sciences. The Michigan State program, largely shaped by David Berlo (a student of Wilbur Schramm) in the late 1950s and 1960s, produced more communication doctorates than any other institution until Berlo's departure in the early 1970s (Rogers 2001). Like many other US communication programs founded in the early postwar decades, Michigan State stressed quantitative training within a psychology-oriented social science approach. Unlike most other programs, however, Michigan State self-consciously blended interpersonal and mass communication research, which elsewhere remained divided along speech- and journalism-derived lines.

In the Facebook era, of course, the interpersonal/mass communication distinction is fading. A body of CMC research most strongly associated with Joseph Walther (1996) has provided the foundation for a series of more recent Michigan State studies of SNSs and online dating self-presentation. The pre-SNS CMC literature, including

Walther's widely employed "hyperpersonal model," explored the effects of technology-related attributes like physical isolation, asynchronicity, and reduced visual cues, on interpersonal communication. Among other findings and predictions, this literature concluded that communication online is conducive to "selective self-presentation" (Walther 2007).

This basic CMC-affordances approach has been updated and widely adopted by SNS scholars, including Walther and other Michigan State colleagues. Indeed, fifteen studies (8%) in the corpus have Michigan State-trained or -employed first authors, far more than any other university – despite the exclusion of Michigan State's non-SNS online dating studies. Among scholars represented in the corpus, the most often cited (Ellison, referenced in 70% of the studies) and third-most cited (Walther, 34%) are both based at Michigan State.

The Michigan State work is methodologically inventive, conceptually rich, and widely cited, even by trained psychologists. Ellison co-authored the major orienting article on SNS research (boyd and Ellison 2007), referenced in about a third (32%) of the corpus. A pair of fascinating experiments, first-authored by Walther (Walther et al. 2008, 2009), used mock Facebook "friends'" appearances and comments to test his and Park's (2002) "warranting" hypothesis – that, in forming impressions, people rely more on other-generated information (e.g. Wall comments or "friend" attractiveness) than self-generated data (e.g. profiles) since the former are harder to manipulate.

The Michigan State literature is unmistakably influenced by psychological currents within and beyond communication. The works draw heavily on psychological social psychology, and a great majority of the journal citations reference psychology and psychology-oriented interpersonal communication titles. One index of the psychological cast of these studies is their frequent focus on the "social capital benefits" of Facebook and other SNSs. In defining "social capital," Ellison and her co-authors awkwardly invoke Bourdieu – without engaging with his critical, power-laced conception of the term (Ellison, Steinfield and Lampe 2007: 1145 and 2011: 875).

Psychology and SNS/self research: a critique

Despite its ingenuity and conceptual yield, the psychology and psychology-influenced work on SNSs and the self offers a narrow view of the topic. Given its dominance in the literature, key psychological assumptions may drown out other relevant aspects of study. I focus here on five overlapping themes in the literature that cumulatively render invisible broader social, economic, historical, and cultural contexts.

Causality

The studies' heavy reliance on correlational survey analysis and experimentation are not intrinsically problematic. They yield important findings that are not easily obtainable via other approaches. But they are employed unreflectively and without sufficient humility about their limitations.

The validity problems inherent in survey research and experimentation are not at issue – nor are the significant complications due to student samples and self-reported SNS behavior. More fundamental is the implicit picture of causality that these studies invoke.

By isolating independent variables to attempt to account for discrete outcomes, this literature implies that SNS selfhood can be explained in cause-and-effect terms. Whether the independent variable is SNS differences or user-narcissism, the suggestion is that social life can be explained by some number of isolated factors. (This assumption creates causality dilemmas in interpreting findings, since personality traits like narcissism may predict SNS behavior or else result from SNS use (Bergman et al. 2011: 710).)

Researchers often concede the artificiality of the lab setting and the fact that correlation is not causation. Nevertheless, research design – and accompanying language like "explains" or "accounts for" – leaves an ontological residue. Social life operates according to a cause-and-effect logic which is, moreover, measurable. As methodological fiction openly acknowledged, there is no problem with these assumptions. But reflexivity is rarely on display in the psychological SNS/self literature.

The fundamental complexity and messiness of social life is, therefore, occluded. In particular, historically emergent economic and cultural factors – in all their elaborate interpenetration – are excluded by default. Since these factors are hard, if not impossible, to measure as quantifiable variables, and resist cause-and-effect reasoning, they are ignored. The resulting picture of social life is grossly attenuated.

The pre-social subject

Even though theoretical resources abound in psychological social psychology to ground individual selfhood in social relations and wider patterns of culture, most of the psychology-oriented literature under review assumes a pre-social subjectivity. Here again methodology plays a role. Most studies treat their subjects as pre-formed individuals whose differences overwhelmingly relate to the psychological traits they already bear.

This account omits the social and cultural sources of these traits. The implication is that subjects pop out of the womb with, say, a positive attitude to self-disclosure. The few studies that examine gender or cultural orientation are a partial exception, but even contrasts like "individualist" and "collectivist" are blunt and decontextualized.

The end of history

These studies also neglect the historical specificity of the patterns that they measure. By treating personality and self-performance as timeless traits and behaviors, they imply that it was always thus. But modern western individualism, for example, is a product of the comparatively recent past – developing from the early modern period onward. The sense that we are each dignified individuals guided by self-defined purposes is even newer, and emerged unevenly across social strata. The quest for self-fulfillment and authenticity spread widely only in the mid-nineteenth century, mixing developments in art, literature, and social thought with a nascent consumer economy. The growth of visual and electronic mass media, celebrity culture, and an advertising-driven consumption economy are all crucial and interrelated backdrops to the self that is performed on Facebook. These are recent changes, but the impression gleaned from the psychological literature is that the modern self is eternal, etched in human nature.

Equality and pluralism

Every individual sampled in the psychology-oriented SNS/self studies was born into a more-or-less stratified society, with patterned inequalities of power and position. Some of that relative privilege or marginality derived from ascribed categorical identities like race and gender for which there is no realistic opt-out. Economic and geographic contingencies helped to determine who has the identity resources – not to mention technological access – to present a desirable image of self. Indeed, SNS self-presentation is especially conducive to status markings and performed privilege.

Power and inequality rarely if ever appear in the psychological work under review. Instead, research subjects are treated as a collection of individuals distinguished mainly by personality or levels of self-esteem.

Technology ex nihilo

The technological affordances of Facebook and other SNSs are widely discussed in this literature, but the sites appear as always already configured. In the typical treatment, individual self-performances – and the impressions formed of those performances by others – are influenced by these sites' architectural features. Several studies discuss privacy settings and creative user adaptations, especially in relation to tensions between privacy, context collapse, and self-disclosure benefits (e.g. Ellison et al. 2011; Vitak 2012).

But these studies neglect the social and economic forces that helped to shape SNSs in the first place. The affordances built into technologies are designed by humans embedded in social contexts. These medium-specific features often have unintended consequences, and users react, adapt, and ultimately reshape technologies through their ongoing interactions. Technologies like SNSs are dynamic, a mix of congealed human action suspended in design, modified by user practice and then reengineered with those practices and other imperatives in mind.

In the case of SNSs, "other imperatives" prominently include the need to attract investment and generate profits. The cultural currents supporting performative self-expression predated Mark Zuckerberg's entrepreneurial pluck; indeed, they helped shape the Web software he initially designed. But Facebook's business model – to peddle self-disclosure to micro-targeting advertisers – requires that semi-public sharing take increasing hold among its worldwide users.

The relationship between technology, economics, and culture is complex: Facebook was informed by, and benefited from, a pre-existing exhibitionist strain in the culture – itself the product of an intertwined, historically emergent mix of cultural and economic factors. Facebook, in turn, has a plain interest in spreading this culture, in part by encouraging more liberal sharing norms through its default settings.

There is no independent variable that can explain this dynamic.

Sociologists struggle too, but their more catholic approach means that the questions are at least posed.

Sociology-oriented studies: a reply

Though they are relatively few, sociologists and sociology-influenced communication scholars in the corpus furnish a response of sorts to the limitations identified in the psychology-oriented literature. They tend to employ diverse methods, emphasize the social self, and ground their analysis in history and relations of power.

Perhaps because of these different assumptions, the sociology-oriented studies are not often cited in the rest of the SNS/self literature. One exception is work by Alice Marwick, a communication-trained assistant professor at Fordham. Marwick is cited in 20 studies (11% of the total), a prominence attributable to the excellence of her work as well as co-authorship with high-profile scholars like boyd (Marwick and boyd 2011) and Ellison (Marwick and Ellison 2012). Based on the inclusion criteria, one of Marwick's articles was classified as "sociology-influenced" (Marwick 2012), which has not yet been cited. The only widely cited item among the sociology-influenced studies is an article by a team of sociologists at Temple (Zhao, Grasmuck, and Martin 2008). That study's general orientation, early publishing date, and prescient focus on Facebook helped to attract eighteen citations (10%). Tellingly, a related study from the same team (Grasmuck, Martin, and Zhao 2009) – this time focused on racial identity displays – has been referenced just twice.

Methods

The trained sociologists in the corpus were far more likely than their psychological counterparts to employ qualitative methods. About two-thirds (64%) of the fourteen empirical studies used only qualitative methods – including six ethnographies and two interview-based works. One study mixed quantitative content analysis with interview techniques, while the remaining four (29%) used quantitative techniques like survey research (one) and content analysis (three).

Of the nine empirical studies by sociology-influenced communication scholars, four employed just qualitative methods (including three ethnographies), while three others relied on quantitative methods (including two surveys). The two remaining articles mixed survey analysis with interviews (one) and focus groups (one).

Overall, the sociology-oriented work was far more likely to employ at least one qualitative method (70%) than the psychology-oriented work (13%). Like all methods, ethnography and open-ended interview-style approaches are partial and imperfect. Findings are far more dependent, for example, on the interpretive summaries generated by researchers. Samples are rarely representative. Methods like these, moreover, have trouble capturing those facets of social life (like international trade or policy making) that are not typically part of everyday lived experience.

But qualitative approaches tend to be more sensitive to the complexity of actual social experience than alternative methods. That same sensitivity to nuance and contradiction means that these studies rarely depend on simple cause-and-effect explanations. They also tend to be more self-reflexive about their own limitations. When supplemented by work focused on wider social and economic forces, qualitative approaches can generate findings more closely matched to the layered and interdependent social world they study.

The social self

It is a core tenet of sociology that individual selfhood is produced within social relations – even if the individualism of the modern West denies those social origins (Elias 1978). George Herbert Mead's (1934) classic account of self-formation – centered on the social process of imagining oneself through others' eyes – is frequently cited in the sociology-oriented SNS/self literature. Mead's work on the self and significant symbols formed the core of the "symbolic interactionist" tradition named by Mead's student Herbert Blumer. Many of the SNS works under review are explicitly indebted to Mead and/or symbolic interactionism (e.g. J. Davis 2010, 2012; Farquhar 2012; Tufekci 2008a).

Crucial to a symbolic interactionist approach is the insight that the self-making process is ongoing, not confined to early childhood or adolescence. The self-concept of a Facebook user, in other words, is constantly revised as she or he makes sense of the reactions of others while posting, chatting, "stalking," and commenting (Grasmuck, Martin, and Zhao 2009: 162). As Eden Litt (2012) has explored in a smart essay, the ambiguous composition of one's SNS audience leads many users to lean much more heavily on their imaginations of that audience – which then doubles back on their self-concepts and presentation choices (see also Marwick and boyd 2011). The "imagined audience" theme is taken in a slightly different direction by

Marwick (2012), who discusses the SNS-enhanced process of "social surveillance." Facebook users, assuming they are being watched by their peers, may internalize the "surveilled gaze" and adapt their self-presentation (and even sense of self) accordingly (381; see also Humphreys 2011: 577).

In her ethnographic study of Myspace, sociologist Jenny Davis (2010) draws on more recent self-oriented work in the symbolic interactionist tradition that emphasizes identity verification (e.g. Burke 2004). She reads her subjects' profile constructions as standing invitations for other users to validate and affirm their self-concepts. "By shaping how they are seen," she writes, "[users] are at the same time able to shape how they see themselves" (Davis 2010: 1116). Common to all these studies is the basic insight that the self is made and re-made through a dynamic process of interpreting others' impressions in SNS interaction – which, moreover, is treated as embedded in offline sociality.

Like so many others in the bibliography, the sociology-oriented studies frequently reference Goffman's dramaturgical approach to self-presentation. The engagement with Goffman's work is, however, notably deeper in many of these studies. A number of works adapt Goffman's situation-specific, audience-tailored theory of face-to-face self-performance to particular SNS features, most often (1) the desegregation of previously discrete audiences and/or (2) the reduction in apparently unintentional, "given-off" cues (e.g. Enli and Thumim 2012; Lewis, Kaufman, and Christakis 2008; Mendelson and Papacharissi 2010). In one especially creative rethinking of Goffman, Bernie Hogan (2010) draws a contrast between self-presentations that occur in synchronous "situations" and those that happen in asynchronous "exhibitions." The world is "not only a stage," he writes, "but also a library and a gallery" (2010: 379). Hogan observes that much SNS activity revolves around the curation of exhibitions, comprised of reproducible "artifacts" like photos, updates, and comments. The curator is not, in the first instance at least, the user, but instead the algorithms (like Facebook's EdgeRank) that select and render visible self-oriented artifacts according to proprietary criteria.

History

Sociology arguably came to self-consciousness as a field trying to make sense of rapid social changes associated with (western) modernity. In that sense, the discipline is fundamentally historical, grappling as it always has with what makes modern life distinctive.

This historical orientation is reflected in the far closer attention paid to modern developments like consumer capitalism in the sociology-inflected SNS/self literature.

Papacharissi and Gibson, for example, embed their discussion of privacy and SNSs in the "urban problem of modernity" (2011: 78). The relative anonymity of city life made certain kinds of privacy easier to maintain, but also helped compel self-disclosure and the performance of a distinctive self in the midst of the faceless crowd.

The growth of an advertising-saturated consumer economy in the late nineteenth century provided an affective repertoire to perform (and adorn) a distinct self. A number of SNS/self works cite scholars like Andrew Wernick (1991) and Zygmunt Bauman (e.g. 2005) to emphasize the premium placed on attention and visibility in consumer-oriented cultures (e.g. Dobson 2012; Hearn 2008; Schwarz 2010). On sites like Facebook, the "threat of invisibility" is often perceived as far more horrifying than the "threat of visibility" – which, as Tania Bucher (2012) observes, Facebook's EdgeRank algorithm exploits by encouraging a "participatory subjectivity" driven by the "constant possibility of disappearing and becoming obsolete" (1164).

One obviously relevant backdrop to SNS self-performance is the wider media culture, which emerged in tandem with a broader set of modern social changes, prominently including the consumer economy. Visual media like film and the glossy magazine co-developed in complicated ways with consumer subjectivity, as models of coveted visibility or as vehicles for anxiety-suffused, aspirational advertising. Sociology-oriented scholars in the SNS literature frequently refer to media-culture antecedents of Facebook self-performance, as well as the ongoing, dynamic interplay between mass-mediated fame and SNS "micro-celebrity" (Marwick and boyd 2011; Litt 2012; Papacharissi 2010; cf. Senft 2008). Mark Andrejevic's (2004, 2007) work on self-disclosure in reality TV and the "interactive" web is often applied to the SNS context (Trottier 2011; Humphreys 2011; Marwick 2012).

Ori Schwarz's brilliant ethnography of young SNS users details the "'borrowed' cultural model of advertisements" in many photographic self-presentations, complete with self-designed logos (2010: 168). Many users of Shox, an Israeli SNS, orient their self-performances around stardom: "successful users speak of themselves as 'celebrities." Friends are assembled on the site according to the "logic of the catalogue," with the stress on physical beauty. Users are presented as "multiple choices, like products of different brands seen synchronically one besides the other on the shelf, a visual economy of abundance" (Schwarz 2010: 175).

A handful of articles stress the significance of relatively recent social and economic shifts that have intensified modern aspects of self. A new "reflexivity," in Giddens's (1991) terms, or "liquid modernity" in Bauman's (2005) more critical take, characterizes the self-making process in the contemporary West (Mendelson and Papacharissi 2010; Robards and Bennett 2011). A few of the sociology-oriented works apply Ernest Sternberg's (1998) argument that that the "ability to present oneself has become a critical economic asset" to SNS self-performance (1998: 5; Litt 2012; Marwick and boyd 2011). Alison Hearn (2008) draws together many of the themes, theories and cultural trends already highlighted in her sweeping account of self-branding on Facebook and elsewhere – a topic addressed by Marwick too in her graduate theses (2005, 2010).[2]

Alone among the 179 works in the corpus, Jenny Davis's (2012) ethnography of Myspace users takes seriously the moral ideal of authenticity. She describes the tension between the labor of self-presentation and the felt demand for "authentic" self-expression. Many users, she found, feel compelled to conceal their labor in order to maintain an "authentic" front. Though Davis does not trace the history of authenticity as a resonant moral ideal, rich philosophical (C. Taylor 1989) and literary (Trilling 1972) studies exist to supplement her analysis. Though almost never cited in the SNS/self literature, scholarship on the history and sociology of the therapeutic ethos – by figures like Jackson Lears, Philip Rieff, Erich Fromm, Warren Susman, Christopher Lasch, and David Riesman – describes the twentieth-century consumer culture's contradictory embrace of the authenticity ethic. Facebook's affordances arguably enhance what I have elsewhere called "calculated authenticity" (Pooley 2010).

Taken together, this sociology-inflected SNS/self literature sharply challenges psychology-influenced work's ahistorical approach. Traits such as narcissism are not just borne by individuals but wax or wane according to broader cultural developments (Mendelson and Papacharissi 2010). One implication is that even Goffman's dramaturgical approach is insufficiently historicized, and that psychological concepts like "self-monitoring" (Snyder 1974) and "public self-consciousness" (Fenigstein, Scheier, and Buss 1975) would be enriched by taking modern promotional culture into account.

Difference

The psychology-oriented literature tends to treat SNS users as generic individuals who bear some mix of otherwise unexamined dispositions and traits. But differences in social life are also patterned along racial, class, and gender lines. Power and agency are unevenly distributed – inequalities which are expressed, challenged, and reproduced on Facebook and other SNSs. Work on these themes, though comparatively more prominent, is still rare within the sociology-influenced SNS/self literature.

Communication scholar Andra Siibak (2009, 2010) has employed quantitative survey and content analysis to study gender on Rate, an Estonian SNS. Among young users she surveyed, girls were especially concerned with appearance and photographic self-portrait. Siibak concluded that girls' SNS selves are more often "built upon the self-beliefs, norms and values that are associated with the traditional female gender role." In a parallel study – a content analysis of males' profile photos in Rate's "Damn I'm Beautiful!" community – Siibak found that appearance-oriented norms, including advertising poses, were also prevalent among male youths. In this group, traditional masculinity mixed with "newer more androgynous forms of masculinity introduced by the consumer culture" (2009: 411). Another quantitative content analysis, this one of MySpace profiles (Magnuson and Dundes 2008), found that female users in a heterosexual relationship were far more likely to highlight their significant other than their male counterparts.

Grasmuck, Martin, and Zhao (2009) mixed content analysis of Facebook profiles with in-person interviews in their study of racial self-presentation. They observe that racial self-identification is excluded from Facebook's core identity fields. Even so, African-American and Latino student-subjects – as well as those with sub-continental Indian ancestry – invested a great deal in their racialized identity claims on Facebook. By contrast, white students and those with Vietnamese ancestry showed far less involvement. The authors read this racial gap as a "certain resistance to the racial silencing of minorities by dominant color-blind ideologies of broader society where direct referencing of race remains taboo" (2009: 175).

Schwarz's Shox ethnography uses Bourdieu's capital/field formulation to study status distinction between user communities. He proposes a new, "corporeal" conception of capital, grounded in body self-representations on the site. For many younger users, trade in sexualized self-imagery is an adaptive strategy by a less-educated group already stigmatized as vulgar. Corporeal capital is the currency they possess – a "last resort in the virtual sphere" (Schwarz 2010: 176). But a group of older, better-educated users marks the boundary of its community, in explicit contrast to the skin-exposing youth, through self-aware parody and direct dismissal. These users prefer text over photos, exchange compliments on higher-status cultural themes, and work to conceal the effort involved in their self-presentational work. With its focus on status and class, Schwarz's study bears little resemblance to the Michigan State social capital literature.

Relations of power, tethered to pre-existing and offline inequalities, may get reinscribed on SNSs. A number of sociology-influenced studies draw on Eszter Hargittai's (e.g. 2008) work on socially rooted disparities of technical skill and access (e.g. Litt 2012; Papacharissi and Gibson 2011). Others point to audience desegregation on ubiquitous sites like Facebook, which often place users in a shared interactive space with authority figures like parents and bosses (e.g. Marwick 2012; Tufekci 2008b).

Common to all these studies is a sensitivity to the uneven topography of social life, as expressed in the dynamic interaction of online and offline worlds.

Technology in context

Scholars with a sociological orientation are far more likely to reference the profit-seeking economic context in which almost all SNSs operate (e.g. Enli and Thumim 2012). Each site's architectural features are designed by engineers within the commercial framework of their employers. For sociology-influenced researchers, this does not mean that a site's affordances dictate user practice; in fact, many studies highlight creative adaptations by users that go on to shape the living technology (e.g. Lewis, Kaufman, and Chistakis 2008; Papacharissi and Gibson 2011). As discussed, wider cultural currents permeating modern selfhood predate the SNS phenomenon by a century or more – and, indeed, helped to inform site designs intended to appeal to a broad user base. Technology, culture, and economics cannot be neatly partitioned, nor can SNS self-oriented activity be considered their collective product (Papacharissi 2010: 306).

In her ethnographic study of Dodgeball, Lee Humphreys (2011) found that users, though savvy and careful about their visibility to other users, were unconcerned about the data-mining surveillance conducted by Google, Dodgeball's owner. As Marwick observes, "Most social media users are less concerned with governments or corporations watching their online activities than key members of their extended network" (2012: 379). A few studies point to the value-producing "labor" invested by SNS users in performing their selves, which SNSs translate into revenue in the form of micro-targeted advertising (e.g. Hearn 2008; Schwarz 2012; cf. Andrejevic 2010). Ripe for analysis in symbolic interactionist terms is the possibility that users' self-concepts are altered as they consume advertisements that they assume reflect their SNS activity.

Bucher's (2012) superb study of Facebook's EdgeRank algorithm – the proprietary formula that filters the content appearing in users' News Feeds – is unusual for its focus on the subtle interplay between technology and self-presentational practices. Facebook's EdgeRank apparently favors status updates that attract comments and other forms of engagement. By dangling the threat of invisibility, Facebook encourages a "participatory subject" through its algorithmic bias. The same filtering logic renders a certain kind of engagement-oriented update more visible, in the process modeling that brand of self-presentation to users.

A second Schwarz study (2012), comprising several SNS-related case studies, develops an argument of similar sophistication. SNS users, already influenced by promotional culture, interact with sites' affordances in such a way that their self-marketing takes on a new character. The ability to record and display durable "objects" – witty status updates, party photos – has helped transform many users into what Schwarz calls the "new hunter-gatherers." Armed with camera-phones and highly attuned to display-worthy experiences, many users live their lives poised to "record and collect valuable moments . . . in order to gain ratings, attention and recognition, and to maintain ties with acquaintances" (2012: 82). Schwarz calls this new attentiveness the "exploitation of the present," the real-time search for recordable experience to display online. The "hunter-gatherer of the everyday" comes to view face-to-face encounters as potential resources for SNS sharing.

Bucher and Schwarz exemplify a sociological approach to SNSs as socially shaped technologies that intensify – even as they alter – existing norms of self-performance. One notable lacuna, however, is memory. Recent changes to Facebook, including the shift to narrative "Timeline" profiles, call out for contributions from the sociology of memory (Olick, Vinitzky-Seroussi, and Levy 2011).

Conclusion

This review – focused on the comparative influence of psychology and sociology within SNS/self research – has neglected the contributions of other disciplines, including communication research that did not meet the "influenced" criteria for either sociology or psychology. The relatively glowing picture of sociology presented here also needs qualification. Despite the promise of the discussed studies, the potential contributions of sociology to SNS work remain mostly unfulfilled. Media research, abandoned in the 1960s, is still an afterthought for most sociologists, despite the obvious centrality of mediated communication to contemporary social life (Peters and Pooley 2012). The discipline's incentive structure frustrates those few scholars taking active interest in media sociology. Publishing outlets are nonexistent; only one among the top twenty ranked departments has an explicit track devoted to media inquiry. In the case of SNS research, relevant streams of scholarship are segregated across at least five relatively insular American Sociological Association (ASA) sections. The rich heritage of work on the sociology of the self (Owens, Robinson, and Smith-Lovin 2010) is begging for more serious application to the SNS context.

This chapter's harsh assessment of psychological work on SNSs and the self might be tempered too. Perhaps it is unrealistic to expect a social psychologist conducting a controlled experiment on Facebook self-disclosure to incorporate the history of western individualism into her analysis. Nevertheless, these broader themes are compatible with mainstream psychological approaches, as evidenced by creative work that draws connections between SNS self-disclosure and the wider culture of mediated celebrity (Stefanone, Lackaff, and Rosen 2012). At the very least, limitations of method and approach could be explicitly articulated.

The study of SNS selfhood would certainly benefit from a great deal more sociology. The discipline's existing marginality is lamentable, but the area – like its object of study – is still young. Sociology has the unique, if quixotic, virtue of attempting to grasp social life as a whole, in all its impossible complexity. A small number of sociologists and sociologically inclined communication scholars are already bringing a different perspective to social media research. They are too few.

Notes

1 Due to space constraints, the full corpus could not be published here. A PDF bibliography of the corpus is available for download at http://jeff-pooley.com/pubs/data/sociology-SNS-self-bibliography.pdf.
2 For reasons discussed, theses and dissertations were not included in the bibliographic analysis.

References

Aalberg, T., and Curran J. (2011) *How Media Inform Democracy: A Comparative Approach*. London: Routledge.

Abbott, A. (2001) *Chaos of Disciplines*. Chicago: University of Chicago Press.

Abel, R. (1987) "The real tort crisis – too few claims." *Ohio State Law Journal* 48: 443–68.

Abu-Lughod, L. (2004) *Dramas of Nationhood: The Politics of Television in Egypt*. Chicago: University of Chicago Press.

Adams, N. G., and Bettis, P. J. (2003) *Cheerleader! An American Icon*. New York: Palgrave Macmillan.

Adorno, T. W. (1981–2) "Transparencies on Film." trans. Thomas Y. Levin. *New German Critique* 24–5: 199–205.

Adorno, T. (2001) *The Culture Industry*. London: Routledge.

Adorno, T. W., and Horkheimer, M. (1977) "The culture industry: enlightenment as mass deception," in James Curran, Michael Gurevitch, and Janet Woollacott (eds), *Mass Communication and Society*. London: Edward Arnold, pp. 349–83.

Adorno, T., and Horkheimer, M. (1996) *Dialectic of Enlightenment*. New York: Verso.

Agar, J. (2003) *The Government Machine: A Revolutionary History of the Computer*. London: MIT Press.

Alexander, J. (2007) *The Civil Sphere*. Oxford: Oxford University Press.

Alexander, J. C., and Smith, P. (2006) "The strong program in cultural sociology: elements of a structural hermeneutics", in J. Alexander, *The Meanings of Social Life*. New York: Oxford University Press, pp. 11–26.

Allen, B. (1997) "Referring to schools of thought: an example of symbolic citations." *Social Studies of Science* 27(6): 937–49.

Allport, G. (1954) *The Nature of Prejudice*. Addison-Wesley.

Al-Mahadin, S. (2011) "Arab feminist media studies: towards a poetics of diversity." *Feminist Media Studies* 11(1): 7–12.

Altheide, D. L. (1976) *Creating Reality: How TV News Distorts Events*. Beverley Hills, CA: Sage.

Amariglio, J., Childers, J., and Cullenberg, S. (eds) (2009) *Sublime Economy: On the Intersection of Art and Economics*. New York: Routledge.

Anderson, A. (2009) "Media, politics and climate change: towards a new research agenda." *Sociology Compass* 3: 166–82.

Anderson, B. (1983) *Imagined Community*. London: Verso.

Anderson, C. W. (2012a) "Towards a sociology of computational and algorithmic journalism." Published online before print December 10, 2012, for *New Media and Society*. Available at http://www.cwanderson.org/?page_id=575, accessed September 2, 2013.

Anderson, C. W. (2012b) *Networking the News: The Struggle to Rebuild Metropolitan Journalism, 1997–2011*. Philadelphia, PA: Temple University Press.

Anderson, C., Bell, E., and Shirky, C. (2012) "Post-industrial journalism: adapting to the present." Columbia Journalism School. Available at http://towcenter.org/

Andrejevic, M. (2004) *Reality TV: The Work of Being Watched*. Lanham, MD: Rowman & Littlefield.

Andrejevic, M. (2006) "Total information awareness: the media version." *Flow* 4(8), available at http://flowtv.org/2006/07/total-information-awareness-the-media-version, accessed September 1, 2013.

Andrejevic, M. (2007) *iSpy: Surveillance and Power in the Interactive Era*. Lawrence: University Press of Kansas.

Andrejevic, M. (2010) "Social network exploitation," in Z. Papacharissi (ed.), *A Networked Self: Identity, Community, and Culture on Social Network Sites*. New York: Routledge, pp. 82–101.

Ang, I. (1985) *Watching Dallas: Soap Opera and the Melodramatic Imagination*. London: Methuen.

Ang, I. (1991) *Desperately Seeking the Audience*. London: Routledge.

Ang, I. (1996) *Living Room Wars: Rethinking Media Audiences for a Postmodern World*. London: Routledge.

Appadurai, A. (1986) "Introduction: commodities and the politics of value," in A Appadurai (ed.), *The Social Life of Things: Commodities in Cultural Perspective*. Cambridge, UK: Cambridge University Press, pp. 3–63.

Aronson, P. (2003) "Feminists or 'postfeminists'? Young women's attitudes toward feminism and gender relations." *Gender & Society* 17(6): 903–22.

Attali, J. (2008) "This is not America's final crisis." *New Perspectives Quarterly* 25(2): 31–3.

Austen, J., and Fraiman, S. (1994) *Northanger Abbey* (Norton Critical Editions). New York: W. W. Norton and Co.

Bacon-Smith, C. (1992) *Enterprising Women: Television Fandom and the Creation of Popular Myth*. Philadelphia, PA: University of Pennsylvania Press.

Baker, C. E. (1995) *Advertising and a Democratic Press*. Princeton, NJ: Princeton University Press.

Baker, P. J. (1973) "The life histories of W. I. Thomas and Robert E. Park." *American Journal of Sociology* 79(2) (September): 243–60.

Banet-Weiser, S. (2004) "Girls rule! Gender, feminism, and nickelodeon." *Critical Studies in Media Communication* 21(2): 119–39.

Banet-Weiser, S. (2007) *Kids Rule! Nickelodeon and Consumer Citizenship*. Durham, NC: Duke University Press.

Bantz, C. R. (1985) "News organization: conflict as a crafted cultural norm." *Communication* 8(2): 225–44.

Barker, M., with Austin, T. (2000) *From Antz to Titanic: Reinventing Film Analysis*. London: Pluto.

Baron, N., and Ling, R. (2007) "Emerging patterns of American mobile phone use: Electronically-mediated communication in transition," in G. Goggin and L. Hjorth (eds), *Mobile Media 2007*. Australia: University of Sydney.

Barry, A., Osborne, T., and Rose, N. (eds) (1996) *Foucault and Political Reason: Liberalism, Neo-Liberalism, and Rationalities of Government*. Chicago: University of Chicago Press.

Bartky, S. L. (1990) *Femininity and Domination: Studies in the Phenomenology of Oppression*. London: Routledge.

Baruh, L. (2004) "Anonymous reading in interactive media." *Knowledge, Technology, & Policy* 17(1): 59–73.

Bateson, G. (1972) *Steps to an Ecology of Mind*. Chicago: University of Chicago Press.

Baudrillard, J. (1988) *Selected Writings*. Ed. Mark Poster. Stanford: Stanford University Press.

Bauman, Z. (2001) "Consuming life." *Journal of Consumer Culture* 1(1): 9–29.

Bauman, Z. (2005) *Liquid Life*. Cambridge, UK: Polity.

Bazerman, C. (1988) "Codifying the social scientific style: the APA Publication Manual as a behaviorist rhetoric," in C. Bazerman (ed.), *Shaping Written Knowledge: The Genre and Activity of the Experimental Article in Science*. Madison: University of Wisconsin Press, pp. 257–77.

Becher, T. (1989) *Academic Tribes and Territories: Intellectual Enquiry and the Cultures of Disciplines*. Milton Keynes, UK: Open University Press.

Bechtel, R., Achelpohl, C., and Akers, R. (1972) "Correlates between observed behavior and questionnaire responses on television viewing," in Comstock et al. (eds), *Television and Social Behavior, Vol. IV: Television in Day to Day Life*. US Government Printing Office, pp. 274–344.

Beck, U. (1992) *Risk Society: Towards a New Modernity*. London: Sage Publications.

Beck, U. (2003) "Rooted cosmopolitanism: emerging from a rivalry of distinctions," in U. Beck, N. Sznaider, and R. Winter (eds), *Global America: The Cultural Consequences of Globalization*. Liverpool: Liverpool University Press, pp. 15–29.

Beck, U., Giddens, A., and Lash, S. (1994) *Reflexive Modernization: Politics, Tradition and Aesthetics in the Modern Social Order*. Palo Alto, CA: Stanford University Press.

Becker, A. B. (2013) "Star power? Advocacy, receptivity, and viewpoints on celebrity involvement in issue politics." *Atlantic Journal of Communication* 21(1): 1–16.

Becker, H. (1962) *Outsiders: Studies in the Sociology of Deviance*. New York: The Free Press.

Becker, R. (2006) *Gay TV and Straight America*. Piscataway: Rutgers University Press.

Beer, D., and Burrows, R. (2007) "Sociology and, of and in Web 2.0: some initial considerations." Sociological Research online. Available at www.socresonline.org.uk/12/5/17.html, accessed December 10, 2012.

Bell, M. (2011) "Feminism and women's film criticism in post-war Britain, 1945–1959." *Feminist Media Studies* 11(4): 399–416.

Benford, R., and Snow, D. (2000) "Framing processes and social movements: an overview and assessment." *Annual Review of Sociology* 26: 611–39.

Benkler, Y. (2006) *The Wealth of Networks: How Social Production Transforms Markets and Freedom*. New Haven, CT: Yale University Press.

Bennett, L. (2008) "Assets under attack: metal theft, the built environment and the dark side of the global recycling market." *Environmental Law and Management* 20: 176–83.

Benson, R. (2004) "Bringing the sociology of media back in." *Political Communication* 21(3): 275–92.

Benson, R. (2009) "What makes news more multiperspectival? A field analysis." *Poetics* 37(5–6): 402–18.

Benson, R. (2013) *Shaping Immigration News: A French-American Comparison*. Cambridge, UK: Cambridge University Press.

Benson, R., and Neveu, E. (eds) (2005) *Bourdieu and the Journalistic Field*. Cambridge, UK: Polity.

Benson, R., and Powers, M. (2011) *Public Media and Political Independence*. Washington, DC: Free Press Research Report.

Benwell, B. (ed.) (2003) *Masculinity and Men's Lifestyle Magazines*. Oxford: Blackwell Publishing.

Benwell, B. (2012) *Postcolonial Audiences: Readers, Viewers, Reception*. London and New York: Routledge.

Berger, P. L., and Luckmann, T. (1966) *The Social Construction of Reality*. New York: Doubleday.

Bergman, S. M., Fearrington, M. E., Davenport, S. W. and Bergman, J. Z. (2011) "Millennials, narcissism, and social networking: what narcissists do on social networking sites and why." *Personality and Individual Differences* 50(5): 706–11.

Best, J. (2001) "Giving it away: the ironies of sociology's place in academia." *The American Sociologist* 32(1): 107–13.

Bielby, D., and Harrington, C. L. (2008) *Global TV: Exporting Television and Culture in the World Market*. New York and London: New York University Press.

Bielby, D. D., and Bielby, W. T. (1996) "Women and men in film: gender inequality among writers in a culture industry." *Gender and Society* 10(3): 248–70.

Bielby, D. D., Harrington, C. L., and Bielby, W. T. (1999). "Whose stories are they? Fan engagement with soap opera narratives in three sites of fan activity." *Journal of Broadcasting & Electronic Media* 43: 35–51. Reprinted in Toby Miller (ed.) (2002) *Television: Critical Concepts in Media and Cultural Studies*. New York: Routledge Press, pp. 101–21.

Bielby, W. T., and Bielby, D. D. (1992) "Cumulative disadvantage in an unstructured labor market: gender differences in the careers of television writers." *Work and Occupations* 19(4): 366–86.

Bijker, W., Hughes, T., and Pinch, T. (1989) *The Social Construction of Technological Systems: New Directions in the Sociology and History of Technology*. London: MIT Press.

Billig, M. (1995) *Banal Nationalism*. London and Thousand Oaks: Sage.

Bin, Z. (1998) "Popular family television and party ideology: the Spring Festival eve happy gathering." *Media, Culture & Society* 20(1): 43–58.

Bird, E. (1992a) *For Enquiring Minds: A Cultural Study of Supermarket Tabloids*. Knoxville: University of Tennessee Press.

Bird, E. (1992b) "Travels in nowhere land: ethnography and the 'impossible' audience." *Critical Studies in Mass Communication* 9: 250–60.

Bird, E. (2003) *The Audience in Everyday Life: Living in a Media World*. New York and London: Routledge.

Blumler, J. (1981) "Mass communication research in Europe: some origins and prospects, in Michael Burgoon (ed.), *Communication Yearbook 5* Transaction Books, pp. 145ff.

Boase, J., and Kobayashi, T. (2012) "Role call – the role of mobiles in relational roles," in: *Mobile Communication Community and & Locative Media: From the Everyday to the Revolutionary*. Presented at the International Communication Association 2012 ICA Mobile Communication Pre-Conference Workshop, ICA, Phoenix, AZ.

Bobo, J. (1995) *Black Women as Cultural Readers*. New York: Columbia University Press.

Boczkowski, P. (2005) *Digitizing the News*. The MIT Press.

Boczkowski, P. J. (2010) *News at Work: Imitation in an Age of Information Abundance*. Chicago: University of Chicago Press.

Boltanski, L. (1999) *Distant Suffering: Morality, Media and Politics*. Cambridge, UK: Polity.

Boltanski, L. (2011) *On Critique*. Cambridge, UK: Polity.

Boltanski, L., and Chiapello, E. (2005) *The New Spirit of Capitalism*. London: Verso.

Bourdieu, P. (1984) *Distinction*. Cambridge, MA: Harvard University Press.

Bourdieu, P. (1993). *The Field of Cultural Production*. New York: Columbia.

Box, R. C. (ed.) (2007) *Democracy and Public Administration*. Armonk, NY: M. E. Sharpe.

boyd, d., and Crawford, K. (2011) Six provocations for Big Data. A Decade in Internet Time: Symposium on the Dynamics of the Internet and Society. OII, Oxford, UK. Available online on http://papers.ssrn.com/sol3/papers.cfm?abstract_id=1926431

boyd, d., and Ellison, N. B. (2007) "Social network sites: definition, history, and scholarship." *Journal of Computer-Mediated Communication* 13(1): 210–30.

Breed, W. (1952) *The Newspaperman, News and Society*. New York: Arno Press.

Breed, W. (1955) "Social control in the newsroom: a functional analysis." *Social Forces* 33(4): 326–35.

Bretl, D. J., and Cantor, J. (1988) "The portrayal of men and women in US television commercials." *Sex Roles* 18 (9/10): 595–609.

Briggs, A., and Burke, P. (2003) *A Social History of the Media: From Gutenberg to the Internet*. Cambridge, UK: Polity.

Brunsdon, C. (1991) "Crossroads: notes on soap opera." *Screen* 22(4): 32–7.

Brunsdon, C. (2000) *The Feminist, the Housewife, and the Soap Opera*. Oxford: Clarendon Press.

Brunsdon, C., and Morley, D. (1978) *Everyday Television*. London: BFI.

Brunsdon, C., D'Acci, J., and Spigel, L. (eds) (1997) *Feminist Television Criticism: A Reader*. Oxford University Press.

Bryant, J. (ed.) (1990) *Television and the American Family*. Mahwah, NJ: Lawrence Erlbaum.

Bucher, T. (2012) "Want to be on the top? Algorithmic power and the threat of invisibility on Facebook." *New Media & Society* 14(7): 1164–80.

Bueno, G. (2002) "La canonización de Marilyn Monroe." *El Catoblepas* 9(2).

Burke, P. J. (2004) "Identities and social structure: the 2003 Cooley-Mead Award address." *Social Psychology Quarterly* 67(1): 5–15.

Burnham, D. (1984) *The Rise of the Computer State*. London: Weidenfeld and Nicholson.

Burrows, L., and Wright, J. (2004) "The discursive production of childhood, identity and health," in J. Evans, B. Davies, and J. Wright (eds), *Body Knowledge and Control: Studies in the Sociology of Physical Education and Health*. New York: Routledge, pp. 83–95.

Burstein, P. (1985) *Discrimination, Jobs, and Politics*. Chicago: University of Chicago Press.

Butsch, R. (2000) *The Making of American Audiences from Stage to Television, 1750 to 1990*. Cambridge, UK: Cambridge University Press.

Butsch, R. (2008) *The Citizen Audience: Crowds, Publics, Individuals*. New York: Routledge.

Butters, S. (1976) "The logic of inquiry of participation observation." in S. Hall and T. Jefferson (eds), *Resistance through Ritual: Youth Subcultures in Post-War Britain*. Hutchinson, pp. 253–72.

Buxton, W. (2008) "From Park to Cressey: Chicago sociology's engagement with media and mass culture," in D. Park and J. Pooley (eds), *The History of Media and Communication Research*, pp. 345–62.

Byars, J. (1991) *All that Hollywood Allows: Re-reading Gender in 1950s Melodrama*. Chapel Hill: University of North Carolina Press.

Caldwell, J. T. (1995) *Televisuality: Style, Crisis, and Authority in American Television*. New Brunswick: Rutgers University Press.

Calhoun, C. (1992) "Sociology, other disciplines, and the project of a general understanding of social life," in T. C. Halliday and M. Janowitz (eds), *Sociology and Its Publics: The Forms and Fates of Disciplinary Organization*. Chicago: University of Chicago Press, pp.137–98.

Calhoun, C. (ed.) (2007) *Sociology in America*. Chicago: University of Chicago Press.

Calhoun, C., Rojek, C., and Turner, B. S. (2005) "Introduction," in C. Calhoun, C. Rojek, and B. S. Turner (eds), *The Sage Handbook of Sociology*. London: Sage.

Cantor, M. (1977) "Women and public broadcasting." *Journal of Communication* 27(1): 14–19.

Cantor, M., and Pingree, S. (1983) *The Soap Opera*. Beverly Hills and London: Sage.

Cantril, H. (1940) *The Invasion from Mars*. Princeton University Press.

Cantril, H., and Allport, G. (1935) *The Psychology of Radio*. Harper and Brothers.

Carey, J. W. (1992) *Communication as Culture: Essays on Media and Society*. New York: Routledge.

Carey, J. W. (2005) "Historical pragmatism and the internet." *New Media & Society* 7(4): 443–55.

Carragee, K. M., and Roefs, W. (2004) "The neglect of power in recent framing research." *Journal of Communication* 54(2): 214–33.

Carson, D., Welsch, J., and Ditmar L. (1994) *Multiple Voices in Feminist Film Criticism*. Minneapolis: University of Minnesota Press.

Carstens, A., and Beck, J. (2005) "Get ready for the gamer generation." *Techtrends* 49(3): 22–5.

Carter, C., and McLaughlin, L. (2011) "The Tenth Anniversary issue of *Feminist Media Studies*" (Editors' Introduction) *Feminist Media Studies* 11(1): 1–5.

Castells, M. (1996) *The Rise of the Network Society*. Oxford: Blackwell.

Castells, M. (2007) "Communication, power and counter-power in the network society." *International Journal of Communication* 1: 238–66.

Castells, M. (2009) *Communication Power*. Oxford: Oxford University Press.

Castells, M. (2012) *Networks of Outrage and Hope*. Cambridge, UK: Polity.

Chambliss, W. (1973) "The saints and the roughnecks." *Society* 11(1): 24–31.

Chaney, D. (1994) *The Cultural Turn: Scene-Setting Essays on Contemporary Cultural History*. London: Routledge.

Chakravartty, P., and Zhao, Y. (eds) (2007) *Global Communications: Toward a Transcultural Political Economy*. Lanham: Rowman & Littlefield.

Chartier, R. (2005a) "Crossing borders in early modern Europe: sociology of texts and literature." Trans. Maurice Elton. *Book History* 8: 37–50.

Chartier, R. (2005b, December 17) "Le droit d'auteur est-il une parenthèse dans l'histoire?" *Le Monde*. Available at www.lemonde.fr/societe/article/2005/12/17/roger-chartier-le-droit-d-auteur-est-il-une-parenthese-dans-l-histoire_722516_3224.html.

Charters, W. W. (1933) *Motion Pictures and Youth*. New York: Macmillan.

Chesley, N. (2005) "Blurring boundaries? Linking technology use, spillover, individual distress, and family satisfaction." *Journal of Marriage and Family* 67: 1237–48.

Chib A.,and Chen,V. H.-H. (2011) "Midwives with mobiles: a dialectical perspective on gender arising from technology introduction in rural Indonesia." *New Media & Society* (May) 13(3): 486–501

Clark, D. (1995) *Negotiating Hollywood: The Cultural Politics of Actors' Labor*. Minneapolis: University of Minnesota Press.

Clemens, E. A. (1997) *The People's Lobby: Organizational Innovation and the Rise of Interest Group Politics in the United States, 1890–1925*. Chicago: University of Chicago Press.

Coates, T.-N. (2009) "*The Cosby Show* and Barack Obama, The Atlantic Blog, January 27. Available at www.theatlantic.com/entertainment/archive/2009/01/the-cosby-show-and-barack-obama/6638/, accessed September 30, 2013.

Cohen, A. A., and Lemish, D. (2005) "When bombs go off the mobiles ring: the aftermath of terrorist attacks," in K. Nyiri (ed.), *A Sense of Place: The Global and the Local in Mobile Communication*. Vienna: Passagen Verlag, pp. 117–28.

Cohen, C. (1963) *The Press and Foreign Policy*. Princeton: Princeton University Press.

Cohen, S. (2002 [1972]) *Folk Devils and Moral Panics*, 3rd edn. Abingdon, UK: Routledge.

Cole, S. (ed.) (2001) *What's Wrong with Sociology?* New Brunswick: Transaction Publishers.

Collett, P. (1987) "The viewers viewed." *Et cetera* 44(3): 245–51.

Collins, R. (2004) *Interaction Ritual Chains*. Princeton: Princeton University Press.

Commission on the Future of Women's Sport (2010) *Prime Time: The Case for Commercial Investment in Women's Sport*. London: Women's Sport and Fitness Foundation.

Comstock, G. et al. (eds) (1972) *Television and Social Behavior*. US Government Printing Office.

Cook, P., with Dodd, P. (1993) *Women and Film: A Sight and Sound Reader*. London: Scarlet Press/Philadelphia: Temple University Press.

Corbett, C. J., and Turco, R. P. (2006) "Sustainability in the motion picture industry." Report prepared for the Integrated Waste Management Board of the State of California http://personal.anderson.ucla.edu/charles.corbett/papers/mpis_report.pdf, accessed September 1, 2013.

Corman, P. (1996) *Left Intellectuals and Popular Culture in Twentieth Century America*. North Carolina University Press.

Cottle, S. (2006) *Mediatized Conflict*. Maidenhead: Open University Press.

Couldry, N. (2003) *Media Rituals*. London: Routledge.

Couldry, N. (2010a) "Sociology and cultural studies: an interrupted dialogue," in J. R. Hall, L. Grindstaff, and M. C. Lo (eds), *Handbook of Cultural Sociology*. New York: Routledge, pp. 77–86.

Couldry, N. (2010b) *Why Voice Matters: Culture and Politics after Neoliberalism*. London: Sage.

Couldry, N. (2012) *Media, Society, World: Social Theory and Digital Media Practice*. Cambridge, UK: Polity.

Couldry, N., and Hepp, A. (2012) "Comparing media cultures," in Frank Esser and Thomas Hanitzsch (eds), *The Handbook of Comparative Communication Research*. London: Routledge, pp. 249–61.

Couldry, N., Hepp, A., and Krotz, F. (2010) (eds) *Media Events in a Global Age*. London: Routledge.

Council of the Inspectors General on Integrity and Efficiency (2009) *A Progress Report to the Present, Fiscal Year 2008* (Sept. 8), www.ignet.gov.

Cranberg, G., Bezanson, R., and Soloski, J. (2001) *Taking Stock: Journalism and the Publicly Traded Newspaper Company*. Ames: Iowa State University Press.

Crane, D. (2000) *Fashion and Its Social Agendas*. Chicago: University of Chicago Press.

Cressey, P. (1938) "The motion picture experience as modified by social background and personality." *American Sociological Review* 3 (August): 516–25.

Critcher, C. (1979) "Sociology, cultural studies and the post-war working class," in John Clarke, Chas Critcher, and Richard Johnson, *Working Class Culture: Studies in History and Theory*. Hutchinson.

Critcher, C. (2003) *Moral Panics and the Media*. Buckingham, UK: Open University.

Crowley, D., and Heyer, P. (2013) "Media," in P. Simonson, J. Peck, R. T. Craig, and J. P. Jackson Jr (eds), *The Handbook of Communication History*. New York and London: Routledge, pp. 58–75.

Crowley, M. (2008) "Post-Racial?" *The New Republic*, March 12. Available at www.newrepublic.com/article/post-racial, accessed September 30, 2013.

Crowther-Heyck, H. (2006) "Patrons of the revolution: ideals and institutions in postwar behavioral science." *Isis* 97: 420–46.

Csikszentmihalyi, M., Larson, R., and Prescott, S. (1977) "The ecology of adolescent activity and experience." *Journal of Youth and Adolescence* 6: 281–94.

Curran, J., Fenton, N., and Freedman, D. (2012) *Misunderstanding the Internet*. London: Routledge.

Cushion, S. (2012) *The Democratic Value of News: Why Public Service Media*. London: Palgrave Macmillan.

D'Acci, J. (1994) "Defining women: television and the case of *Cagney and Lacey*." Chapel Hill, NC: University of North Carolina Press.

Dalton, R., Scarrow, S., and Cain, B. (2003) "New forms of democracy? Reform and transformation of democratic institutions," in B. Cain, R. Dalton, and S. Scarrow (eds), *Democracy Transformed? Expanding Political Opportunities in Advanced Industrial Democracies*. Oxford: Oxford University Press, pp. 1–20.

Davis, J. (2010) "Architecture of the personal interactive homepage: constructing the self through MySpace." *New Media & Society* 12(7): 1103–119.

Davis, J. L. (2012) "Accomplishing authenticity in a labor-exposing space." *Computers in Human Behavior* 28(5): 1966–73.

Dayan, D. (2010) "Beyond media events: disenchantment, derailment, disruption," in N. Couldry, A. Hepp, and F. Krotz (eds) *Media Events in a Global Age*. London: Routledge, pp. 23–31.

Dayan, D., and Katz, E. (1992) *Media Events: The Broadcasting of History*. Harvard University Press.

de Lauretis, T. (1984) *Alice Doesn't: Feminism, Semiotics, Cinema*. The Association of American University Presses.

de Sola Pool, I. (1971) "The social impact of the telephone." Cambridge, MA: MIT Press.

Delia, J. (1987) "Communication research: a history," in C. R. Berger and S. H. Chaffee (eds), *Handbook of Communication Science*. Newbury Park, CA: Sage, pp. 20–98.

DeLisle, J. (2008) "'One world, different dream': the contest to define the Beijing Olympics," in M. E. Price and D. Dayan (eds), *Owning the Olympics: Narratives of the New China*. Ann Arbor: The University of Michigan Press.

Delli Carpini, M., and Williams, B. (2011) *After Broadcast News*. Cambridge, UK: Cambridge University Press.

Denzin, N. K. (1992) *Symbolic Interactionism and Cultural Studies*. Cambridge, MA: Blackwell.

Deuze, M. (2007) *Media Work*. Cambridge, UK and Malden, MA: Polity.

De Vany, A. S. (2003) *Hollywood Economics: How Extreme Uncertainty Shapes the Film Industry*. New York: Routledge.

DiMaggio, P. J., and Powell, W. W. (1983) "The Iron Cage revisited: institutional isomorphism and collective rationality in organizational fields." *American Sociological Review* 48(2): 147–60.

Doane, M. A. (1987) *The Desire to Desire: The Woman's Film of the 1940s.* Bloomington: Indiana University Press.

Doane, M. A., Mellencamp, P., and Williams, L. (eds) (1984) *Re-Vision: Essays in Feminist Film Criticism.* Los Angeles: American Film Institute.

Dobson, A. S. (2012) "'Individuality is everything': 'autonomous' femininity in MySpace mottos and self-descriptions." *Continuum* 26(3): 371–83.

Dohrn-van Rossum, G. (1992) *History of the Hour: Clocks and Modern Temporal Orders.* Chicago: University of Chicago.

Dominick, J., and Rauch, G. (1972) "The image of women in network TV commercials." *Journal of Broadcasting* 16(3): 259–65.

Donnelly, J. (1986) "International human rights: a regime analysis," *International Organization* 40(3) (Summer): 599–642.

Donner, J. (2008) "Research approaches to mobile use in the developing world: a review of the literature." *The Information Society* 24: 140–59.

Donner, J. (2009) "Blurring livelihoods and lives: the social uses of mobile phones and socioeconomic development." *Innovations: Technology, Governance, Globalization* 4(1): 91–101.

Douglas, S. (1994) *Where the Girls Are: Growing Up Female with the Mass Media.* New York: Three Rivers Press (a division of Random House).

Douglas, S. (2010) *The Rise of Enlightened Sexism: How Popular Culture Took Us from Girl Power to Girls Gone Wild.* New York: St Martin's Press.

Dow, B. (1992) "Feminism and femininity in Murphy Brown." *Southern Communication Journal* 57(2): 143–55.

Dow, B. (1996) *Primetime Feminism: Television, Media Culture, and the Women's Movement since 1970.* University of Pennsylvania Press, Philadelphia.

Dow, B. (2002) "Ally McBeal, Lifestyle feminism, and the politics of personal happiness." *The Communication Review* 5(4): 259–64.

Downie, L. Jr, and Schudson, M. (2009) "The reconstruction of American journalism." *Columbia Journalism Review*, posted on October 19. Available at: http://www.cjr.org/reconstruction/the_reconstruction_of_american.php?page=all.

Dreier, P. (1979) "The case for transitional reforms." *Social Policy* 9(4): 5–16.

Dreier, P. (1982) "Capitalists vs. the media: an analysis of an ideological mobilization among business leaders." *Media, Culture & Society* 4: 111–32.

Du Gay, P., and Pryke, M. (2002) *Cultural Economy: Cultural Analysis and Commercial Life.* London and Thousand Oaks: Sage.

Durkheim, E. (1938) *The Rules of the Sociological Method.* New York: The Free Press.

Durkheim, E. (1995) *The Elementary Forms of Religious Life.* Glencoe, IL: The Free Press.

Dutton, W., and Naiona, F. (2003) "The social dynamics of wireless on September 11: reconfiguring access," in A. M. Noll (ed.), *Crisis Communication*. Lanham, MD: Rowan and Littlefield, pp. 69–82.

Dyer, R. (1986) *Heavenly Bodies: Film Stars and Society*. New York: St Martin's Press.

Dyson, E., Gilder, G., Keyworth, G. and Toffler, A. (1994) *Cyberspace and the American Dream: A Magna Carta for the Knowledge Age*. Version 1.2. Available at Progress and Freedom Foundation pff.org/issues-pubs/futureinsights/fi1.2magnacarta.html.

Eagle, N., Pentland, A. (Sandy), and Lazer, D. (2009) "Inferring friendship network structure by using mobile phone data." Proceedings of the National Academy of Sciences of the United States of America 106(36): 15274–8.

Earls, M. (2003) "Advertising to the herd: how understanding our true nature challenges the ways we think about advertising and market research." *International Journal of Market Research* 45(3): 311–37.

Eco, U. (1987) *Travels in Hyperreality: Essays*, trans. William Weaver. London: Picador.

Economist (2012, November 10) "More than just a game."

Edwards, P. N. (1995) "From 'impact' to social processes: computers in society and culture," in G. Jasanoff (ed.), *Handbook of Science and Technology Studies*. London: MIT Press.

Elias, N. (1978) *The Civilizing Process*. New York: Blackwell.

Elias, N. (1992) *Time: An Essay*. Oxford: Blackwell.

Ellison, N. B. et al. (2011) "Negotiating privacy concerns and social capital needs in a social media environment," in S. Trepte and L. Reinecke (eds), *Privacy Online: Perspectives on Privacy and Self-disclosure in the Social Web*. New York: Springer, pp. 19–32.

Ellison, N. B., Steinfield, C., and Lampe, C. (2007) "The benefits of Facebook 'friends': social capital and college students' use of online social network sites." *Journal of Computer-Mediated Communication* 12(4): 1143–68.

Ellison, N. B., Steinfield, C., and Lampe, C. (2011) "Connection strategies: social capital implications of Facebook-enabled communication practices." *New Media & Society* 13(6): 873–92.

Emirbayer, M., and Mische, A. (1998) "What is agency?" *American Journal of Sociology* 103: 962–1023.

Enli, G. S., and Thumim, N. (2012) "Socializing and self-representation online: exploring Facebook." *Observatorio* (OBS*) 6(1): 87–105.

Entman, R. (2004) *Projections of Power: Framing News, Public Opinion and US Foreign Policy*. Chicago: University of Chicago.

Epstein E. J. (1973) *News from Nowhere*. New York: Random House.

Erens, P. (ed.) (1990) *Issues in Feminist Film Criticism*. Bloomington: Indiana University Press.

Ericson, R., Baranek, P., and Chan, J. (1989) *Negotiating Control: A Study of News Sources*. Open University Press.

Eriksen, T. H. (2001) Øyeblikkets tyranni: rask og langsom tid i infor-masjonssamfunnet [Tyranny of the moment: fast and slow time in the information age] Oslo: Aschehoug.

Eyal, G. (2010) "Spaces between fields," in Phil Gorski (ed.), *Pierre Bourdieu and Historical Analysis*. Durham, NC: Duke University Press.

Farquhar, L. (2012) "Performing and interpreting identity through Facebook imagery." *Convergence: The International Journal of Research into New Media Technologies*.

Faye, C. (2012) "American social psychology: examining the contours of the 1970s crisis." *Studies in the History and Philosophy of Biological and Biomedical Sciences* 43(2) (June): 514–21.

Feenberg, A. (2002) *Transforming Technology*. New York: Oxford University Press.

Feenberg, A. (2010) *Between Reason and Experience*. Cambridge, MA: MIT Press.

Feenberg, A., and Freedman, M. (2001) *When Poetry Ruled the Streets: The French May Events of 1968*. New York: SUNY Press.

Feenberg, A., and Grimes, S. (2009) "Rationalising play: a critical theory of digital gaming." *The Information Society* 25(2): 105–18.

Fenigstein, A., Scheier, M. F., and Buss, A. H. (1975) "Public and private self-consciousness: assessment and theory." *Journal of Personality and Social Psychology* 43(4): 522–7.

Ferree, M. M., Gamson, W., Gerhards, J., and Rucht, D. (2002) *Shaping Abortion Discourse: Democracy and the Public Sphere in Germany and the United States*. Cambridge, UK: Cambridge University Press.

Figley, C. R., and Jones, R. (2008) "The 2007 Virginia Tech shootings: identification and application of lessons learned." *Traumatology* 14: 4–7.

Fischer, C. (1992) *America Calling: A Social History of the Telephone*. Berkeley: University of California Press.

Fishman, M. (1980) *Manufacturing the News*. Austin: University of Texas Press.

Fiske, J. (1992) "Audiencing: a cultural studies approach to watching televi-sion." *Poetics* 41: 345–59.

Fitter, M. (1979) "Towards more 'natural' interactive systems." *International Journal of Man-Machine Studies* 11(3): 339–50.

Fligstein, N., and McAdam D. (2012) *A Theory of Fields*. Oxford: Oxford University Press.

Flint, J (2005) "As critics carp, HBO confronts ratings decline." *Wall Street Journal* 8 June, B1.

Foucault, M. (1995) *Discipline and Punish*. New York: Vintage.

Fourcade, M. (2009) *Economists and Societies: Discipline and Profession in the United States, Britain, & France, 1890s to 1990s*. Princeton, NJ: Princeton University Press.

Fraser, N. (1992) "Rethinking the public sphere: a contribution to the critique of actually existing democracy", in C. Calhoun (ed.), *Habermas and the Public Sphere*. Cambridge, MA: The MIT Press, pp. 109–42.

Freedland, J. (2013, March 9) "Danny Boyle: champion of the people." *Guardian*, www.guardian.co.uk/film/2013/mar/09/danny-boyle-queen-olympics-film.

Freiberger, P., and Swain, M. (1984) *Fire in the Valley: The Making of the First Personal Computers*. London: McGraw-Hill.

Frosh, P., and Wolfsfeld, G. (2007) "ImagiNation: News discourse, nationhood and civil society." *Media, Culture and Society* 29(1): 105–29.

Fuchs, C. (2011) "New Media, Web 2.0 and surveillance." *Sociology Compass* 5(2): 134–47.

Fuchs, S. (2001) "Beyond agency." *Sociological Theory* 19(1): 24–40.

Fuller, K. (1996) *At the Picture Show: Small Town Audiences and the Creation of Movie Fan Culture*. Smithsonian Institution Press

Fung, R. (1991) "Looking for my penis: the eroticized Asian in gay video porn," in Bad Object-Choices (ed.), *How Do I Look? Queer Film and Video*. Seattle: Bay Press, pp. 145–68.

Gajjala, R. (2002) "An interrupted postcolonial/feminist cyberethnography: complicity and resistance in the 'cyberfield.'" *Feminist Media Studies* 2(2): 177–93.

Gajjala, R. (ed.) (2012) *Cyberculture and the Subaltern: Weavings of the Virtual and Real*. Plymouth, UK: Lexington Books.

Gallup, G., and Rae, S. (1940) *The Pulse of Democracy*. New York: Simon & Schuster.

Gamble, S. (2001) *The Routledge Companion to Feminism and Postfeminism*, 2nd edn. London and New York: Routledge.

Gamson, J. (1998) *Freaks Talk Back: Tabloid Talk Shows and Sexual Nonconformity*. Chicago: University of Chicago Press.

Gamson, W. (2004) "On a sociology of the media." *Political Communication* 21(3): 305–7.

Gamson, W. A., and Modigliani, A. (1989) "Media discourse and public opinion on nuclear power: a constructionist approach." *American Journal of Sociology* 95(1): 1–37.

Gandy, O. H., Jr (1989) "The surveillance society: information technology and bureaucratic control." *Journal of Communication* 39(3): 61–76.

Gans, H. (1972) "The famine in American mass-communications research: Comments on Hirsch, Tuchman and Gecas." *American Journal of Sociology* 77: 697–705.

Gans, H. (1979) *Deciding What's News: A Study of CBS Evening News, NBC Nightly News, Newsweek, and Time*. New York: Pantheon Books.

Gans, H. (2011) "Multiperspectival news revisited: journalism and representative democracy," *Journalism* 12: 3–13.

Gans, H. (2012) "Against culture versus structure." *Identities* 19(2): 125–34.

García Canclini, N. (2004) *Diferentes, desiguales y desconectados: Mapas de interculturalidad*. Barcelona: Editorial Gedisa.

Gary, B. (1999) *The Nervous Liberals: Propaganda Anxieties from World War I to the Cold War*. Columbia University Press.

Genz, S., and Brabon, B. A. (2009) *Postfeminism: Cultural Texts and Theories*. Edinburgh: Edinburgh University Press.

Gergen, K. J. (1973) "Social psychology as history." *Journal of Personality and Social Psychology* 26(2): 309–20.

Gergen, K. (1992) *The Saturated Self: Dilemmas of Identity in Contemporary Life*. New York: Basic Books.

Gergen, K. J. (2009) *Relational Being: Beyond Self and Community*. Oxford: Oxford University Press.

Gibson, C., and Lennon, E. (1999, February) *Historical Census on the Foreign-born Population of the United States: 1850–1990*. Working Paper. Washington, DC: US Bureau of the Census.

Giddens, A. (1990) *The Consequences of Modernity*. Cambridge, UK: Polity.

Giddens, A. (1991) *Modernity and Self-identity: Self and Society in the Late Modern Age*. Palo Alto, CA: Stanford University Press.

Gieber, W. (1956) "Across the desk: a study of 16 *Telegraph* editors," *Journalism Quarterly* 27: 423–32.

Gieber, W. (1964) "News is what newspapermen make it," in L. A. Dexter and D. M. White (eds), *People, Society and Mass Communications*. New York: Free Press, pp. 172–82.

Gilbert, J. (1986) *A Cycle of Outrage: America's Reaction to Juvenile Delinquency in the 1950s*. New York: Oxford University Press.

Gill, R. (2003) "From sexual objectification to sexual subjectification: the resexualization of women's bodies in the media." *Feminist Media Studies* 3(1): 100–5.

Gill, R. (2007a) "Postfeminist media culture: elements of a sensibility." *European Journal of Cultural Studies* 10(2): 147–66.

Gill, R. (2007b) *Gender and the Media*. Cambridge, UK: Polity.

Gillespie, M. (1995) *Television, Ethnicity and Cultural Change*. London: Routledge.

Gilroy, P. (2004) *After Empire: Melancholia or Convivial Culture*. London: Routledge.

Ginsburg, F., Abu-Lughod, L., and Larkin, B. (eds) (2002) *Media Worlds: Anthropology on New Terrain*. Berkeley: University of California Press.

Gitlin T. (1978) "Media sociology: the dominant paradigm." *Theory and Society* 6(2): 205–53.

Gitlin, T. (1980) *The Whole World is Watching: Mass Media in the Making and Unmaking of the New Left*. Berkeley: University of California Press.

Gitlin, T. (1983) *Inside Prime Time*. London: Routledge.

Glander, T. (2000) *Origins of Mass Communications Research during the American Cold War: Educational Effects and Contemporary Implications*. Mahwah, NJ: Lawrence Erlbaum.

Gledhill, C. (1978) "Recent developments in feminist criticism." *Quarterly Review of Film Studies* 3(4): 457–93.

Gledhill, C. (1992) "Speculations on the relationship between soap opera and melodrama." *Quarterly Review of Film and Video* 14 (1/2): 103–24.

Glennie, P., and Thrift, N. (2009) *Shaping the Day: A History of Timekeeping in England and Wales 1300–1800*. Oxford: Oxford University Press.

Goffman, E. (1959) *The Presentation of Self in Everyday Life*. Garden City, NY: Doubleday.

Goffman, E. (1967) *Interaction Ritual: Essays on Face-to-Face Behavior*. New York: Pantheon.

Goffman, E. (1974) *Frame Analysis: An Essay on the Organization of Experience*. Cambridge, MA: Harvard University Press.

Goldberg, S. (2013, February 13) "Daryl Hannah leads celebrity keystone XL protest at White House gates." *Guardian*, available at www.guardian.co.uk/environment/2013/feb/13/daryl-hannah-keystone-xl-protest-obama, accessed September 2, 2013.

Golding, P., and Elliott, P. (1979) *Making the News*. Addison Wesley Longman.

Goldman, R., Heath, D., and Smith, S. L. (eds) (1991) "Notes on commodity feminism." *Critical Studies in Media Communication* 8: 333–51.

Golumbia, D. (2009) "Games without play." *New Literary History* 40.

Goodings, L. (2011) "The dilemma of closeness and distance: a discursive analysis of wall posting in MySpace." *Forum Qualitative Sozialforschung/Forum Qualitative Social Research* 12(3).

Gordon, C. (ed.). (1980) *Power-Knowledge: Selected Interviews and Other Writings, 1972–1977/Michel Foucault*. Brighton: Harvester Press.

Gordon, E., and Silva, A. de S. e (2011) *Net Locality: Why Location Matters in a Networked World*, 1st edn. Oxford: Wiley-Blackwell.

Gordon, T., and Verna, M. E. (1978) *Mass Communication Effects and Processes: A Comprehensive Bibliography, 1950–1975*. Sage.

Gorz, A. (1980) *Farewell to the Working Class*. London: Pluto.

Gouldner, A. (1976) *The Dialectic of Ideology and Technology*. New York: Seabury Press.

Gramsci, A. (1978) *Selections from the Prison Notebooks of Antonio Gramsci*. Trans. Quentin Hoare and Geoffrey Nowell-Smith. New York: International Publishers.

Grasmuck, S., Martin, J., and Zhao, S. (2009) "Ethno-racial identity displays on Facebook." *Journal of Computer-Mediated Communication* 15(1): 158–88.

Gray, A. (1992) *Video Playtime: The Gendering of a Leisure Technology*. London: Routledge.

Gray, A., Campbell, J., Erickson, M., Hanson, S., and Wood, H. (eds) (2007) *CCCS Selected Working Papers, Vols 1 and 2*. Abingdon, UK: Routledge

Gray, H. (1989) "Television, black Americans and the American dream." *Critical Studies in Mass Communication* 6: 376–86.

Gray, H. (1993) "Black and white and in color." *American Quarterly* 45: 467–72.

Gray, H. (2004) *Watching Race: Television and the Struggle for Blackness.* Minneapolis: University of Minnesota Press.

Greenwood, J. D. (2004) *The Disappearance of the Social in American Social Psychology.* Cambridge, UK: Cambridge University Press.

Greve, H. R., Pozner, J., and Rao, H. (2006) "Vox populi: resource partitioning, organizational proliferation, and the cultural impact of the insurgent microradio movement." *The American Journal of Sociology* 112: 802–37.

Grieveson, L. (2004) *Policing Cinema: Movies and Censorship in Early Twentieth-Century America.* Berkeley: University of California Press.

Grindstaff, L. (2002) *The Money Shot: Trash, Class, and the Making of TV Talk Shows.* Chicago: University of Chicago Press.

Grindstaff, L., and West, E. (2006) "Cheerleading and the gendered politics of sport." *Social Problems* 54(4): 500–18.

Grindstaff, L., and West, E. (2010) "Hands on hips, smiles on lips! Gender, race, and the performance of 'spirit' in cheerleading." *Text & Performance Quarterly* 30(2): 143–62.

Grindstaff, L., and West, E. (2011) "Post-feminism and the 'new cheerleader' media icon." Paper presented at the International Communication Association, Boston, MA.

Grindstaff, L., and West, E. (2012) "Will the real 'F' word please stand up? 'Feminism' and 'femininity' in contemporary media iconography." Paper presented at the American Sociological Association, Denver CO, August 17–20.

Grossman, L. (2006, December 13) "Time's Person of the Year: You." *Time.* Available at time.com/time/magazine/article/0,9171,1570810,00. html.

Habermas, J. (1971) *Knowledge and Human Interests.* Boston: Beacon Press.

Habermas, J. (1987a) *Toward a Rational Society.* Cambridge, UK: Polity.

Habermas, J. (1987b) *The Theory of Communicative Action* (vol. 2): *Lifeworld and System.* Boston: Beacon Press.

Habermas, J. (1989 [1962]) *The Structural Transformation of the Public Sphere,* trans. Thomas Burger. Cambridge, MA: The MIT Press.

Habermas, J. (1996) *Between Facts and Norms: Contributions to a Discourse Theory of Law and Democracy.* Cambridge, MA: The MIT Press.

Habermas, J. (2006) "Political communication in media society: does democracy still enjoy an epistemic dimension? The impact of theory on empirical research." *Communication Theory* 16: 411–26.

Hains, R. (2009) "Power feminism mediated: girl power and the commercial politics of change." *Women's Studies in Communication* 32(1): 89–113.

Hains, R. (2012) *Growing Up with Girl Power: Girlhood on Screen and in Everyday Life.* New York: Peter Lang.

Hall, E. J., and Rodriguez, M. S. (2003) "The myth of postfeminism." *Gender & Society* 17(6): 878–902.

Hall, S. (1973) *Encoding and Decoding in the Television Discourse*. Birmingham: CCCS.

Hall, S. (1980) "Encoding/decoding," in Stuart, Hall, Dorothy Hobson, Andrew Lowe, and Paul Willis (eds), *Culture, Media, Language*. London: Unwin Hyman, pp. 107–17.

Hall, S. (1997) *Representation: Cultural Representations and Signifying Practices*. London: Sage.

Hall, S., and Jefferson, T. (1976) *Resistance through Ritual: Youth Subcultures in Post-war Britain*. Hutchinson.

Hall, S., Critcher, C., Jefferson, T., Clarke, J., and Roberts, B. (1978) *Policing the Crisis: Mugging, the State, and Law and Order*. London: Palgrave Macmillan.

Hallin, D. C., and Mancini, P. (2004) *Comparing Media Systems: Three Models of Media and Politics*. New York: Cambridge University Press.

Hallin, D. C., and Mancini, P. (2012) *Comparing Media Systems Beyond the Western World*. Cambridge, UK: Cambridge University Press.

Hampton, K. N., Sessions, L. F., and Her, E. J. (2011) "Core networks, social isolation, and new media." *Information, Communication & Society* 14: 130–55.

Hansen, M. (1994) *Babel and Babylon: Spectatorship in American Silent Film*. Cambridge, MA: Harvard University Press.

Haralovich, M. B., and Rabinovitz, L. (eds) (1999) *Television, History, and American Culture*. Durham and London: Duke University Press.

Hardt, M., and Negri, T. (2000) *Empire*. Cambridge, MA: Harvard.

Hargittai, E. (2008) "The digital reproduction of inequality," in D. B. Grusky (ed.), *Social Stratification: Class, Race, and Gender in Sociological Perspective*. Boulder, CO: Westview Press, pp. 936–44.

Hargittai, E., and Litt, E. (2011) "The Tweet smell of celebrity success: explaining variation in Twitter adoption among a diverse group of young adults." *New Media and Society* 13(15): 824–42.

Harrington, C. L., and Bielby, D. (1995) *Soap Fans: Pursuing Pleasures and Making Meaning in Everyday Life*. Philadelphia: Temple University Press

Harrison, K., and Cantor, J. (1997) "The relationship between media consumption and eating disorders." *Journal of Communication* 47(1): 40–67.

Hartley, J. (1987) "Invisible fictions: television audiences, paedocracy, pleasure." *Textual Practice* 1(2): 121–38.

Haskell, M. (1974 [1987]) *From Reverence to Rape: The Treatment of Women in the Movies*. Chicago: University of Chicago Press.

Hastorf, A., and Cantril, H. (1954) "They saw a game: a case study." *Journal of Abnormal and Social Psychology* 49(1) (January): 129–34.

Havens, T. (2000) "'The biggest show in the world': race and the global popularity of *The Cosby Show*." *Media, Culture and Society* 22: 371–91.

Havens, T. (2011) "Inventing universal television: global television fairs as tournaments of value," in B. Moeran and J. Strandgaard Pedersen (eds), *Negotiating Values in the Creative Industries: Fairs, Festivals and Competitive Events*. Cambridge and London: Cambridge University Press.

Havens, T. (2012) "Minority television trade as cultural journey: the case of New Zealand's bro'town," in B. E. Smith-Shomade (ed.), *Watching While Black: Centering the Television of Black Audiences*. Piscataway: Rutgers University Press.

Havens, T., Lotz, A., and Tinic, S. (2009) "Critical media industry studies: a research approach." *Communication, Culture & Critique* 2: 234–53.

Hays, S. (1994) "Structure and agency and the sticky problem of culture." *Sociological Theory* 12(1) (March): 57–72.

Hearn, A. (2008) "Variations on the branded self: theme, invention, improvisation and inventory," in D. Hesmondhalgh and J. Toynbee (eds), *The Media and Social Theory*. New York: Routledge, pp. 194–210.

Hebdige, D. (1979) *Subculture: the Meaning of Style*. London and New York: Methuen.

Heclo, H. (1978) "Issue networks and the executive establishment," in A. King (ed.), *The New American Political System*. Washington, DC. American Enterprise Institute, pp. 87–124.

Herman, E. S., and Chomsky, N. (1988) *Manufacturing Consent*. New York: Pantheon.

Hesmondhalgh, D. (2008) "Cultural and creative industries," in T. Bennett (ed.), *The SAGE Handbook of Cultural Analysis*. London and Thousand Oaks, CA: Sage, pp. 552–69.

Hesmondhalgh, D. (2010) "Media industry studies, media production studies," in J. Curran (ed.), *Media and Society*, 5th edn. London and New York: Bloomsbury.

Hesmondhalgh, D. (2012) *Cultural Industries*, 2nd edn. London and Thousand Oaks, CA: Sage.

Hesmondhalgh, D., and Baker, S. (2011) *Creative Labour: Media Work in Three Cultural Industries*. New York and London: Routledge.

Hesmondhalgh, D., and Toynbee, J. (eds) (2008) *The Media and Social Theory*. London: Routledge.

Hill, A. (2005) *Reality TV: Audiences and Factual Television*. London and New York: Routledge.

Hill Collins, P. (1986) "Learning from the outsider within: the sociological significance of black feminist thought." *Social Problems* 33(6): S14–S32.

Hill Collins, P. (2000) *Black Feminist Thought: Knowledge, Consciousness, and the Politics of Empowerment*, 2nd edn. New York and London: Routledge.

Hilmes, M. (ed.) (2007) *NBC: America's Network*. Berkeley: University of California.

Hirsch, P. (1972) "Processing fads and fashions: an organization-set analysis of cultural industry system." *American Journal of Sociology* 77: 639–59.

Hirsch, P. (2000) "Cultural industries revisited." *Organization Science* 11: 356–61.

Hobson, D. (1982) *Crossroads, the Drama of a Soap Opera.* London: Methuen.

Hoffner, C., and Cantor, J. (1991) "Perceiving and responding to mass media characters," in J. Bryant and D. Zillmann (eds), *Responding to the Screen: Reception and Reaction Processes.* Hillsdale, NJ: Lawrence Erlbaum Associates, pp. 63–101.

Hogan, B. (2010) "The presentation of self in the age of social media: distinguishing performances and exhibitions online." *Bulletin of Science, Technology & Society* 30(6): 377–86.

Hollows, J., and Moseley, R. (eds) (2006) *Feminism in Popular Culture.* Oxford and New York: Berg.

Holmes, S., and Jermyn, D. (eds) (2004) *Understanding Reality Television.* London and New York: Routledge.

Holmwood, J. (2010) "Sociology's misfortune: disciplines, interdisciplinarity and the impact of audit culture." *British Journal of Sociology* 61: 639–58.

Holt, J., and Perren, A. (2009) *Media Industries: History, Theory, and Method.* Oxford: Wiley-Blackwell.

Hoover, S. M., Schofield Clark, L., and Alter, D. F. (eds) (2004) *Media, Home, and Family.* New York: Routledge.

Hughes, N., and Lonie, S. (2007) "M-PESA: mobile money for the 'unbanked' turning cellphones into 24-hour tellers in Kenya." *Innovations: Technology, Governance, Globalization* 2(1–2): 63–81.

Humphreys, L. (2011) "Who's watching whom? A study of interactive technology and surveillance." *Journal of Communication* 61(4): 575–95.

Humphreys, S. (2008) "Ruling the virtual world: governance in massively multiplayer online games." *European Journal of Cultural Studies* 11(2): 149–71.

Hunt, D. (1997) *Screening the Los Angeles "Riots."* Cambridge, UK: Cambridge University Press.

Huntington, S. (2011) *The Clash of Civilizations and the Remaking of World Order.* New York: Simon and Schuster.

Illich, I. (1971) *De-schooling Society.* Harmondsworth: Penguin.

Illouz, E. (2003) *Oprah Winfrey and the Glamour of Misery.* New York: Columbia University Press.

Isber, C., and Cantor, M. (1975) "Report of the Task Force on Women in Public Broadcasting." Corporation for Public Broadcasting, Washington, DC.

Ishii, K. (2006) "Implications of mobility: the uses of personal communication media in everyday life." *Journal of Communication* 56: 346–65.

Ito, M. (2005) "Mobile phones, Japanese youth and the replacement of social contact," in R. Ling and P. Pedersen (eds), *Mobile Communications: Renegotiation of the Social Sphere.* London: Springer, pp. 131–48.

Jacobs, N. (1959) *Culture for the Millions? Mass Media in Modern Society.* Beacon Press.

Jacobs, R. (2000) *Race, Media and the Crisis of Civil Society: From Watts to Rodney King*. Cambridge, UK: Cambridge University Press.

Jacobs, R. N. (2009) "Culture, the public sphere, and media sociology: a search for a classical founder in the work of Robert Park." *American Sociologist* 40: 149–66.

Jacobs, R. (2012) "Entertainment media and the aesthetic public sphere," in J. Alexander, R. Jacobs, and P. Smith (eds), *Oxford Handbook of Cultural Sociology*. New York: Oxford University Press, pp. 318–42.

Jacobs, R. and McKernan, B. (unpublished manuscript) "Global Media, Culture, and Critique: British and Australian News Narratives about American Television".

Jacobs, R., and Townsley, E. (2011) *The Space of Opinion: Media Intellectuals and the Public Sphere*. New York: Oxford University Press.

Jacobs, R., and Wild, N. (forthcoming) "A cultural sociology of *The Daily Show* and *The Colbert Report*." *American Journal of Cultural Sociology* 1: 69–95.

Jensen, R. (2007) "The digital provide: information (technology), market performance and welfare in the South Indian fisheries sector." *The Quarterly Journal of Economics* 122: 879–924.

Jhally, S., and Lewis, J. (1992) *Enlightened Racism: The Cosby Show, Audiences, and the Myth of the American Dream*. Boulder, CO: Westview Press.

Johns, J. (2006) "Video games production networks: value capture, power relations and embeddedness," *Journal of Economic Geography* 6(2): 151–80.

Johnson, P., Sears, D., and McConahay, J. (1971) "Black invisibility, the press, and the Los Angeles riots." *American Journal of Sociology* 76: 698–721.

Johnson, R. (1986/7) "What is cultural studies anyway?" *Social Text* 16: 38–80.

Johnson, V. E. (2008) *Heartland TV: Prime-time Television and the Struggle for US Identity*. New York and London: New York University Press.

Jowett, G., Jarvie, I., and Fuller, K. (1996) *Children and the Movies: Media Influence and the Payne Fund Controversy*. Cambridge, UK: Cambridge University Press.

Jurgenson, N., and Ritzer, G. (2012) "The internet, Web 2.0, and beyond," in G. Ritzer (ed.), *The Wiley-Blackwell Companion to Sociology*. New York: Wiley-Blackwell, pp. 626–48.

Kannis, P. (1991) *Making Local News*. Chicago: University of Chicago Press.

Kaplan, E. A. (ed.) (1978) *Women in Film Noir*. London: British Film Institute.

Kaplan, E. A. (1983) *Women and Film: Both Sides of the Camera*. London: Methuen.

Karim, K. (2002) "Making sense of the 'Islamic peril': journalism as cultural practice," in B. Zelizer and S. Allan (eds), *Journalism after September 11*. London: Routledge, pp. 101–16.

Katz, E. (1957) "The two-step flow of communication, an up-to-date report on an hypothesis." *Public Opinion Quarterly* 21(1): 61–78.

Katz, E. (1963) "The diffusion of new ideas and practices," in Wilbur Schramm (ed.), *The Science of Human Communication*. Basic Books, pp. 77–93.

Katz, E. (1983) "Return of the humanities and sociology." *Journal of Communication* 33: 51–2.

Katz, E. (2009) "Why sociology abandoned communication." *American Sociologist* 40: 167–74.

Katz, E., and Lazarsfeld, P. (1955) *Personal Influence: The Part Played by People in the Flow of Mass Communication*. The Free Press.

Katz, E., and Liebes, T. (2007) "'No more peace!': how disaster, terror and war have upstaged media events." *International Journal of Communication* 1: 157–66.

Katz, E., and Pooley, J. (2008) "Further notes on why American sociology abandoned mass communication research." *Journal of Communication* 58: 767–86.

Katz, E., Blumler, J., and Gurevitch, M. (1973/4) "Uses and gratifications research." *Public Opinion Quarterly* 37(4) (Winter): 509–23.

Katz, J. E., and Rice, R. E. (2002) "The telephone as an instrument of faith, hope, terror and redemption: America, 9-11." *Prometheus* 20: 247–53.

Kavoori, A. and Chadha, K. (2009) "The cultural turn in international communication." *Journal of Broadcasting & Electronic Media* 53(2): 336–46.

Keane, J. (2008) *The Life and Death of Democracy*. New York: Simon & Schuster.

Keck, M., and Sikkink, K. (1998) *Activists Beyond Borders: Advocacy Networks in International Politics*. Ithaca: Cornell University Press.

Keller, M. (2007) *America's Three Regimes: A New Political History*. New York: Oxford University Press.

Kilbourne, J. (1999) *Can't Buy My Love: How Advertising Changes the Way We Think and Feel*. New York: Simon & Schuster.

Kim, M.-J. and Chung, A. Y. (2005) "Consuming orientalism: images of Asian American women in multicultural advertising." *Qualitative Sociology* 28(1): 67–91.

Kirkpatrick, D. (2010) *The Facebook Effect: The Real Inside Story of Mark Zuckerberg and the World's Fastest-Growing Company*. London: Virgin.

Kirkpatrick, G. (2004) *Critical Technology*. London: Ashgate.

Kirkpatrick, G. (2008) *Technology and Social Power*. Basingstoke: Palgrave.

Kirkpatrick, G. (2011) *Aesthetic Theory and the Video Game*. Manchester: Manchester University Press.

Kleis Nielsen, R. (2012) *Ten Years that Shook the Media World: Big Questions and Big Trends in International Media Developments*. Oxford: Reuters Institute for the Study of Journalism.

Kompare, D. (2006) "Publishing flow: DVD box sets and the reconception of television." *Television and New Media* 7: 335–60.

Kornhauser, W. (1959) *The Politics of Mass Society.* The Free Press.

Kreps, G. L., and Maibach, E. W. (2008) "Transdisciplinary science: the nexus between communication and public health." *Journal of Communication* 588: 723–48.

Kuhn, A. (1982) *Women's Pictures: Feminism and Cinema.* London: Routledge and Kegan Paul.

Kuipers, G. (2011) "Cultural globalization as the emergence of a transnational cultural field: transnational television and national media landscapes in four European countries." *American Behavioral Scientist* 55(5): 541–57.

Lamont, M. (2009) *How Professors Think: Inside the Curious World of Academic Judgment.* Cambridge, MA: Harvard University Press.

Lamont, M., and Thévenot, L. (eds) (2000) *Comparative Cultural Sociology.* Cambridge, UK: Cambridge University Press.

Landes, D. S. (1983) *Revolution in Time: Clocks and the Making of the Modern World.* Cambridge, MA: Belknap.

Larkin, B. (2008) *Signal and Noise: Media, Infrastructure, and Urban Culture in Nigeria.* Durham and London: Duke University Press.

Lash, S., and Lury, C. (2007) *Global Culture Industry.* Cambridge, UK: Polity.

Latham, K. (2009) "Media, the Olympics and the search for the 'real China.'" *The China Quarterly* 197: 25–43.

Latour, B. (2005) "From Realpolitik to Dingpolitik, or how to make things public," in B. Latour and P. Weibel (eds), *Making Things Public: Atmospheres of Democracy.* Oxford: Oxford University Press, pp. 14–41.

Laurel, B. (1993) *Computers as Theatre.* Addison-Wesley

Law, J. (2009) "Actor network theory and material semiotics," in Bryan S. Turner (ed.), *The New Blackwell Companion to Social Theory.* Oxford: Wiley-Blackwell, pp. 141–58.

Lazarsfeld, P., Berelson, B., and Gaudet, H. (1944) *The People's Choice: How the Voter Makes up his Mind in a Presidential Campaign.* Columbia University Press.

Leblanc, L. (1999) *Pretty in Punk: Girls' Gender Resistance in a Boys' Subculture.* Rutgers University Press.

Lee, C.-C., Man Chan, J., Pan, Z. and So, C. Y. K. (2000) "National prisms of a 'global media event,'" in J. Curran and M. Gurevitch (eds), *Mass Media and Society*, 3rd edn. London: Arnold, pp. 295–309.

Lengermann, P. M., and Niebrugge-Brantley, J. (2002) "Back to the future: settlement sociology, 1885–1930." *The American Sociologist* 33(3): 5–20.

Lenhart, A. (2009) *Teens and Sexting.* A Pew Internet & American Life Project Report.

Lenhart, A., Ling, R., Campbell, S., and Purcell, K. (2010) *Teens and Mobile Phones.* Washington, DC: Pew Research Center.

Leno, J. (2008, May 1) "Jay Leno's green garage." *Popular Mechanics* http://www.popularmechanics.com/cars/jayleno/green-garage/4261712, accessed October 4, 2013..

Leuchtenburg, W. (1995) *The Supreme Court Reborn*. New York: Oxford University Press.

Levine, R.V. (1998) *A Geography of Time: The Temporal Misadventures of a Social Psychologist, or How Every Culture Keeps Time Just a Little Bit Differently*. New York: Basic.

Levy, S. (1984) *Hackers: Heroes of the Digital Revolution*. Harmondsworth: Penguin

Lewin, K. (1951) *Field Theory in Social Science*. New York: Harper & Row.

Lewis, B. (2003) *What Went Wrong? The Clash between Islam and Modernity in the Middle East*. New York: Harper.

Lewis, K., Kaufman, J., and Christakis, N. (2008) "The taste for privacy: an analysis of college student privacy settings in an online social network." *Journal of Computer-Mediated Communication* 14(1): 79–100.

Lichter, R. S., Lichter, L. S., and Rothman, S. (1994) *Prime Time: How TV Portrays American Culture*. Washington, DC and Lanham, MD: Regnery Publishers.

Licoppe, C. (2004) "Connected presence: the emergence of a new repertoire for managing social relationships in a changing communications technoscape." *Environment and Planning: Society and Space* 22: 135–56.

Licoppe, C. (2007) "Co-proximity events: weaving mobility and technology into social encounters," in K. Nyiri (ed.), *Towards a Philosophy of Telecommunications Convergence*. Budapest: T-Mobile.

Lie, J., and Abelmann, N. (1999) "The 1992 Los Angeles riots and the 'black–Korean conflict,'" in K. Kim (ed.), *Koreans in the Hood: Conflict with African-Americans*. Baltimore: Johns Hopkins University Press, pp. 75–90.

Liebes, T., and Kampf, Z. (2009) "From black and white to shades of gray: Palestinians in the Israeli media during the Second Intifada." *International Journal of Press/Politics* 14(4): 434–53.

Liebes, T., and Katz, E. (1993) *The Export of Meaning: Cross-Cultural Readings of Dallas*. Cambridge, UK: Polity.

Lindlof, T. (ed.) (1987) *Natural Audiences: Qualitative Research of Media Uses and Effects*. Ablex.

Ling, R. (1997) "'One can talk about common manners!'" The use of mobile telephones in inappropriate situations," in L. Haddon (ed.), *Themes in Mobile Telephony Final Report of the COST 248 Home and Work Group*. Stockholm: Telia.

Ling, R. (2004) *The Mobile Connection: The Cell Phone's Impact on Society*. San Francisco: Morgan Kaufmann.

Ling, R. (2008a) "Mobile communication and teen emancipation," in G. Goggin and L. Hjorth (eds), *Mobile Technologies: From Telecommunications to Media*. New York: Routledge.

Ling, R. (2008b) *New Tech, New Ties: How Mobile Communication is Reshaping Social Cohesion.* Cambridge, MA: MIT Press.

Ling, R. (2012a) *Taken for Grantedness: The Embedding of Mobile Communication into Society.* Cambridge, MA: MIT Press.

Ling, R. (2012b) "Mobile phones and digital *Gemeinschaft*: social cohesion in the era of cars, clocks and mobile phones," in *Local and Mobile: Linking Mobilities, Mobile Communication and Locative Media.* Presented at the Local and Mobile: Linking mobilities, mobile communication and locative media, Raleigh, NC.

Ling, R. (2012c) "From Ubicomp to Ubiex(pectations)," in 11th ICMB Conference on Adoption, Use and Effect of Mobile Systems and Applications (21–22 June). Presented at the 11th ICMB Conference on adoption, use and effect of Mobile Systems and Applications, Delft.

Ling, R., Baron, N., Lenhart, A., and Campbell, S. (2010) "'Girls text really weird': cross-gendered texting among teens." Association of Internet Researchers.

Ling, R., Bertel, T., and Sundsøy, P. (2012) "The socio-demographics of texting: an analysis of traffic data." *New Media & Society* 14: 280–97.

Lippmann, W. (1997 [1922]) *Public Opinion.* New York: The Free Press.

Litt, E. (2012) "Knock, knock. Who's there? The imagined audience." *Journal of Broadcasting & Electronic Media* 56(3): 330–45.

Livingstone, S. (2005) *Audiences and Publics.* Intellectual Press

Livingstone, S. (2009) "On the mediation of everything." *Journal of Communication* 59(1): 1–18.

Livingstone, S., and Lunt, P. (1994) *Talk on Television: Audience Participation and Public Debate.* London and New York: Routledge.

Livingstone, S., and Press, A. (2006) "Taking audience research into the age of new media: old problems and new challenges," in M. White, J. Schwoch, and D. Goankar (eds), *Cultural Studies and Methodological Issues.* London: Basil Blackwell, pp. 175–200.

Loomis, B., and Cigler, A. (1998) "Introduction: the changing nature of interest group politics," in A. Cigler and B. Loomis (eds), *Interest Group Politics,* 5th edn. Washington, DC: CQ Press, pp. 1–32.

Lopes, P. (2009) *Demanding Respect: The Evolution of the American Comic Book.* Philadelphia: Temple University Press.

Lorber, J. (2006) "Shifting paradigms and challenging categories." *Social Problems* 53(4): 448–53.

Lorde, A. (1984) *Sister Outsider.* Berkeley, CA: Crossing Press.

Lotz, A. (2001) "Postfeminist television criticism: rehabilitating critical terms and identifying postfeminist attributes." *Feminist Media Studies* 1(1): 105–21.

Lotz, A. D. (2006) *Redesigning Women: Television after the Network Era.* Urbana and Chicago: University of Illinois Press.

Lowney, K. (1999) *Baring Our Souls: TV Talk Shows and the Religion of Recovery.* New York: Aldine de Gruyter.

Lu, X. (2009) "Ritual, television, and state ideology: rereading CCTV's 2006 Spring Festival gala," in Y. Zhu and C. Berry (eds), *TV China*. Bloomington: Indiana University Press, pp. 111–25.

Lull, J. (1990) *Inside Family Viewing*. Comedia.

Macdonald, M. (2003) *Exploring Media Discourse*. London: Arnold.

Madigan, R., Johnson, S., and Linton, P. (1995) "The language of psychology: APA style as epistemology." *American Psychologist* 50(6): 428–36.

Mahapatra, B. et al. (2012) "HIV risk behaviors among female sex workers using cell phones for client solicitation in India." *Journal of AIDS and Clinical Research* S1: 14.

Magnuson, M. J., and Dundes, L. (2008) "Gender differences in 'social portraits' reflected in MySpace profiles." *CyberPsychology & Behavior* 11(2): 239–41.

Malinowski, B. (1922) *Argonauts of the Western Pacific*. Routledge

Manga, J. (2003) *Talking Trash: The Cultural Politics of Daytime Talk Shows*. New York: New York University Press.

Manin, B. (1997) *The Principles of Representative Government*. Cambridge, UK: Cambridge University Press.

Manza, J., and Brooks, C. (2012) "How sociology lost public opinion: a genealogy of a missing concept in the study of the political." *Sociological Theory* 30(2): 89–113.

Marcus, G. (1995) "Ethnography in/of the world system: the emergence of multi-sited ethnography." *Annual Review of Anthropology* 24: 95–117.

Marcuse, H. (1964) *One-Dimensional Man*. London: RKP.

Marcuse, H. (1978) *The Aesthetic Dimension*. London: Macmillan.

Marcuse, H. (1998 [1941]) "Some social implications of modern technology," in Douglas Kellner (ed.), *Collected Papers of Herbert Marcuse, Vol. One: Technology, War and Fascism*. London: Routledge, pp. 41–65.

Martin, J. L. (2003) "What is field theory?" *American Journal of Sociology* 109: 1–49.

Martín-Barbero, J. (2003) "Proyectos de modernidad en América Latina." *Metapolítica* 29: 35–51.

Marwick, A. (2005) "Selling your self: identity online in the age of a commodified internet." MA. University of Washington.

Marwick, A. (2010) "Status update: celebrity, publicity and self-branding in Web 2.0." PhD. New York University.

Marwick, A. (2012) "The public domain: surveillance in everyday life." *Surveillance & Society* 9(4): 378–93.

Marwick, A. E., and boyd, d. (2011) "I tweet honestly, I tweet passionately: Twitter users, context collapse, and the imagined audience." *New Media & Society* 13(1): 114–33.

Marwick, A., and Ellison, N. B. (2012) "'There isn't wifi in Heaven!' Negotiating visibility on Facebook memorial pages." *Journal of Broadcasting & Electronic Media* 56(3): 378–400.

Marx, K. (1994 [1852]) *The Eighteenth Brumaire of Louis Bonaparte*. New York: International Publications.

Maxwell, R. (1996) "Out of kindness and into difference: the values of global market research." *Media, Culture & Society* 18(1): 105–26.

Maxwell, R. (ed.) (2001) *Culture Works*. Minneapolis: University of Minnesota Press.

Maxwell, R., and Miller, T. (2012) *Greening the Media*. New York: Oxford University Press.

Mayer, V. (2003) *Producing Dreams, Consuming Youth: Mexican Americans and Mass Media*. New Brunswick, NJ: Rutgers University Press.

Mayer, V. (2011) *Below the Line: Producers and Production Studies in the New Television Economy*. Durham, NC: Duke University Press.

Mayer, V., Banks, M., and Caldwell, J. T. (2009) *Production Studies: Cultural Studies of Media Industries*. New York and Abingdon: Routledge.

Mayne, J. (1990) *The Woman at the Keyhole: Feminism and Women's Cinema*. The Association of American University Presses.

Mayne, J. (1993) *Cinema and Spectatorship*. London and New York: Routledge.

Maynes, M. J. (1982) "Foreword," in R. Johnson, G. McClennan, B. Schwartz, and D. Sutton (eds), *Making Histories: Studies in History Writing and Politics*. Minneapolis: University of Minnesota Press, pp. 4–6.

McCain, Thomas (ed.) (1982) Qualitative Methods issue. *Journal of Broadcasting* (Fall) 26(4).

McCarthy, A. (2001) *Ambient Television: Visual Culture and Public Space*. Durham, NC: Duke University Press.

McChesney, R. W. (2013). *Digital Disconnect: How Capitalism Is Turning the Internet Against Democracy*. New York: New Press.

McChesney, R. W., and Bellamy Foster, J. (2003) "The commercial tidal wave." *Monthly Review* 54(10): 1–16.

McCraw, T. (1984) *Prophets of Regulation*. Cambridge, MA: Harvard University Press.

McCubbins, M., and Schwartz, T. (1984) "Congressional oversight overlooked: police patrols versus fire alarms." *American Journal of Political Science* 28: 165–79.

McCurdy, P. (2012) "Social movements, protest and mainstream media." *Sociology Compass* 6: 244–55.

McGuigan, J. (1992) *Cultural Populism*. London: Routledge.

McGuire, W. J. (1976) "The yin and yang of progress in social psychology: seven koan," in L. H. Strickland, F. E. Aboud, and K. J. Gergen (eds), *Social Psychology in Transition*. New York: Plenum Press, pp. 33–49.

McKercher, C., and Mosco, V. (eds) (2007) *Knowledge Workers in the Information Society*. Lanham: Lexington.

McNeill, A. (1996) *Total Television*, 4th edn. New York: Penguin Books.

McPhail, T. L. (2009) "Introduction to development communication," in

Thomas L. McPhail (ed.), *Development Communication: Reframing the Role of the Media*. Malden: Wiley-Blackwell, pp. 1–20.

McQuail, D. (1969) *Towards a Sociology of Mass Communications*. London: Collier-Macmillan.

McQuail, D. (1972) *Sociology of Mass Communications: Selected Readings*. Penguin.

McQuail, D. (2008) *Mass Communication Theory*. London: Sage.

McRobbie, A. (1977) *Jackie: An Ideology of Adolescent Femininity*. Birmingham: CCCS, University of Birmingham.

McRobbie, A. (2004) "Postfeminism and popular culture." *Feminist Media Studies* 4(3): 255–64.

McRobbie, A. (2009) *The Aftermath of Feminism: Gender, Culture, and Social Change*. London and Los Angeles: Sage.

Mead, G. H. (1934) *Mind, Self and Society*. Chicago: University of Chicago Press.

Medvetz, T. (2012) *Think Tanks in America*. Chicago: University of Chicago Press.

Meehan, E. (2002) "Gendering the commodity audience: critical media research, feminism, and political economy," in E. Meehan and E. Riordan (eds), *Sex and Money: Feminism and Political Economy in the Media*. Minneapolis and London: University of Minnesota Press, pp. 209–22.

Meehan, E. R., and Riordan, E. (eds) (2001) *Sex and Work: Feminism and Political Economy in the Media*. Minneapolis: University of Minnesota Press.

Mellancamp, P. (1995) *A Fine Romance: Five Ages of Film Feminism*. Philadelphia: Temple University Press.

Mendelson, A. L., and Papacharissi, Z. (2010) "Look at us: collective narcissism in college student Facebook photo galleries," in Z. Papacharissi (ed.), *A Networked Self: Identity, Community, and Culture on Social Network Sites*. New York: Routledge, pp. 251–73.

Metz, C. (1975) "The imaginary signifier." *Screen* 16(2): 14–76.

Metz, C. (1986) *The Imaginary Signifier: Psychoanalysis and the Cinema*. Bloomington: Indiana University Press.

Meyer, D. S., and Tarrow, S. (1998) "A movement society: contentious politics for a new century," in D. S. Meyer and S. Tarrow (eds), *The Social Movement Society*. Lanham, MD: Rowman and Littlefield, pp. 1–29.

Meyrowitz, J. (1985) *No Sense of Place: The Impact of Electronic Media on Social Behavior*. Oxford, UK: Oxford University Press.

Miège, B. (1989) *The Capitalization of Cultural Production*. New York: International General.

Miliband, R. (1977) *Marxism and Politics*. New York: Oxford University Press.

Miller, T. (2009) "Cybertarians of the world unite: you have nothing to lose but your tubes!" in P. Snickars and P. Vondereau (eds), *The YouTube Reader*. Stockholm: National Library of Sweden, pp. 424–40.

Miller, T. (2010) "Film and society," in James Curran (ed.), *Media and Society*, 5th edn. London: Bloomsbury Academic, pp. 18–37.

Miller, T. (2012) "Being 'accountable': TV audiences and surveillance," in Göran Bolin (ed.), *Cultural Technologies: The Shaping of Culture in Media and Society*. London: Routledge, pp. 87–102

Miller, T., Govil, N., McMurria, J., Maxwell, R., and Wang, T. (2005) *Global Hollywood 2*. London: British Film Institute.

Mills, C. Wright (1959) *The Sociological Imagination*. New York: Oxford University Press.

Mische, A. (2008) *Partisan Publics: Communication and Contention across Brazilian Youth Activist Networks*. Princeton: Princeton University Press.

Mitchell, A. M. (1929) *Children and the Movies*. Chicago: University of Chicago Press.

Modleski, T. (1990) *Loving with a Vengeance: Mass-Produced Fantasies for Women*. New York: Routledge.

Moeran, B. (2010) "The book fair as a tournament of values." *Journal of the Royal Anthropological Institute* 16: 138–54.

Moeran, B., and Strandgaard Pedersen, J. (2011) "Introduction," in B. Moeran and J. Strandgaard Pedersen (eds), *Negotiating Values in the Creative Industries: Fairs, Festivals, and Competitive Events*. Cambridge and New York: Cambridge University Press.

Molotch, H., and Lester, M. (1974) "News as purposive behaviour: on the strategic use of routine events, accidents and scandals." *American Sociological Review* 33: 101–12.

Monk, A., Carroll, J., Parker, S., and Blythe, M. (2004) "Why are mobile phones annoying?" *Behavior and Information Technology* 23(1): 33–41.

Morley, D. (1986) *Family Television: Cultural Power and Domestic Leisure*. London: Comedia.

Morris, N., and Waisbord, S. (eds) (2001) *Media and Globalization: Why the State Matters*. Rowman and Littlefield.

Morrison, D. E. (1998) *The Search for a Method: Focus Groups and the Development of Mass Communication Research*. University of Luton Press.

Mosco, V. (2004) *The Digital Sublime*. Cambridge, MA: MIT Press.

Mosco, V., and McKercher, C. (2008) *The Laboring of Communication: Will Knowledge Workers of the World Unite?* Lanham: Lexington.

Mosco, V., McKercher, C., and Huws, U. (eds) (2010) *Getting the Message: Communications Workers and Global Value Chains*. London: Merlin Books.

Mosley, R. and Read, J. (2002) "Having it Ally": Popular television (post-) feminism." *Feminist Media Studies* 21: 231–49.

Mukherjee, R. (2003) "Between enemies and traitors: black press coverage of September 11 and the predicament of national 'others,'" in S. Chermak, F. Bailey, and M. Brown (eds), *Media Representations of September 11*. Westport, CT: Praeger, pp. 29–46.

Mulvey, L. (1975) "Visual pleasure and narrative cinema." *Screen* 16(3): 6–18.

Mumford, L. (1934) *Technics and Civilization*. San Diego: Harvest.

Munsterberg, H., and Lansdale, A. (2001 [1916]) *Hugo Munsterberg on Film: The Photoplay: A Psychological Study and Other Writings*. Abingdon, UK: Routledge.

Murdock, G. (1973) "Political deviance: the press presentation of a militant mass demonstration," in S. Cohen and J. Young (eds), *The Manufacture of News Production: A Reader*. Beverly Hills: Sage Publications, pp. 206–25.

Murray, S., and Ouellette, L. (2009) *Remaking Television Culture*. New York and London: New York University Press.

Murthy, D. (2012) *Twitter: Social Communication in the Twitter Age*. Cambridge, UK: Polity.

Naficy, H. (1993) *The Making of Exile Cultures: Iranian Television in Los Angeles*. Minneapolis: University of Minnesota Press.

The Nation (2013, February 22) "DiCaprio calls on Yingluck to ban ivory trade." The Nation, available at www.nationmultimedia.com/national/ DiCaprio-calls-on-Yingluck-to-ban-ivory-trade-30200375.html, accessed September 1, 2013.

National Science Foundation (2011) Doctorate recipients from US universities 2011. Arlington, VA: National Science Foundation. Available at: www.nsf.gov/statistics/sed/digest/2011/, accessed September 2, 2013.

Negri, A. (2007) *Goodbye Mister Socialism*. Paris: Seuil.

Negroponte, N. (1995) *Being Digital*. London: Coronet.

Neville, R. (1971) *Playpower*. London: Paladin.

Newcomb, H., and Hirsch, P. (1983) "Television as a cultural forum." *Quarterly Review of Film* 8: 45–55.

Nichols, B. (1981) *Ideology and the Image: Social Representation in the Cinema and Other Media*. Bloomington: Indiana University Press.

Nickerson, R. S. (1976) "On conversational interaction with computers," Proceedings of the ACM/SIGGRAPH workshop, Pittsburgh.

Nielsen, R. (2012) "Is 'post-industrial journalism' a US-only phenomenon, or are the lessons worldwide?" Nieman Lab. Available at www.niemanlab. org/2012/12/is-post-industrial-journalism-a-u-s-only-phenomenon-or-are-the-lessons-worldwide/, accessed on September 3, 2013.

Nightingale, V. (1993) "What's ethnographic about ethnographic audience research?" in Graeme Turner (ed.), *Nation, Culture, Text: Australian Cultural and Media Studies*. London and New York: Routledge, pp. 164–78.

Ogan, C. L., Bashir, M., Camaj, L. et al. (2009) "Development communication: the state of research in an era of ICTs and globalization." *Gazette* 71(8): 655–70.

Olick, J. K., Vinitzky-Seroussi, V., and Levy, D. (2011) "Introduction," in J. K. Olick, V. Vinitzky-Seroussi, and D. Levy (eds), *The Collective Memory Reader*. New York: Oxford University Press, pp. 3–62.

Ong, A. (2006) *Neoliberalism as Exception: Mutations in Citizenship and Sovereignty*. Durham, NC: Duke University Press.

Orgad, S. (2008) "'Have you seen Bloomberg?' Satellite news channels as agents of the new visibility." *Global Media and Communication* 4(3): 301–27.

Orgad, S. (2009a) "The survivor in contemporary culture and public discourse: a genealogy." *The Communication Review* 12(2): 132–61.

Orgad, S. (2009b) "Watching how others watch us: the Israeli media's treatment of international coverage of the Gaza war." *The Communication Review* 12(3): 250–61.

Orgad, S. (2011) "Proper distance from ourselves: the potential for estrangement in the mediapolis." *International Journal of Cultural Studies* 14(4): 401–21.

Orgad, S. (2012) *Media Representation and the Global Imagination.* Cambridge, UK: Polity.

Ouellette, L., and Hay, J. (2008) *Better Living Through Reality TV.* Oxford: Wiley-Blackwell.

Owens, T. J., Robinson, D. T., and Smith-Lovin, L. (2010) "Three faces of identity." *Annual Review of Sociology* 36(1): 477–99.

Pan, Z. (2010) "Enacting the family-nation on a global stage: an analysis of CCTV's spring festival gala," in M. Curtin and H. Shah (eds), *Re-Orienting Global Communication: India and China Beyond Borders.* Urbana-Champaign, IL: University of Illinois Press, pp. 240–59.

Papacharissi, Z. (2010) "Conclusion: a networked self," in Z. Papacharissi (ed.), *A Networked Self: Identity, Community, and Culture on Social Network Sites.* New York: Routledge, pp. 304–18.

Papacharissi, Z., and Gibson, P. L. (2011) "Fifteen minutes of privacy: privacy, sociality, and publicity on social network sites," in S. Trepte and L. Reinecke (eds), *Privacy Online: Perspectives on Privacy and Self-disclosure in the Social Web.* New York: Springer.

Papathanassopoulos, S. (2007) "Financing public service broadcasters in a new era," in E. de Bens (ed.), *Media Between Culture and Commerce.* Chicago: University of Chicago Press/Intellect Books, pp. 151–66.

Parameswaran, R. (1999) "Western romance fiction as English-language media in postcolonial India." *Journal of Communication* 49(3): 84–105.

Parameswaran, R. (2001) "Feminist media ethnography in India: exploring power, gender, and culture in the field." *Qualitative Inquiry* 7(1): 69–103.

Parameswaran, R. (2002) "Reading fictions of romance: gender, sexuality, and nationalism in postcolonial India." *Journal of Communication* 52(4): 832–51.

Parameswaran, R. (2004) "Global queens, national celebrities: tales of feminine triumph in post-liberalization India." *Critical Studies in Media Communication* 21(4): 346–70.

Parekh, B. (2000) *Rethinking Multiculturalism: Cultural Diversity and Political Theory.* Basingstoke: Palgrave.

Park, D. (2008) "The two-step flow vs. the lonely crowd: conformity and the media in the 1950s," in D. Park and J. Pooley (eds), *The History of Media and Communication Research*, pp. 251–68.

Park, D., and Pooley, J. (eds) (2008) *The History of Media and Communication Research: Contested Memories*. New York: Peter Lang.

Park, R. (1904 [1972]) *The Crowd and the Public*. Chicago: University of Chicago Press.

Park, R. (1922) *The Immigrant Press and its Control*. Harper and Bros.

Park, R. (1923) "The natural history of the newspaper." *American Journal of Sociology* 29(3) (Nov.): 273–89.

Park, R., and Burgess, E. (1921) *Introduction to the Science of Sociology*. Chicago: University of Chicago Press.

Patel, S. (ed.) (2010) *The ISA Handbook of Diverse Sociological Traditions*. London: Sage Publications.

Patterson, S. (1978) "The semi-sovereign congress," in A. King (ed.), *The New American Political System*. Washington, DC: American Enterprise Institute, pp. 125–77.

Peck, J. (2008) *The Age of Oprah: Cultural Icon for the Neoliberal Era*. Paradigm Publishers.

Pendakur, M. (1990) *Canadian Dreams and American Control*. Toronto: Garamond.

Penley, C. (ed.) (1988) *Feminism and Film Theory*. New York: Routledge.

Penley, C. (1989) *The Future of an Illusion: Film, Feminism, and Psychoanalysis*. Minneapolis: University of Minnesota Press.

Peters, J. D., and Pooley, J. (2012) "Media and communications," in G. Ritzer (ed.), *The Wiley-Blackwell Companion to Sociology*. New York: Wiley-Blackwell, pp. 402–17.

Peterson, R. A. (1990) "Why 1955? Explaining the advent of rock music." *Popular Music* 9: 97–116.

Peterson, R. A., and Anand, N. (2004) "The production of culture perspective." *Annual Review of Sociology* 30: 311–34.

Petras, J., and Veltmeyer, H. (2011) *Social Movements in Latin America: Neoliberalism and Popular Resistance*. Basingstoke: Palgrave Macmillan.

Pew Foundation [Project for Excellence in Journalism] (2012) State of the media report. Available at: http://stateofthemedia.org/2011/overview-2/key-findings/.

Pfau, M. (2008) "Epistemological and disciplinary intersections." *Journal of Communication* 58(4): 597–602.

Pickering, M. (2001) *Stereotyping: The Politics of Representation*. New York: Palgrave.

Piette, John D., and Kerr, E. A. (2006) "The impact of comorbid chronic conditions on diabetes care." *Diabetes Care* 29(3): 725–31.

Pinch, T. (2010) "The invisible technologies of Goffman's sociology from the merry-go-round to the internet." *Technology and Culture* 51(2): 409–24.

Piore, M. J., and Sabel, C. F. (1984) *The Second Industrial Divide: Possibilities for Prosperity*. New York: Basic Books.

Pitcher, K. (2006) "The staging of agency in 'Girls Gone Wild.'" *Critical Studies in Media Communication* 23(3): 200–18.

Pooley, J. (2006) "Fifteen pages that shook the field: *Personal Influence*, Edward Shils, and the remembered history of mass communication research." *The Annals of the Academy of Political and Social Science* 608, November.

Pooley, J. (2010) "The consuming self: from flappers to Facebook," in M. Aronczyk and D. Powers (eds), *Blowing Up the Brand*. New York: Peter Lang Publishing, pp. 71–89.

Pooley, J., and Katz, E. (2008) "Further notes on why American sociology abandoned mass communication research." *Journal of Communication* 58(4): 767–86.

Posner, R. (1997) "The rise and fall of administrative law." *72 Chicago Kent Law Review*: 953–63.

Poster, M. (1995) *The Second Media Age*. Cambridge, UK: Polity

Poster, M. (2006) *Information Please!* Durham, NC: Duke University Press.

Powers, M. (2013) *Humanity's Publics: NGOs, Journalism, and the International Public Sphere*. Unpublished dissertation in Media, Culture, and Communication, New York University.

Press, A. L. (1991) *Women Watching Television: Gender, Class, and Generation in the American Television Experience*. Philadelphia: University of Pennsylvania Press.

Press, A. L. (2010) "Feminism? That's so seventies!" in C. M. Scharff and R. Gill (eds), *New Femininities: Postfeminism, Neoliberalism, and Subjectivity*. London: Palgrave, pp. 117–33.

Press, A. L. (2011) "Feminism and media in the postfeminist era: what to make of the 'feminist' in feminist media studies." *Feminist Media Studies* 11(1): 107–14.

Press, A. L. (2012) "The price of motherhood: feminism and cultural bias." *Communication, Culture, and Critique* 5: 119–24.

Press, A. L. (2013) "Fractured feminism: articulations of feminism, sex, and class by reality TV viewers," in L. Ouellette (ed.), *A Companion to Reality Television*. New York: Wiley-Blackwell.

Press, A. L. (in press) "Feminism LOL: Media Culture and 'feminism on the ground' in a postfeminist age." Manuscript in progress

Press, A. L., and Cole, E. R. (1999) *Speaking of Abortion: Television in the Lives of Women*. Chicago: University of Chicago Press.

Press, A. L., and Tripodi, F. (in press) "Feminism in a postfeminist world: who's hot – and why we care – on the collegiate 'Anonymous Confession Board,'" in C. Carter, L. McLaughlin, and L. Steiner (eds), *The Routledge Companion to Media and Gender*. New York: Routledge.

Probyn, E. (1990) "New traditionalism and postfeminism: TV does the home." *Screen* 31(2): 147–59.

Projansky, S. (2001) *Watching Rape: Film and Television in Postfeminist Culture*. New York and London: New York University Press.

Punathambekar, A. (in press) *From Bombay to Bollywood: The Making of a Global Media Industry*. New York and London: New York University Press.

Putnam, R. (1998) *Bowling Alone*. New York: Simon & Schuster.

Radway, J. (1984) *Reading the Romance: Women, Patriarchy, and Popular Literature*. Chapel Hill: University of North Carolina Press.

Radway, J. (1988) "Reception study: ethnography and the problems of dispersed audiences and nomadic subjects." *Cultural Studies* 2(3): 359–76.

Radway, J. (2008) "What's the matter with reception study? Some thoughts on the disciplinary origins, conceptual constraints, and persistent viability of a paradigm," in P. Goldstein and J. L. Machor (eds), *New Directions in American Reception Study*. New York: Oxford University Press.

Rakow, L. F., and Navarro, V. (1993) "Remote mothering and the parallel shift: women meet the cellular telephone." *Critical Studies in Mass Communication* 10: 144–57.

Ranciere, J. (2009) *The Emancipated Spectator*. London: Verso.

Rapping, E. (1994) *Media-tions: Forays into the Culture and Gender Wars*. Boston: South End Press.

Raz, J. (1994) *Ethics in the Public Domain*. Oxford: Clarendon Press.

Rheingold, H. (2002) *Smart Mobs*. Cambridge, MA: Perseus.

Rhines, J. A. (1996) *Black Film/White Money*. New Brunswick: Rutgers University Press.

Robards, B., and Bennett, A. (2011) "MyTribe: post-subcultural manifestations of belonging on social network sites." *Sociology* 45(2): 303–17.

Roberts, B. (1976) "Naturalistic research into subcultures and deviance," in S. Hall and T. Jefferson, *Resistance through Rituals: Youth Subcultures in Post-War Britain*. Hutchinson, pp. 243–52.

Robertson, C., Sawford, K., Daniel, S. L. et al. (2010) "Mobile phone-based infectious disease surveillance system, Sri Lanka." *Emerging Infectious Diseases* 16(10): 1524.

Robinson, G. (2011) "Thoughts on Lazarsfeld's New York 'radio studies' from the perspective of 2010," in Charles T. Salmon (ed.), *Communication Yearbook* 35: 29–44.

Robson, W. (1998) *Management Information Systems*. London: Pitman Press.

Rodríguez, A. (1999) *Making Latino News: Race, Language, Class*. Thousand Oaks, CA: Sage.

Rodriguez, C. (1997) *Latin Looks: Images of Latinas and Latinos in US Media*. Boulder, CO: Westview Press.

Rodriguez, C. (2004) *Heroes, Lovers and Others: The Story of Latinos in Hollywood*. Washington, DC: Smithsonian Institution Press.

Rogers, E. (1994) *A History of Communication Study: A Biographical Approach*. New York: The Free Press.

Rogers, E. M. (2001) "The Department of Communication at Michigan State University as a seed institution for communication study." *Communication Studies* 52(3): 234–48.

Rose, J. (2003) *On Not Being Able to Sleep: Psychoanalysis and the Modern World*. Princeton, NJ: Princeton University Press.

Rose, N. (2006) "Governmentality." *Annual Review of Law and Social Science* 2: 83–104.

Rosen, C. (2007) "Summer. Virtual friendship and the new narcissism." *The New Atlantis*, pp. 15–31. Available at: www.thenewatlantis.com/publica tions/virtual-friendship-and-the-new-narcissism, accessed 8 January 2013.

Rosen, J. (2002) "September 11 in the mind of American journalism", in B. Zelizer and S. Allen (eds), *Journalism After September 11*. London: Routledge, pp. 27–35.

Rosen, M. (1974) *Popcorn Venus: Women, Movies, and the American Dream*. New York: Avon Books.

Rosen, R. (2000) *The World Split Open: How the Modern Women's Movement Changed America*. New York: Viking.

Rosenberg, B., and White, D. (eds) (1957) *Mass Culture: The Popular Arts in America*. The Free Press

Rosenberg, M. (1979) *Conceiving the Self*. New York: Basic Books.

Rosenfeld, R. (2010) "Sociology: a view from the diaspora." *British Journal of Sociology* 61(4): 666–70.

Ross, C. et al. (2009) "Personality and motivations associated with Facebook use." *Computers in Human Behavior* 25(2): 578–86.

Ross, K. (1996) *Black and White Media: Black Images in Popular Film and Television*. Cambridge, UK: Polity.

Ross, K. (2009) *Gendered Media: Women, Men and Identity Politics*. Lanham, MD: Rowman & Littlefield.

Rossi, P. (1959) "Four landmarks in voting research," in E. Burdick and A. J. Brodbeck (eds), *American Voting Behavior*. The Free Press, pp. 5–54.

Rowlatt, J. (2009, March 6) "Justin does Dallas!" *BBC News*, available at www.bbc.co.uk/blogs/ethicalman/2009/03/justin_does_dallas.html, accessed September 1, 2013.

Ruccio, D. F. and Amariglio, J. (2003) *Postmodern Moments in Modern Economics*. Princeton: Princeton University Press.

Ruch, A. (2009) "World of Warcraft: service or space?" *Game Studies* 9(2): 1.

Ruddock, A. (2008) "Media studies 2.0? Binge drinking and why audiences still matter." *Sociology Compass* 2(1): 1–15.

Ryfe, D. (2012) *Can Journalism Survive? An Inside Look at American Newsrooms*. Cambridge, UK: Polity.

Sacks, H. (1995) *Lectures on Conversation. Vols. I and II*. Ed. Gail Jefferson. Malden: Blackwell.

Saha, A. (2012) "Beards, scarves, halal meat, terrorists, forced marriage': television industries and the production of 'race.'" *Media, Culture and Society* 34(4): 424–38.

Said, E. (2003 [1978]) *Orientalism*. London: Penguin.

Samuel, R. (1981) *People's History and Socialist Theory*. Routledge and Kegan Paul.

Santhanam, L. H., and Rosenstiel, T. (2011) "Why US newspapers suffer more than others." *The State of the News Media* 2010, October. Available at http://stateofthemedia.org/2011/mobile-survey/international-newspaper-economics/, accessed September 3, 2013.

Sassen, S. (2006) *Territory, Authority, Rights: From Medieval to Global Assemblages*. Princeton: Princeton University Press.

Scannell, P. (1996) *Radio, Television and Modern Life*. Cambridge, MA: Wiley-Blackwell.

Scharff, C. (2011) *Repudiating Feminism: Young Women in a Neoliberal World*. Farnham: Ashgate.

Schiller, H. I. (1989) *Culture, Inc.: The Corporate Takeover of Public Expression*. New York: Oxford University Press.

Schiller, D. (2007) *How to Think About Information*. Champaign: University of Illinois Press.

Schippers, M. (2002) *Rockin' Out of the Box: Gender Manuevering in Alternative Hard Rock*. Piscataway, NJ: Rutgers University Press.

Schlesinger, P. (1978) *Putting Reality Together: BBC News*. Constable.

Schlesinger, P. (1991) *Media, State, and Nation: Political Violence and Collective Identities*. London: Sage.

Schlesinger, P., and Tumber, H. (1994) *Reporting Crime: The Media Politics of Criminal Justice*. Oxford, UK: Clarendon Press.

Schneiderman, B. (1997) *Designing the User Interface: Strategies for Effective HCI*. Boston: Addison-Wesley.

Schofield Clark, L. (2003) *From Angels to Aliens: Teenagers, the Media, and the Supernatural*. New York: Oxford University Press.

Schramm, W. (1983) "Unique perspective of communications research." *Journal of Communication* 33: 6–17.

Schudson, M. (1989) "The sociology of news production." *Media, Culture & Society* 11: 263–82.

Schudson, M. (1998) *The Good Citizen: A History of American Civic Life*. New York: The Free Press.

Schudson, M. (2002) "What's unusual about covering politics as usual?" in B. Zelizer and S. Allan (eds), *Journalism After September 11*. New York: Routledge, pp. 36–47.

Schudson, M. (2004) "The place of sociology in the study of political communication." *Political Communication* 21(3): 271–3.

Schudson, M. (2008) *Why Democracies Need an Unlovable Press*. Cambridge, UK: Polity.

Schudson, M. (2010) "Political observatories, databases, and news in the emerging ecology of public information." *Daedalus* 139(2) (Spring): 100–9.

Schwarz, O. (2010) "On friendship, boobs and the logic of the catalogue: online self-portraits as a means for the exchange of capital." *Convergence: The International Journal of Research into New Media Technologies* 16(2): 163–83.

Schwarz, O. (2012) "The new hunter-gatherers: making human interaction productive in the network society." *Theory, Culture & Society* 29(6): 78–98.

Scott, J. (2005) "Sociology and its others: reflections on disciplinary specialisation and fragmentation." *Sociological Research Online* 10(1) (March).

Seale, C. (2003) *Media and Health*. London: Sage.

Seipp, D. J. (2006) "Our law, their law, history, and the citation of foreign law." *Boston University Law Review* 86: 1417–46.

Seiter, E. (1999) *Television and New Media Audiences*. Oxford and New York: Oxford University Press.

Sender, K. (2012) *The Makeover: Reality Television and Reflexive Audiences*. New York and London: New York University Press.

Senft, T. M. (2008) *Camgirls: Celebrity and Community in the Age of Social Networks*. New York: Peter Lang.

Sennett, R. (2006) *The Culture of the New Capitalism*. New Haven, CT: Yale University Press.

Sewell, William H. Jr (1992) "A theory of structure: duality, agency and transformation." *American Journal of Sociology* 98: 1–29.

Sewell, William H. Jr (2005) *Logics of History*. Chicago: University of Chicago Press.

Shah, H. and Thornton, M. (2004) *Newspaper Coverage of Interethnic Conflict: Competing Visions of America*. Thousand Oaks, CA: Sage.

Shattuc, J. (1997) *The Talking Cure: TV Talk Shows and Women*. New York: Routledge.

Sherif, M. (1977) "Crisis in social psychology: some remarks about breaking through the crisis." *Personality and Social Psychology Bulletin* 3: 368–82.

Shively, J. (1990) *Cowboys and Indians: The Perception of Western Films among American Indians and Anglo-Americans*. Palo Alto, CA: Stanford University Press.

Shively, J. (2009) "Cowboys and indians: perceptions of western films among American Indians and Anglos," in Toby Miller (ed.), *The Contemporary Hollywood Reader*. London: Routledge, pp. 409–20.

Shohat, E., and Stam, R. (eds) (2003) *Multiculturalism, Postcoloniality, and Transnational Media*. New Brunswick, NJ: Rutgers University Press.

Shome, R., and Hegde, R. S. (2002a) "Culture, communication, and the challenge of globalization." *Critical Studies in Media Communication* 19(2): 172–89.

Shome, R., and Hegde, R. S. (2002b) "Postcolonial approaches to communication: charting the terrain, engaging the intersections." *Communication Theory* 12(3): 249–70.

Shore, Elena (2004) "Ho Chi Minh Protests." Pacific News Service, available at http://02e1137.netsolhost.com/Villages/Asian/politics_law/archives/pns_hochiminh_protests_0504.asp, accessed September 1, 2013.

Sigal, L. V. (1973) *Reporters and Officials: The Organization and Politics of Newsmaking*. New York: D. C. Heath.

Sigelman, L. (1973) "Reporting the news: an organizational analysis." *American Journal of Sociology* 79(1): 132–51.

Siibak, A. (2009) "Constructing the self through the photo selection – visual impression management on social networking websites." *Cyberpsychology: Journal of Psychosocial Research on Cyberspace* 3(1).

Siibak, A. (2010) "Constructing masculinity on a social networking site: the case-study of visual self-presentations of young men on the profile images of SNS *Rate*." *Young* 18(4): 403–25.

Silverman, K. (1988) *The Acoustic Mirror: The Female Voice in Psychoanalysis and Cinema*. Bloomington, IN: Indiana University Press.

Silverstone R. (1994) *Television and Everyday Life*. London: Routledge.

Silverstone, R. (1999) *Why Study the Media*. London: Sage.

Silverstone, R. (2005) "Mediation and communication," in C. Calhoun, C. Rojek, and B. Turner (eds), *The SAGE Handbook of Sociology*. London: Sage, pp. 188–207.

Silverstone, R. (2007) *Media and Morality: On the Rise of the Mediapolis*. Cambridge, UK: Polity.

Simonson, P. (ed.) (2006) *The Annals of the American Academy of Political and Social Science* (November) 608(1): special issue on *Personal Influence*.

Skocpol, T. (1999) "Advocates without members: the recent transformation of American civic life," in T. Skocpol and M. Fiorina (eds), *Civic Engagement in American Democracy*. Washington, DC: Brookings Institution Press, pp. 461–509.

Small, A., and Vincent, G. (1894) *An Introduction to the Study of Society*. New York: American Book Company.

Smelser, N. (ed.) (1988) *Handbook of Sociology*. Newbury Park, CA: Sage.

Smith, M., and Yanacopulos, H. (2004) "The public faces of development: an introduction." *Journal of International Development* 16(5): 657–64.

Smith, P., Mahdavi, J., Caralho, M., et al. (2008) "Cyberbullying: its nature and impact in secondary school pupils." *Journal of Child Psychology and Psychiatry* 49: 376–85.

Smith, T. (2012) *Barack Obama, Post-Racialism, and the New Politics of Triangulation*. New York: Palgrave Macmillan.

Smith-Shomade, B. E. (2007) *Pimpin' Ain't Easy: Selling Black Entertainment Television*. London: Routledge.

Smulovitz, C., and Peruzzotti, E. (2000) "Societal accountability in Latin America." *Journal of Democracy* 11 (October): 147–58.

Smythe, D. (2004) "The consumer's stake in radio and television," in J. D. Peters and P. Simonson (eds), *Mass Communication and American Social Thought: Key Texts, 1919–1968*. Lanham: Rowman & Littlefield, pp. 318–28.

Snow, C. P. (1987) *The Two Cultures and a Second Look: An Expanded Version of the Two Cultures and the Scientific Revolution*. Cambridge: Cambridge University Press.

Snyder, M. (1974) "Self-monitoring of expressive behavior." *Journal of Personality and Social Psychology* 30(4): 526–37.

Sobieraj, S. (2011) *Soundbitten: The Perils of Media-Centered Political Activism* New York: New York University Press.

Soloski, J. (2005) "Taking stock redux: corporate ownership and journalism of publicly traded newspaper companies," in Robert G. Picard (ed.), *Corporate Governance of Media Companies*. Jönkoping, Sweden: JIBS Research Reports.

Spears, N., Royne, M., and Van Steenburg, E. (2013) "Are celebrity-heroes effective endorsers? Exploring the link between hero, celebrity, and advertising response." *Journal of Promotion Management* 19(1): 17–37.

Spigel, L. (1992) *Make Room for TV*. Chicago: University of Chicago Press.

Spigel, L., and Mann, D. (eds) (1992) *Private Screenings: Television and the Female Consumer*. Minneapolis: University of Minnesota Press.

Sreberny, A. (2008) "The analytic challenges of studying the Middle East and its evolving media environment." *Middle East Journal of Culture and Communication* 1: 8–23.

Stacey, J., and Thorne, B. (1985) "The missing feminist revolution in sociology." *Social Problems* 32(4): 301–16.

Stahler-Sholk, R., Vanden, H., and Kuecker, G. (eds) (2008) *Latin American Social Movements in the Twenty-first Century: Resistance, Power, and Democracy*. Lanham, MD: Rowman & Littlefield.

Staiger, J. (2005) *Media Reception Studies*. New York: New York University Press.

Starr, P. (2004) *The Creation of the Media*. New York: Basic Books.

Steele, S. (2008) "Obama's post-racial promise," *Los Angeles Times*, November 5.

Stefanone, M. A., Lackaff, D., and Rosen, D. (2012) "The relationship between traditional mass media and 'social media': reality television as a model for social network site behavior." *Journal of Broadcasting & Electronic Media* 54(3): 508–25.

Steinmetz, G. (2004) "Odious comparisons: incommensurability, the case study, and 'small N's' in sociology." *Sociological Theory* 22(3): 371–400.

Sternberg, E. (1998) "Phantasmagoric labor: the new economics of self-presentation." *Futures* 30(1): 3–21.

Stice, E., and Shaw, H. (1994) "Adverse effects of the media portrayed thin-ideal on women and linkages to bulimic symptomatology." *Journal of Social and Clinical Psychology* 13(3): 288–308.

Stouffer, S. (1953) "PR and the social sciences 1952–1962." *Public Relations Journal* (Jan.): 9–11, 34–6.

Stouffer, S. et al. (1949) *The American Soldier: Studies in Social Psychology in World War II* (4 vols). Princeton: Princeton University Press.

Straubhaar, J. D. (2007) *World Television: From Global to Local*. London: Sage.

Strayer, D. L., and Johnston, W.A. (2001) "Driven to distraction: dual-task studies of simulated driving and conversing on a cellular telephone." *Psychological Science* 12: 462–6.

Strayer, D. L., Drews, F. A., and Crouch, D. J. (2006) "A comparison of the cell phone driver and the drunk driver." *Human Factors* 48: 381–92.

Sugrue, T. (2010) *Not Even Past: Barack Obama and the Burden of Race.* Princeton: Princeton University Press.

Sundsøy, P. R., Ling, R., Bjelland, J., Canright, G., and Engø-Monsen, K. (2012) The activation of social networks in the wake of the 22 July Oslo bombing. Presented at the NSNA XXXII Conference, Redondo Beach, CA.

Swidler, A. (1986) "Culture in action: symbols and strategies." *American Sociological Review* 51: 273–86.

Tasker, Y., and Negra, D. (eds) (2007) *Interrogating Postfeminism: Gender and the Politics of Popular Culture.* Durham and London: Duke University Press.

Taylor, C. (1989) *Sources of the Self: The Making of the Modern Identity.* Cambridge, MA: Harvard University Press.

Taylor, E. (1989) *Prime-Time Families: Television Culture in Postwar America.* Berkeley and Los Angeles: University of California Press.

Tesler, M., and Sears, D. O. (2010) *Obama's Race: The 2008 Election and the Dream of a Post-Racial America.* Chicago: University of Chicago Press.

Thelen, K. (1999) "Historical institutionalism in comparative politics." *Annual Review of Political Science* 2: 369–404.

Thomas, W. I. (1914) "The Prussian-Polish situation: an experiment in assimilation." *American Journal of Sociology* 19(5) (March): 624–39.

Thompson, E. P. (1967) "Time, work discipline and industrial capitalism." *Past and Present* 38: 65–97.

Thompson, J. B. (1984) *Studies in the Theory of Ideology.* Cambridge, UK: Polity.

Thompson, J. B. (1995) *The Media and Modernity: A Social Theory of the Media.* Cambridge, UK: Polity.

Thompson, J. B. (2005) "The new visibility." *Theory, Culture & Society* 22(6): 31–51.

Thornham, S. (ed.) (1999) *Feminist Film Theory. A Reader.* Edinburgh: Edinburgh University Press.

Tierney, J. (2008) "Where have all the bigots gone?" New York Times Tierney Lab Blog. Available at http://tierneylab.blogs.nytimes.com/2008/11/07/where-have-all-the-bigots-gone/?_r=0, accessed September 30, 2013.

Tilly, C. (2004) *Social Movements, 1768–2004.* Boulder, CO: Paradigm Publishers.

Toffler, A. (1983) *Previews and Premises.* New York: William Morrow.

Tomaselli, K. G. (2009) "Repositioning African media studies: thoughts and provocations." *Journal of African Media Studies* 1(1): 9–21.

Tomlinson, A. (1996) "Olympic spectacle: opening ceremonies and some paradoxes of globalization." *Media, Culture & Society* 18(4): 583–602.

Tomlinson, J. (1999) *Globalization and Culture*. Chicago: University of Chicago Press.

Torres, S. (2003) "Black, white, and in color: television and black civil rights." Princeton: Princeton University Press

Townsley, E. (2012) "Media intellectuals, the public sphere, and the story of Barack Obama in 2008," in J. Alexander, R. Jacobs, and P. Smith (eds), *Oxford Handbook of Cultural Sociology*. New York: Oxford University Press, pp. 284–317.

Trilling, L. (1972) *Sincerity and Authenticity*. Cambridge, MA: Harvard University Press.

Trottier, D. (2011) "A research agenda for social media surveillance." *Fast Capitalism* 8(1).

Tuchman, G. (1976) "Telling stories." *Journal of Communication* 26: 93–7.

Tuchman, G. (1978) *Making News: A Study in the Construction of Reality*. New York: The Free Press.

Tuchman, G. with Fortin, N. (1989) *Edging Women Out: Victorian Novelists, Publishers, and Social Change*. New York: Routledge.

Tuchman, G., Daniels, A. K., and Benet, J. W. (1978) *Hearth and Home: Images of Women in the Mass Media*. Oxford University Press.

Tucker, L. (1997) "Was the revolution televised? Professional criticism about *The Cosby Show* and the essentialization of black cultural expression." *Journal of Broadcast and Electronic Media* 41: 90–108.

Tufekci, Z. (2008a) "Grooming, gossip, Facebook and Myspace." *Information, Communication & Society* 11(4): 544–64.

Tufekci, Z. (2008b) "Can you see me now? Audience and disclosure regulation in online social network sites." *Bulletin of Science, Technology & Society* 28(1): 20–36.

Tulloch, J., and Zinn, J. O. (2011) "Risk, health and the media." *Health, Risk & Society* 13(1): 1–16.

Tumber, H. (1999) "Introduction," in *News: A Reader*. New York: Oxford University Press, pp. xv–xix.

Tumber, H. (2000) "Introduction: academic at work," in H. Tumber (ed.), *Media Power, Professionals and Policies*. London: Routledge, pp. 1–12.

Tumber, H. (2006) "Journalists at work – revisited." *Javnost – the Public* 13(3): 57–68.

Tunstall, J. (ed.) (1970) *Media Sociology*. Urbana, IL: University of Illinois Press.

Tunstall, J. (1971) *Journalists at Work*. London: Constable.

Turkle, S. (1995) *Life on the Screen*. London: Simon and Schuster.

Turkle, S. (2011) *Alone Together: Why We Expect More from Technology and Less from Each Other*. New York: Basic Books.

Turner, B. S. (2012) "Sociology in the USA and beyond: A half-century decline?" *Journal of Sociology* 48(4): 364–9.

Turner, F. (2006) *From Counter-Culture to Cyber-Culture*. University of Chicago Press.

Turner, J. (2006) "American sociology in chaos: differentiation without integration." *American Sociologist* 37(2): 15–29.

Turner, S. P., and Turner, J. H. (1990) *The Impossible Science: An Institutional Analysis of American Sociology*. London: Sage.

Turow, J. (1997) *Media Systems in Society: Understanding Industries, Strategies, and Power*, 2nd edn. White Plains, NY: Longman.

Turow, J. (2005) "Audience construction and culture production: marketing surveillance in the digital age." *Annals of the American Academy of Political and Social Science* 597: 103–21.

Turow, J. (2011) *The Daily You: How the New Advertising Industry is Defining Your Identity and Your Worth*. New Haven, CT: Yale University Press.

Tyler, I., and Gill, R. (in press) "Postcolonial girl: migrant audibility and intimate activism." *Interventions: International Journal of Post-Colonial Studies*.

United Nations Conference on Trade and Development (2013, May 15) "Trade in creative products reached new peak in 2011, UNCTAD figures show." Available at http://unctad.org/en/pages/newsdetails.aspx?Original VersionID=498&Sitemap_x0020_Taxonomy=UNCTAD%20Home

Usher, N. (2010) "Goodbye to the news: how out-of-work journalists assess enduring news values and the new media landscape." *New Media & Society* 12(6): 911–28.

Vaidhyanathan, S. (2011) *The Googlization of Everything (and Why We Should Worry)*. Berkeley and Los Angeles: University of California Press.

Van Aelst, P., and Walgrave, S. (2002) "New media, new movements? The role of the internet in shaping the 'anti-globalization' movement." *Information, Communication & Society* 5(4): 465–93.

Vieweg, S., Palen, L., Liu, S. B., Hughes, A. L., and Sutton, J. N. (2008) *Collective Intelligence in Disaster: Examination of the Phenomenon in the Aftermath of the 2007 Virginia Tech Shooting*. University of Colorado.

Vilhelmson, B. (1999) "Daily mobility and the use of time for different activities: the case of Sweden." *GeoJournal* 48: 177–85.

Virno, P. (2004) *Grammar of the Multitude*. New York: Semiotext(e).

Vitak, J. (2012) "The impact of context collapse and privacy on social network site disclosures." *Journal of Broadcasting & Electronic Media* 56(4): 451–70.

Vliegenthart, R., and Van Zoonen, E. A. (2011) "Power to the frame: bringing sociology back to frame analysis." *European Journal of Communication* 26(2): 101–15.

Waisbord, S. (2002) "Journalism, risk and patriotism," in B. Zelizer and S. Allan (eds), *Journalism after September 11*. New York: Routledge, pp. 201–19.

Waisbord, S. (2013) *Reinventing Professionalism: News and Journalism in Global Perspective*. Cambridge, UK: Polity.

Wajcman, J. (2008) "Life in the fast lane? Towards a sociology of technology and time." *British Journal of Sociology* 59(1): 59–77.

Walgrave, S., Bennett, L., Van Laer, J., and Breunig, C. (2011) "Multiple engagements and network bridging in contentious politics: digital media use of protest participants." *Mobilization* 16(3): 325–49.

Walker, J. (1983) "The origins and maintenance of interest groups in America." *American Political Science Review* 77 (June): 390–406.

Wallstein, K. (2007) "Agenda setting and the blogosphere: an analysis of the relationship between mainstream media and political blogs." *Review of Policy Research* 24: 567–87.

Walther, J. B. (1996) "Computer-mediated communication: impersonal, interpersonal, and hyperpersonal interaction." *Communication Research* 23(1): 3–43.

Walther, J. B. (2007) "Selective self-presentation in computer-mediated communication: hyperpersonal dimensions of technology, language, and cognition." *Computers in Human Behavior* 23(5): 2538–57.

Walther, J. B., and Parks, M. R. (2002) "Cues filtered out, cues filtered in: computer-mediated communication and relationships," in M. L. Knapp and J. A. Daly (eds), *Handbook of Interpersonal Communication*. Thousand Oaks, CA: Sage, pp. 529–63.

Walther, J. B. et al. (2008) "The role of friends' appearance and behavior on evaluations of individuals on Facebook: are we known by the company we keep?" *Communication Theory* 34(1): 28–49.

Walther, J. B., Van Der Heide, B., Hamel, L. M., and Shulman, H. C. (2009) "Self-generated versus other-generated statements and impressions in computer-mediated communication." *Communication Research* 36(2): 229–53.

Wang, Y. (2008) "Agency: the internal split of structure." *Sociological Forum* 23(3) (Sept.): 481–502.

Wardle, C., and West, E. (2004) "The press as agents of nationalism in the Queen's Golden Jubilee: how British newspapers celebrated a media event." *European Journal of Communication* 19(2): 195–214.

Wartella, E. (1996) "The history reconsidered," in Everett E. Dennis and Ellen Wartella (eds), *American Communication Research – The Remembered History*. Mahwah, NJ: Lawrence Erlbaum, pp. 169–80.

Wasko, J. (ed.) (2005) *A Companion to Television*. Malden: Blackwell.

Wasko, J., Murdock, G., and Sousa, H. (eds) (2011) *The Handbook of Political Economy of Communications*. Malden: Blackwell.

Wasko, J., Phillips, M., and Meehan, E. R. (eds) (2001) *Dazzled by Disney: The Global Disney Audiences Project*. London: Leicester University Press.

Wayne, M. (2003) *Marxism and Media Studies: Key Concepts and Contemporary Trends*. London: Pluto Press.

Weaver, D., and Wilhoit, C. Cleveland (1996) *The American Journalist in the 1990s*. Mahwah, NY: Lawrence Ehrlbaum.

Weber, M. (2005) "Remarks on technology and culture." Trans. Beatrix Zumsteg and Thomas M. Kemple. Ed. Thomas M. Kemple. *Theory, Culture & Society* 22(4): 23–38.

Wellman, B. (2002) "Little boxes, glocalization, and networked individualism," in M. Tanabe, P. van den Besselaar, and T. Ishida (eds), *Digital Cities II: Computational and Sociological Approaches*. Berlin: Springer, pp. 10–25.

Wellman, B., and Rainie, L. (2012) *Networked: The New Social Operating System*. Cambridge, MA: MIT Press.

Werbach, K., and Hunter, D. (2012) *For the Win: How Game Thinking Can Revolutionize your Business*. Philadelphia: Wharton Digital Press.

Wernick, A. (1991) *Promotional Culture: Advertising, Ideology, and Symbolic Expression*. Newbury Park, CA: Sage.

Westlund, O. (2011) *Cross-Media News Work: Sensemaking of the Mobile Media (R)evolution*. Göteborg: University of Göthenburg.

White, D. M. (1950) "The 'gate keeper': a case study in the selection of news." *Journalism Quarterly* 27: 383–90.

Williams, B., and Delli Carpini, M. X. (2011) *After Broadcast News: Media Regimes, Democracy, and the New Information Environment*. Cambridge, UK: Cambridge University Press.

Williams, L. (2001) *Playing the Race Card: Melodramas of Black and White from Uncle Tom to O. J. Simpson*. Princeton: Princeton University Press.

Williams, R. (1977) *Marxism and Literature*. London: Oxford University Press.

Williams, R. (2003 [1974]) *Television: Technology and Cultural Form*. London: Routledge Classics.

Williams, R. (2006 [1980]) "Base and superstructure in Marxist cultural theory," in M. Durham and D. Kellner (eds), *Media and Cultural Studies Keyworks*, rev. edn. Oxford: Blackwell, pp. 130–43.

Wilson, P., and Stewart, M. (eds) (2008) *Global Indigenous Media: Cultures, Poetics, and Politics*. Durham and London: Duke University Press.

Winnicott, D. (1971) *Playing and Reality*. London: Tavistock Press.

Wolff, J. (1999) "Cultural studies and the sociology of culture." *Contemporary Sociology* 28(5): 499–507.

Wolfsfeld, G. (1997) *Media and Political Conflict: News from the Middle East*. Cambridge: Cambridge University Press.

Wood, Gaby (2009, June 7) "'I'm a little bit of a nerd.'" *Guardian*, available at www.guardian.co.uk/film/2009/jun/07/interview-daryl-hannah, accessed September 1, 2013.

Wood, H. (2011) *Talking with Television: Women, Talk Shows, and Modern Self-Reflexivity*. Urbana, IL: University of Illinois Press.

Wood, H., and Skeggs, B. (eds) (2011) *Reality Television and Class*. London: Palgrave Macmillan.

Young, Alford A., Jr (2012) "Rethinking the relationship of African American men to the street", in J. Alexander, R. Jacobs and P. Smith (eds), *Oxford Handbook of Cultural Sociology*. New York: Oxford University Press, pp. 343–4.

Yu, H. (2011) "Doing Chinese media studies: a reflection on the field's history and methodology." *Media International Australia* 138: 66–79.

Yúdice, G. (2002) *El recurso de la cultura: Usos de la cultura en la era global.* Barcelona: Editorial Gedisa.

Zelizer, B. (2004) *Taking Journalism Seriously: News and the Academy.* Thousand Oaks: Sage.

Zelizer, B. (2009) "Journalism and the academy," in K. Wahl-Jorgensen and T. Hanitzsch (eds), *The Handbook of Journalism Studies.* New York: Routledge, pp. 29–41.

Zerubavel, E. (1979) *Patterns of Time in Hospital Life: A Sociological Perspective.* Chicago: University of Chicago Press.

Zerubavel, E. (1985) *Hidden Rhythms: Schedules and Calendars in Social Life.* Berkeley: University of California.

Zhao, S., Grasmuck, S., and Martin, J. (2008) "Identity construction on Facebook: Digital empowerment in anchored relationships." *Computers in Human Behavior* 24(5): 1816–36.

Zwass, V. (1992) *Management Information Systems.* London: Brown Publishers.

Index